Dangerous Offenders

Dangerous Offenders

THE ELUSIVE TARGET OF JUSTICE

Mark H. Moore
Susan R. Estrich
Daniel McGillis
William Spelman

Harvard University Press
Cambridge, Massachusetts, and London, England   1984

LIBRARY OF CONGRESS CATALOGING IN PUBLICATION DATA
Main entry under title:

Dangerous offenders.

　Includes index.
　1. Criminal justice, Administration of — United States.
　2. Crime and criminals — United States.　　3. Violent crimes —
United States.　　I. Moore, Mark Harrison.
KF9223.D36　1985　　　　345.73′05　　　　84-9148
ISBN 0-674-19065-3　　　　347.3055

Preface

WE BEGAN work on this project with markedly different perspectives on the subject of "dangerous offenders," based at least partly on our different academic training. Moore and Spelman are policy analysts, Estrich is a lawyer, and McGillis a psychologist. We also differed in our basic ideological orientations. What united us was an interest in imagining just and effective responses to the public concern about crime and a special curiosity about the potential of proposals designed to focus the attention of the criminal justice system on "dangerous" offenders. What surprised us was that over the course of eighteen months of observation, reading, and deliberation, we developed a shared conception of how the criminal justice system should focus on dangerous offenders. This book reflects that shared conception.

We had the benefit of advice, information, and counsel from an exceptionally wise, well-informed, and talented group of collaborators. Philip B. Heymann and Lloyd Ohlin of Harvard Law School and Cheryl Martorana and Robert Burkhart of the National Institute of Justice created the opportunity for us to do the work and provided support and encouragement. Phil Heymann, in particular, lent his wisdom, charm, and intelligence at the early stages of the project when the problems were being defined and the personal relations developed. The success of the project owes much to his careful nurturing.

We benefited enormously from the counsel of a steering committee that met three times with us over the course of the project funded by the National Institute of Justice, which laid the basis for this book. This group included Superintendent Richard Brzeczek of the Chicago Police Department, Professor Alfred Blumstein, Professor Alan Dershowitz, Dr. Peter Greenwood, Assistant Attorney General D. Lowell Jensen, Professor John Monahan, Professor Lloyd Ohlin, Assistant Attorney General Jonathan C. Rose, Professor Alan Stone, Professor James Q. Wilson, and Professor Marvin Wolfgang. Some special consultants who also attended these meetings and gave us the benefit of their knowledge and advice were Shirley Melnicoe of the National Institute of Justice, on policing; Professor Daniel Freed of Yale University Law School, on bail; Dr. Park E. Dietz and Dr. Robert Fein, on the mental health system; Dr. Alden Miller, on the juvenile justice system; Edward Rendell and John Rieck, on prosecutorial policies; and Robert Mostoeller, on legal defense of career criminals.

The book draws heavily on papers prepared for a conference of academics and practitioners held under the auspices of the NIJ grant. Those who prepared papers were Alfred Blumstein, Barbara Boland, Ken Carlson, Jacqueline Cohen, John Eck, Floyd Feeney, Ken Feinberg, Brian Forst, William Gay, John Goldkamp, Peter Greenwood, John Monahan, Lloyd Ohlin, Michael Sherman, Michael Smith, Mary Toborg, Paul Tracy, and Marvin Wolfgang. In addition, David Nemecek, director of the FBI's National Crime Information Center, gave a lucid account of national criminal justice records. Other active discussants included Thomas Atkins, the Honorable Richard Banks, the Honorable William B. Bryant, Zachary Carter, the Honorable Julian Houston, Dennis Nowicki, David Nurco, the Honorable Rudolph Pierce, Walter Prince, Oliver Revell, Harry Tischler, John Rieck, Dr. Henry Steadman, and William Weld.

Several reviewers advised us on an early draft of the book. Professors Franklin Zimring, Albert Reiss, and Stanton Wheeler all made helpful comments and criticisms. Professor Reiss's comments in particular were incisive and thorough. The final product owes much to these careful efforts to set us straight.

We also benefited from very competent and resourceful administrative assistance. Anita B. Moulton, administrative officer of the Program in Criminal Justice at the Kennedy School of Government, kept all of the various aspects of the project moving smoothly: she was the true manager of the project. She was assisted by Diana Murray and Nancy Sawdon, who assumed most of the burden of typing, and by Natalie Burnett, who assisted Susan Estrich.

Contents

Figures

Tables

Dangerous Offenders

Introduction

IDEAS THAT SHAPE public policy fit the temper of their times. Otherwise they lack the currency to legitimate and guide governmental action. The idea that the criminal justice system might control crime more effectively by focusing its efforts on dangerous offenders is one of these.

The idea is a compelling one because it addresses the major problems currently confronting the criminal justice system — public concern about crime and overflowing prisons. Americans are sufficiently afraid of crime to keep ranking it among the most urgent of social concerns. However, there is no room in the prisons to accommodate the increasing number of offenders that the system is committed to punishing. Therefore it seems only sensible to reserve the limited space for the offenders who most deserve punishment and whose incapacitation would do the most good to society by reducing crime in the future.

Two questions then arise. Do some offenders commit more violent crimes more often than other offenders? If so, can this group be identified? Recent social science studies suggest that such offenders do exist. Persuasive evidence has been compiled indicating that serious criminal offending is highly concentrated: 5 percent of criminal offenders account for half of the serious violent crime in the United States.[1] Moreover, the worst 1 percent of offenders commit crimes at such a high rate (more than fifty serious offenses per year) that simply incapacitating them would justify their imprisonment, even if there were no other justification such as deterrence, rehabilitation, or simple justice.[2]

This finding is not practically significant unless we can distinguish the high-rate offenders from others. Recent studies have made progress in this area as well. On the basis of personal characteristics such as prior criminal conduct, previous drug abuse, and unemployment record, offenders can be separated into groups that have dramatically different average rates of offending.[3] Moreover, although there is necessarily some error in the assignment of offenders to high-rate and low-rate groups, these errors are less frequent than with previous methods. So the idea of giving special attention to dangerous offenders assumes a freshness and a degree of scientific sophistication that enhance its common-sense appeal.

The idea also has broad philosophical appeal. To those on the right of the political spectrum, focusing on dangerous offenders reestablishes the idea that individuals should be held responsible for their acts. It recognizes that some people are truly incorrigible and are not the victims of social circumstances. And it celebrates the role of the criminal justice system in affirming the values of the community by punishing those who have most flagrantly violated its rules.

To those on the left, the appeal of such a focus is far less obvious. Indeed, in many ways, the idea is anathema to those who view criminal offenders as victims of social circumstance and therefore susceptible to rehabilitation and to those who worry about the public passion for revenge that might be unleashed by a moralistic crusade against unusually dangerous offenders. However, the idea is interesting even to those on the left, because a selective focus might limit rather than expand the use of socially sanctioned punishment. Moreover, it could also be used to introduce more explicit standards and guidelines into criminal justice decision making. Both features are appealing in a world where preferred liberal policies, such as pursuit of economic and social justice and rehabilitation of prisoners, have become tarnished, and where many alternative responses involve broader, less restrained measures against criminal offenders. Both liberals and conservatives have reasons to agree that prisons could best be used to incapacitate dangerous offenders.

Such a policy also has the proper relationship to existing institutional capabilities. It is neither so far from current practice as to be utopian nor so close that it offers no prospects for noticeable improvements. Indeed, the current situation with regard to prison capacity and sentencing policies makes the whole idea of a selective focus nearly inevitable. It is not surprising, then, that throughout the country, judges, district attorneys, and police executives are using the discretion vested in their office to concentrate on career criminals. Judges are urged to shift from rehabilitative sentencing (in which prison sentences are determined by a prisoner's prospects for rehabilitation) or meting out "just deserts" (in which prison sentences are determined by the seriousness of the conviction offense) to a concept of selective incapacitation (in which prison sentences are lengthened for those deemed unusually dangerous and shortened for others).[4] Prosecutors' offices are developing career criminal units designed to assure that repeat offenders will be prosecuted to the full measure of the law by restricting plea bargaining, moving cases expeditiously to trial, and maintaining close relations with victims and witnesses to protect the strength of their cases.[5] The police are experimenting with "perpetrator-oriented patrols" targeted on suspected high-rate offenders, "felony augmentation" programs providing enhanced investigative efforts in cases involving criminal recidivists, and "robbery case enhancement" programs designed to improve the quality of the evidence in robbery cases that are likely to involve dangerous offenders.[6] And conferences are being held to build commitment to and share information about managing such programs.[7]

This apparent headlong rush to create a special focus on dangerous offenders seems irresponsible to those who think that social policies should be built on a foundation of well-established facts and a careful, widely shared deliberation of their broadest implications. Important questions about the justice and effectiveness of a selective focus on dangerous offenders remain unanswered. Indeed, viewed from some perspectives, it is a shocking idea. As a philosophy of sentencing, it attacks a fundamental principle of justice; offenders are punished for having a bad character and for presenting future risks to the society as well as for present crimes. Moreover, some offenders inevitably will be incorrectly identified and unjustly punished. As a strategy for prosecutors and police, selective policies risk the presumption of innocence, and they create a situation in which *ad hominem* motivations might have license to grow to corrupt investigative and prosecuting agencies.

Nor is it clear that these risks of injustice will be balanced by large reductions in crime. There are many reasons to suspect that the practical benefits in reducing crime will be marginal at best. Perhaps offending is less concentrated in a small percentage of offenders than it now appears. Perhaps our discriminating capabilities are weaker than they now seem. Perhaps those who are imprisoned will be replaced by other, equally dangerous offenders. Perhaps our institutions already focus attention on dangerous offenders, and little more can be gained by simply labeling our implicit policy.

And what of the long-run risks to the institutions and ideology of the criminal justice system? In the past, when we assumed that offenders were much like the rest of us, we could rely on a deliberate and measured response from our criminal justice system. In the future the idea that we are beset by unusually dangerous offenders may foster such zeal among criminal justice officials and the general citizenry that the system will become immoderate. The risks of injustice and corruption, balanced against possibly marginal crime control benefits, do not add up to a strong argument for sharpening the focus of the system. In the absence of a full debate and much more information, this view of the likely consequences of focusing on dangerous offenders must be taken seriously. Reckless disregard of these possibilities seems irresponsible to those who criticize this current trend.

However, to those who understand that public policy in a democracy is generally shaped by some combination of circumstance and fashion — occasionally informed by facts, reason, and a sense of proportion — the current trends in criminal justice policy are quite endurable. Indeed, the situation creates important responsibilities and opportunities. Like most social policies, the policy of giving special attention to dangerous offenders is developing too quickly to allow us to answer all questions in advance but slowly enough to allow us to learn from experience and make adjustments as we go along. The intellectual and social challenge, then, is to develop a framework for evaluating that experience and for using it to guide the evolution of the policy.[8] To do this we must find what social values are at stake in the evolving policy, imagine the many different ways that the system could be more discriminating with respect to dangerousness, and identify the key uncertainties that must be resolved (or simply tolerated). That is the purpose of this book.

The book is divided into two parts. Part I is concerned primarily with the general issues that arise as the society considers the benefits and risks of a more selective focus on unusually dangerous offenders. Part II is concerned with more particular questions about how that focus might be created and made operational at each stage of the criminal justice system — sentencing, pretrial detention, prosecution, and investigation. Slightly different questions of justice and efficacy are raised at each stage. To a degree, the discussion in Part II explicates the general idea of selective policies and makes such proposals practical and concrete. This is, of course, valuable in itself. But the more particular discussion also contributes to our broader understanding of what is at stake in encouraging a more selective focus.

In the concluding chapter we offer our judgments about selective policies. Is a sharpened focus on dangerous offenders just? Can such a policy be effective in managing the problem of crime? Which applications seem particularly valuable and which risky? What are the long-term risks to social institutions? And what uncertainties must be monitored and resolved as the policy evolves?

I

SELECTIVE
JUSTICE

1

Public Danger and the Problem of Crime

AMERICA IS ASSAILED by crime. In 1982 three out of ten American households reported that in that year they had been victimized at least once by criminal offenses.[1] Not surprisingly, Americans are also afraid. One half of the people living in metropolitan areas are afraid to go out alone at night.[2] A palpable sense of public danger infects American communities, particularly its cities.

This sense of danger invigorates proposals to concentrate on dangerous offenders. But unless selective policies seem likely to lessen the public's sense of danger, there is little to balance against the risks to justice that such policies might entail. Without a more specific notion of what sorts of offenses are being committed and who the offenders are, it is hard to know whether the policies are on or off target. So a clear-eyed sense of the nature and magnitude of the crime problem and the role of dangerous offenders in it is essential to any responsible appraisal of the proposals.

THE CRIME PROBLEM

The most obvious feature of the problem is criminal victimization. Robberies, assaults, and burglaries leave victims in their wake. The victims are often in pain and frightened. They are also often the poorer for their experience. While many of their losses are concentrated in the moments, days, and weeks immediately following an attack, some important consequences linger. Sometimes physical injuries suffered in a criminal attack become permanent disabilities. If an uninsured victim sustains financial loss from stolen property, medical payments, and continuing disability, the attack may result in long-lasting financial hardship. And if the attack was particularly traumatic, involving injury or sexual attack at home, the victim may invest time and money in elaborate precautions that fail, despite the investment, to restore the comfortable sense of security the victim enjoyed before the attack.

But it is not just victims who are affected. Their families and friends also experience losses through empathy and economic interdependence. Others in the community who hear of the victimization do not experience the same emotional or financial losses, but they may feel threatened by the prospect of similar victimization and may take time-consuming and expensive actions to protect themselves or to avoid the problem altogether.

From Figure 1, which represents these different aspects of the crime problem, it is easy to see why it is not simply a problem of criminal victimization. Criminal victimization may be defined as the short-run costs inflicted on the victims themselves — the upper left box in the figure. But there are substantial costs associated with each of the other boxes as well — with the long-run effects on victims and with both short- and long-run effects on nonvictims. Indeed, if many people are afflicted by fear, and if the material and emotional consequences of fear are large enough, criminal victimization may be the smaller piece of the overall problem.

But there is something more as well. Society's response to crime is exaggerated out of proportion to the actual consequences, compared to its response to other threats to physical and economic well-being. This exaggeration may not be irrational or inappropriate; it may be understandable and important that citizens react somewhat disproportionately

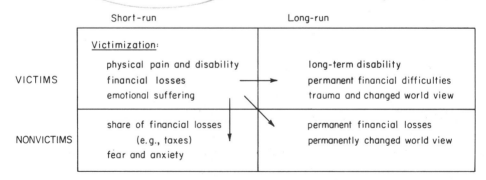

Figure 1   The effects of victimization.

to criminal attacks. We think that some crimes and offenders are particularly terrifying because they reveal the fragility of the conventions that secure ordinary social interactions against fears and worries. Once confidence in these conventions has been breached, much of the behavior that society would regard as mildly annoying disorder suddenly acquires a sinister aspect. So it is the occurrence of crimes and the existence of people who break society's rules that lead us to exaggerate our fears and make us feel vulnerable. Since such fears are natural and inevitable, and since they create significant and real consequences even if exaggerated, it is important to ensure that our social response dampens rather than exacerbates this tendency.

Our definition of the crime problem is critical to our efforts to understand the source of the public's fears and to formulate a social policy. Whether we consider the crime problem to consist primarily of victimization, or of reasonable fears among victims and others, or of the slightly exaggerated sense of public danger that now haunts our cities, each conception has important consequences for determining what offenses and offenders should become the primary targets of crime control policies.

Traditional conceptions of the crime problem emphasize criminal victimization; the victim's extent of loss determines the seriousness of a crime. If the attack was violent, the offense is considered more serious than if no violence occurred. If the property losses were large, either in absolute terms or in terms of the victim's capacity to absorb them, then the crime is worse than if the losses were small. The only information that is considered relevant is what happens to the victim. Missing from this conception of the crime problem, however, is the part played by the relationship between offender and victim, and the intentions and character of the offender.

In a conception of the crime problem that includes (or even emphasizes) public fear, the accounting of the seriousness of a crime is different, because not all criminal offenses have the same capacity to stimulate fear among the general citizenry. Domestic assaults, for example, often produce terrible consequences for the victims; indeed, there must be something especially terrifying about being locked into a relationship with a violent spouse. In terms of victimization, domestic assaults would loom large in any overall conception of the crime problem. Yet these crimes do not threaten the general population; the risk is localized. As a result, they do not produce much fear. This is not to say that domestic assaults are unimportant, of course. Both our sense of justice and our sensitivity to the special quality of victimization and fear in a domestic setting require a determined governmental response to such crimes.

Robberies and burglaries, on the other hand, which usually involve strangers, tend to create fears in the general population because they seem arbitrary and unpredictable. If we think of the crime problem as consisting of generalized fear as well as victimization, then robbery and burglary become more important relative to domestic assaults. If we include the component of fear, we must look at crimes a little differently than if we concentrated exclusively on victimization. The relationship of the offender to the victim and the location of the offense become important, as well as the character of the victimization, because these characteristics determine how widely fear may spread.

If one expands this conception of the crime problem still more to include the heightened sense of public vulnerability, then our accounting of offenses and offenders shifts once again. The sense of public danger is created not only by the objective risks of victimization, losses, and fear, but also by a sense that unrestrained malevolence lies behind the crimes. If we imagine that crimes are committed by callous, determined, and malevolent offenders, we are likely to feel more vulnerable than if we thought crimes were the consequence of provocative circumstances or were committed by offenders much like the rest of us. If we feel beset by violent predators, even small incidents of disorder become alarming, for they seem to offer a warning that attack is imminent. Thus obscene graffiti seems to reveal broad hostility just under the surface of public decorum, and the taunts of teenagers become the prelude to a mugging.

The purposes of this chapter are to explore the dimensions of the crime problem as it is defined by victimization, fear, and public vulnerability, to consider the appropriateness of including or excluding one or more aspects of the problem, and to discover the implications of the different views of the crime problem in judging the relative importance of different kinds of offenses and offenders.

CRIMINAL VICTIMIZATION

The core of the crime problem, criminal victimization, produces tangible losses to victims and establishes the objective basis for fear and the sense of vulnerability. The core of victimization, in turn, is physical injury, and in its worst form, death. We begin our analysis of criminal victimization, then, with murder.

In 1980, according to statistics compiled by the Federal Bureau of

Investigation, about 23,000 Americans were murdered.[3] This translates into a murder rate of 10.2 per 100,000; citizens over the age of twelve have a 1 in 10,000 chance of being murdered each year. The number of homicides has risen each year with the growth in the population, but the rate has been stable for the last decade. Although a 1 in 10,000 chance is not very large, most of us would both notice and be quite unhappy about the imposition of a new risk of this magnitude.

Of course, murder is a very rare crime. More people are the victim of violent offenses that occasionally lead to serious injury, such as robbery, assault, and rape. The Census Bureau, which conducts an annual survey of crime victims, estimates that 6 million rapes, robberies, and assaults were committed in 1980.[4] The FBI, relying on officially reported crimes, indicated that in 1980, 570.5 of every 100,000 Americans — roughly 1 in 200 — were the victim of one of these crimes.[5]

All of these crimes involved an explicit threat of violence, and rape always involves both violence and injury. But broken bones, lost teeth, cuts, or bruises occurred in only about 33 percent of the 5.9 million rapes, robberies, and assaults that occurred in 1980, and most of these injuries were minor.[6] Of those who were injured, only 26.2 percent went to the hospital, and of those, only about 18 percent were admitted for inpatient care.[7] In other words, fewer than 5 percent of the victims of violent crime — about 93,000 people — were hospitalized for injuries suffered in violent crimes. The remainder suffered only cuts and bruises.

If serious physical injury is a rare consequence of criminal victimization, the potential for such injury is ever-present. The threat of violence is explicit in every robbery, rape, and assault, but it is implicit in many property offenses. Indeed, if a victim confronts a burglar in his home, an incident that began as a property crime can quickly become violent. If a woman holds tightly to her purse, and the would-be purse snatcher then hits her, a larceny escalates into a robbery. This potential for escalation exists in virtually all crimes, because any crime is a violation of the rules, inviting surprise, indignation, and retaliation from victims and from witnesses who observe the offense. No doubt, many offenders prefer to use stealth and finesse rather than force, and of these, many will flee rather than use violence when stealth has failed. But most offenders, even those who commit property crimes, seem to threaten force — if not to secure the fruits of their crime, then to guarantee their escape. Otherwise, offenders would be too vulnerable to self-righteous victims.

Offenders' explicit or implicit threats of violence have immediate psychological consequences for victims. If victims resist, their chances of physical injury increase significantly.[8] On the other hand, if they yield to explicit or implied threats, they suffer a less obvious, but no less real, consequence. They feel humiliated and powerless in a situation they feel they ought to be able to control.[9] This psychological trauma, which is slightly different from fear, may have long-run consequences. But during the crime a victim experiences it as a significant and immediate loss of self-esteem. So how much of the immediate cost of victimization comes in the form of physical injury, and how much in the form of trauma and humiliation, may depend on the size of the offender's threats relative to the victim's will to resist.

These observations are significant for judgments about which crimes contribute most to the costs of victimization. If violence and physical injury are considered much more important than economic losses, there is a natural tendency to accord the greatest importance to murder, assault, and robbery rather than to burglaries and larcenies because the first group accounts for the largest portion of physical injury and explicit threats of violence. If we consider the implicit threat of violence against victims to be important, however, and understand that many property crimes have this characteristic, then there is a smaller difference between the crimes with actual violence, or an explicit threat of violence, and other crimes, for a great many offenses carry both the potential for violence and an implicit threat of it. Indeed, if we think of burglaries as holding the potential for violence, and if we add burglaries to rapes, robberies, and assaults, then the number of people threatened by violence increases from 570 of every 100,000 Americans, to 2,239 per 100,000.[10] In this accounting, then, about two out of every hundred Americans experienced a criminal victimization that contained a risk or an implied threat of physical injury.

So far we have been discussing risks and threat of physical injury as the principal aspects of criminal victimization. Consider now risks of economic loss, which are much more frequent than either physical injury or explicit threats of force. Victimization surveys indicate that burglaries and thefts occur five to six times more frequently than personal crimes such as robbery and assault.[11] Moreover, the aggregate losses caused by these crimes are enormous, on the order of $5 billion per year.[12] Several facts reduce the import of this staggering sum, however. For one, the average property loss is less than $100. Many of the larger losses result from auto theft,[13] and in half of these, the car is recovered without damage shortly after the offense.[14] Of the remaining large losses, many are covered by insurance.[15] Although property losses tend to be small, they are extremely widespread. And in any given burglary or theft, there is a small but real chance that the victim will suffer a serious and irrecoverable financial setback.

It is worth keeping in mind that *property* losses result from violent crimes as well as from property offenses. Robberies produce physical injury, psychological trauma, *and financial loss.* Murders and assaults may also bring about significant financial loss through medical payments and lost income. However, the economic losses to victims from property crimes amount to much more. Indeed, because the takes in robbery are so small, and serious physical injuries in robberies and assaults so rare, the economic losses from property crimes such as burglary, larceny, and auto theft are about fifteen times those associated with violent crimes.

In sum, we can think of criminal victimization as consisting of actual physical injury, risk of injury, psychological trauma caused by explicit or implicit threats of force, and economic losses from stolen property, medical expenses, and lost income. Table 1 offers some rough indications of the magnitudes of these losses contributed by different sorts of offenses. The overall toll is significant: 23,000 people killed, another 90,000 injured seriously enough to require hospitalization, over 10 million victims of explicit or implicit threats; $5 billion in property losses, and $290 million in medical payments. The obvious seriousness of the violent offenses is offset to a degree by the greater prevalence of property crimes. So even if we restrict our attention to the narrow issue of short-run losses to victims, it is not clear which offenses should be taken most seriously. On balance, we would put robbery at the top of our list because it involves both violence and property losses, and it occurs often. Burglary and larcenies from the person also seem important because they risk violence and happen often.

THE FEAR OF CRIME

Given the toll of criminal victimization, it is not surprising that Americans are afraid. Two of every five Americans report that they are highly fearful of becoming victims of violent crimes.[16] In the Rocky Mountain states 27 percent of the residents say they worry constantly about burglary; 13 percent worry constantly about being mugged.[17] Between 40 and 50 percent are afraid to walk alone at night within a mile of their home, some 13 percent are afraid to walk alone during the daytime, and an astonishing 16 percent do not feel safe in their own homes at night. Levels of fear

Table 1. Dimensions and magnitude of victimization by type of offense.

Nature of offense	Physical injury (in thousands)				Intimidation and threat (in thousands)			Nonrecovered economic losses (in millions of dollars)		
					Explicit					
	Death	Inpatient care	Emergency room care	Minor injury	Deadly weapon	No weapon	Implicit	Medical expenses	Value of time lost from work	Theft/Damage
Rape and sexual assault	0.6	2.9	17.4	63.1	49.0	118.7	0	8.1	5.2	3.9
Robbery	4.6	30.0	93.5	281.5	533.5	651.1	0	60.0	34.2	101.6
Assault	17.8	56.5	292.5	1052.7	1550.7	3093.1	0	220.9	91.8	44.9
Burglary	0	0	0	0	0	0	5377.0	0	51.0	966.3
Larceny	0	0	0	0	0	0	194.0	0	65.5	2422.4
Auto theft	0	0	0	0	0	0	0	0	39.3	929.5
Total	23.0	89.4	403.4	1397.3	2133.2	3862.9	5571.0	289.0	287.0	4468.6

Sources: U.S. Bureau of the Census, Criminal Victimization in the United States, 1980 (Washington, D.C.: U.S. Department of Justice, Bureau of Justice Statistics, 1982), 22, 57, 60, 61, 63, 64, 68, 69; U.S. Department of Justice, Federal Bureau of Investigation, Uniform Crime Reports for the United States, 1980 (Washington, D.C.: U.S. Government Printing Office, 1981), 13, 174.

are considerably higher today than they were twenty years ago but, like crime rates, the levels have stabilized since the mid-1970s.[18]

That people are afraid is a fact. Whether this fear should be considered an important part of the crime problem is a question. One reason to think it should be is that fear imposes significant costs on individuals and the society at large. Although most psychologists consider small doses of fear and anxiety to be healthy, excessive fears have been repeatedly linked to mental illness, both as causes and results.[19] When anxiety continues for a long time, it can induce serious medical problems as well. Very anxious people are more susceptible to ulcers and infectious diseases and may even be more likely to contract cancer.[20]

But fear imposes economic costs as well, such as the cost of security measures. The home security industries are booming, accounting for $2.6 billion in receipts in 1977.[21] Between 25 and 40 percent of big-city residents change their door locks every few years. Smaller, but still significant, proportions report buying burglar alarms, automatic timers for lights and appliances, bars for their windows, and other devices.[22] The Pinkerton detective agency patrols some fifty neighborhoods throughout the country, at the behest (and substantial expense) of neighborhood residents.[23] And 35 to 45 percent of Americans report owning a handgun, rifle, or shotgun for protection.[24]

Other costs are those of avoiding the possibility of victimization. Most people limit their activities somewhat because of risks of crime. Two of every three residents of Kansas City avoid some parts of the city because of the high risks of victimization there. In Michigan, 66 percent report that they will not go to certain places for fear of crime. And half of the citizens of Atlanta stay home at night; when they must go out, one-third take someone with them for protection.[25]

Subways, downtown areas, and parks are perceived to be particularly dangerous. In Philadelphia, 77 percent of the black adults in households with seventeen-year-old boys said they were making more efforts than before to avoid the subways; the teenage sons agreed that the subways were the most dangerous places.[26] Most residents of Detroit avoid going downtown because of the risks of crime.[27] Residents of a middle-class Seattle community rated a local park as one of the most dangerous places and avoided it.[28]

A third area of costs is insurance. Each year some 150 million Americans pay premiums of $11 billion to insurance companies for protection covering burglary, theft, or vandalism of their homes; 10 to 20 percent of adults report having increased their coverage in recent years as a result of fears of burglary.[29] Recognizing that people are more afraid of mugging than of burglary, a Florida insurance company began offering mugging insurance in 1981. It was immediately besieged with applications.[30]

There is evidence that these anticrime measures can be effective in reducing victimization. A frail old man will not be mugged in a dark alley if he stays home and watches television every night. Police estimate that people can cut the risks of burglary in half or better by installing timers, bars, locks, and alarms.[31] And if a person pays the premiums on her homeowner's policy, a burglary will be much less costly when it occurs. But these security arrangements have some additional costs. As more citizens invest in protective efforts, some at least may be self-defeating, by creating social conditions in which real crime and the fear of crime flourish. If many people avoid going out, there will be fewer people on the street, resulting in less of the informal surveillance and intervention that keep streets safe and orderly.[32]

Similarly, the man who buys a gun to protect his home is more likely to turn it on himself or his family than on a burglar or robber.[33] Barred windows are a fire hazard, and burglar alarms a nuisance — 90 percent of all alarms are false, set off by unwitting family members, innocent neighbors, or pets.[34] And even the most reliable protective devices may stimulate greater fears by providing a constant reminder of the threat of crime. If a citizen resets a burglar alarm every time he leaves his house for the corner store, he can hardly avoid thinking about the risks that induced him to buy it. And the more often his burglar alarm goes off, the more often his neighbors are reminded of the risks of crime.

Insurance, too, may foster crime. Those who are insured may make fewer efforts to protect themselves, knowing they will be reimbursed for any losses.[35] With a decline in private efforts to control crime, and with no offsetting increase in publicly supported crime control efforts, opportunities for committing crimes, particularly property crimes, may well increase. And because some property crimes become violent, the pattern of violent crimes will also be influenced.

Eventually, as we all hunker down in our well-defended homes, confident that any losses will be covered by insurance and suspicious of those few who continue to use the streets, the basic fabric of the society will start to unravel. We will feel less responsible for helping one another and for establishing safe conditions in our communities. At that stage we will be in desperate straits indeed. Because of the direct effect of crime-created stress on the quality of life, and because of the indirect effects on crime levels and social cohesiveness of fearful reactions to crime, fear of crime is, by itself, a serious social problem. In our estimation, it merits as much attention as the problem of victimization.

This view influences our ideas about which crimes are serious, because not all crimes that result in serious victimization create widespread fear. Although people express worries about all kinds of crime, violent or potentially violent crimes are clearly the most feared. Some 40 percent of Americans report that they are "very worried" about being mugged, while far fewer are "very worried" about burglary or simple theft, even though victimization reports indicate that burglaries and thefts are five to seven times more frequent than robberies.[36] Districts that are widely regarded as high crime areas are those with high rates of violent crimes; the aggregate crime rates in these areas tend to be no higher than anywhere else.[37] And people who fear the prospects of a burglary often note that it is the possibility of a violent confrontation with the burglar that makes them so fearful.[38]

Clearly people's fears focus on the risks of physical violence rather than on financial losses, and their fears are disproportionate to the risks of victimization. Why are the fears disproportionately high? The answer to this question, of the sources of the sense of public danger, sheds additional light on the offenses and offenders that are the most important to control.

THE SENSE OF PUBLIC DANGER

Our peace of mind depends upon the good intentions of strangers. In numerous everyday actions we assume that the people we meet will obey the rules we ourselves obey. When walking down a crowded street, the average adult avoids looking at the people he passes and presumes they will pay little attention to him; when jostling onto a bus or maneuvering in traffic, we treat the people who walk or drive near us as though they were relatively predictable billiard balls rather than human beings with minds of their own. Moreover, we presume that others will treat us in the same way. As sociologist Erving Goffman has put it,

> In driving and walking, the individual conducts himself — or rather his vehicular shell — so that the direction, rate, and resoluteness of his proposed course will be readable . . . By providing this cultural prefigurement and committing himself to what it foretells, the individual makes himself into something that others can read and predict from; by employing this device at proper

strategic junctures — ones where his indicated course will be perceived as a promise or warning or threat but not as a challenge — he becomes something to which they can adapt without loss of self-respect.[39]

These rules seem to be necessary if people are to share a crowded environment with a minimum of fear and stress.

The illusion of predictability is shattered when one is robbed or assaulted. It is brought home clearly that at least some strangers do not play by the usual rules, and that others' actions are not so predictable and sensible as one may have thought. The cues that once indicated safety in a situation or place suddenly seem valid no longer. As a result, the cues themselves seem to inspire fear.

Nathan Glazer has pointed out that the graffiti on New York subway cars produce anxiety and fear in the rider:

> He is assaulted continuously, not only by evidence that every subway car has been vandalized, but by the inescapable knowledge that the environment he must endure for an hour or more a day is uncontrolled and uncontrollable, and that anyone can invade it to do whatever damage and mischief the mind suggests . . . While I do not find myself consciously making the connection between the graffiti makers and the criminals who occasionally rob, rape, assault, and murder passengers, the sense that all are part of one world of uncontrollable predators seems inescapable. Even if the graffitists are the least dangerous of these, their ever-present markings serve to persuade the passenger that, indeed, the subway is a dangerous place . . . [40]

Other small disturbances may also suggest a dangerous environment: unruly youngsters, dilapidated buildings, loud music, conspicuous use of alcohol or drugs. And there is evidence that these "incivilities" are more important in provoking fear of crime than the real risks of victimization. For example, the level of fear in fifteen Boston housing projects was strongly associated with the level of incivilities; there was no such correlation between crime rates and fear. Most of the tenants considered vandalism, teen gangs, and harassment to be the biggest crime problems in the project. Likewise, feelings of vulnerability among residents of Atlanta and Chicago were more closely associated with their perception of neighborhood problems such as barking dogs and trash on the streets than with reported crime rates.[41]

This phenomenon of minor incidents triggering fear of serious crime is not confined to urban areas. Small towns and suburbs may be even more likely to react to disorder. In a small California town residents suddenly became panicked about rampant crime in the streets. An examination of their complaints revealed that their concern stemmed from a marijuana arrest at the high school and from teenage activities such as cruising and hanging out. These offenses are not particularly serious by themselves, but they are tangible signs that all is not well in the neighborhood. When people are constantly reminded that their world is not fully under control, they begin to fear violence.

CONCLUSIONS

The crime problem can be considered as victimization, as fear, or as the sense of public danger. Each view adds to an overall conception of the problem by pointing to an element that can be separately managed. In many public policy deliberations about crime, victimization is emphasized over the other aspects of the problem. This is because victimization is tangible and concrete while the other aspects are more ephemeral, and because the most effective and only responsible way of reducing fear and the sense of public danger is to reduce the real victimization. In still other discussions, the crime problem is seen not as a complicated set of consequences of criminal victimization, but instead as a simple problem of justice — of enforcing current laws fairly and equitably without worrying too much about the social benefits of such activity.

Clearly, these conceptions of the crime problem differ. They suggest different priorities as to both objectives and methods of criminal justice policy. But what seems somewhat surprising and important is that no matter which perspective is adopted, certain dangerous offenders always seem to be at the center of the problem. If one thinks about crime as primarily a problem of victimization, then those who commit violent crimes become the most important targets. If one thinks about the problem as primarily one of fear, then those who commit crimes of violence among strangers are the most important targets. And if one thinks about the problem as the sense of public danger, the most important targets are the hardened offenders who commit crimes violently, often, and wantonly and who establish the background against which minor incivilities are perceived as major threats. Even if we view the crime problem as simple justice, dangerous offenders would probably be at the center. If an interest in justice focused attention on violent, premeditated acts, dangerous offenders would be the target. If justice focused on those who were particularly callous and unimpressed by social obligations, then persistent dangerous offenders would once again be central. As one circumnavigates the problem, different offenses and offenders come in and out of view, but what stays in view are determined and persistent offenders.

In our view, the crime problem is best seen as a composite of each of these varied dimensions: as victimization, as fear, as a sense of public danger lurking behind mere disorder, and as a problem of justice for victims, offenders, and the broader community. Much is included in this conception beyond dangerous offenders, but they are never wholly out of the picture and are often near the center.

2

Dangerous Offenders

TO MANY PEOPLE the crime problem is easily understood: it is created by dangerous people who scorn the rights of fellow citizens and who neither respect nor fear the law. The solution seems equally clear: imprison the dangerous until they are no longer a threat.[1]

The sheer crudity of this view offends others. Who should be considered dangerous? How can we recognize such people? And for how long will they be imprisoned?[2] Moreover, the confidence expressed by this view that crimes are the products of evil intentions rather than of enraging circumstances, and the indifference to the role of broad and unjust social processes in creating dangerous offenders, signal naiveté about the social misery that is swept into the criminal justice system.[3] And the casual recourse to imprisonment ignores the costs of creating vast buildings and complex bureaucracies whose sole purpose is to idle criminal offenders.[4]

Yet for all its crudity and for all its potential for political and rhetorical excess, the notion that *some portion* of the crime problem can be justly and effectively handled by concentrating imprisonment on dangerous offenders may reflect some important truths. In fact, the major error in viewing the crime problem as caused by dangerous offenders is probably in seeing it exclusively in these terms. Many criminal offenses may be produced by circumstances rather than evil intentions and by people who are quite ordinary in their values and orientations to the society.[5] Moreover, despite disappointments in the results of rehabilitation, the hope survives that dangerous offenders may be persuaded (through rehabilitation or deterrence) to abandon their criminal careers.[6] Thus we do not claim that we can solve the crime problem simply by incapacitating dangerous offenders.

But it would be an error to assume that all offenders are equally deserving of compassion or equally responsive to rehabilitation. For, if the system does not single out the dangerous offenders from all offenders, the dangerous ones will be treated more leniently and with greater optimism than they deserve, and the less serious offenders will be treated more harshly and with less optimism than is merited.[7] If this occurs, the criminal justice system will operate less justly and less economically than it otherwise could.

This chapter will place the idea of focusing on unusually dangerous offenders in the context of a broader view of crime, the criminal justice system, and alternative crime control policies. The reasons for reaching for this broader perspective are first, to find out what questions of justice arise if we focus on dangerous offenders; second, to tutor our intuitions about what portion of the crime problem and what portion of the workload of the criminal justice system involve this group; and third, to arrive at a tolerably just and practically useful definition of dangerous offenders.

CRIME, CRIMINAL LIABILITY, AND IDEOLOGY

Theories of crime have more than academic importance; beyond intellectual enlightenment, they guide social conceptions of just and effective responses to crime. If, for example, we considered that crime was caused by desperate poverty, unequal economic opportunity, or provocative circumstances, then we would think it unjust, as well as ineffective, to incapacitate the offenders. Such offenders would be nothing more than victims of circumstances. If, on the other hand, we located the engine of criminal offenses in the incorrigible character of offenders (and temporarily ignored, as either practically or morally irrelevant, the question of what shaped character) then incapacitation would make more sense and seem more just.

No matter how narrowly conceived, however, most empirical theories of crime eventually transcend even these broad domains and enter the realm of ideology, for there is something about the subject of crime and criminal punishment that engages our broadest ideological conceptions of human nature and the role of the state. Indeed, it is probably more accurate to view our favored theories of crime, criminal liability, and crime control as deriving from prior ideological commitments rather than from any special investigation of the nature of crime. Those who view humans as the products of their environments, and who deem the state a benefactor when it guarantees entitlements but a grave threat when it enforces social obligations, tend to think that crime is caused by circumstance and to urge that the society respond not by enforcing laws sternly but by expanding opportunities. On the other hand, those who believe that people fashion themselves and their deeds and that the state's fundamental role is to impose responsibilities designed to protect freedom for others view crime as the responsibility of the offender, to which the best response is a dose of punishment backed by the moral authority of the state. Anything less undermines the principles of the society and leaves its citizens vulnerable to those who have placed themselves outside the moral order.

We illustrate the close connections among theories of crime, notions of criminal responsibility, and ideology simply to acknowledge that any discussion of crime and control policy inevitably invokes these broad considerations. They cannot be kept out. They particularly intrude in any discussion that puts criminal offenders, and even more significantly, differences among offenders near the center of its concerns. Indeed, the very concepts of dangerous offenders and selective incapacitation strike at the heart of some liberal conceptions of crime. Selective policies seem to imply first, that offenders, not circumstances, cause crime; second, that individuals differ in their propensity for offending, and that these differences are large enough and permanent enough to be worth reflecting in the decisions of the criminal justice system; third, that broad social processes are causally insignificant or morally irrelevant in shaping these differential motivations for offending and should therefore be ignored; and fourth, that the risks to fairness or due process of focusing on dangerous offenders are either nonexistent, easily controlled, or small enough to be compensated for by other benefits.

We cannot wholly escape the apparent ideological bias inherent in investigating the potential of selective policies. But we can develop a theory of crime that allows us to talk about the concept of dangerous offenders without losing a sense that crimes may be caused by factors other than the evil intentions of bad people and that there may be many effective responses to crime in addition to imprisoning dangerous offenders. Our conception is that dangerous offenders are a noteworthy component of the crime problem, but that they are only a portion of the problem, that many offenders caught up in the criminal justice system are not in any important sense dangerous.

A CONCEPTION OF CRIMINAL OFFENDING

According to our conception, offenses are caused by three factors: the motivations of offenders, the opportunities for criminal offending, and their capacities to commit offenses. To a degree, one can think of motivation as an individual characteristic. People have stronger or weaker desires for economic gain, more or less passion to be expressed, and more or less commitment to living within a set of community obligations. But there is no reason to assume *a priori* that these characteristics are permanent, nor to assume that they are forced on people through inexorable social processes, rather than consciously acquired by individuals fashioning themselves from the material of their past experience. Whatever the exact machinery, we can imagine people as having broad intentions and purposes that not only define their general character but also guide their actions in specific circumstances.

Although the broad, lasting influences on character are the most commonly noted and debated, transient influences can also shape character. Temporary anger brought on by months of unemployment can both motivate and seem to justify crimes. A gang of criminally inclined friends can tempt a teenager into criminal activities for as long as he is in their company.[8] Stimulants can alter motivation for even briefer periods. Drugs, alcohol, even unusually provocative situations may all momentarily disinhibit otherwise responsible people.[9] Of course, drugs, alcohol, and provocative situations can act *consistently* as well as intermittently on an offender's motivation.[10] The point is that there are short-term as well as long-term influences on individuals' motivations.

While motivation and character can be conceived as internal and as under the individual's control to some extent, *opportunities* are external and are shaped primarily by broad social processes. Branch banks, convenience stores, all-night gas stations, and houses that are empty all day—all these increase the opportunities for robbery and burglary. High-rise apartments, which turn hallways into anonymous streets in every respect except accessibility to patrolling police, may broaden the opportunities for rapes, assaults, and robberies.[11] The shift from neighborhood bars in which the regulars keep peace through informal social controls to more anonymous bars in which only the bartender's sawed-off shotgun maintains order, or the increasing strife between divorced couples over joint property and child visitation rights create circumstances that spawn expressive violence.[12] Even if motivations for offending among the population remained constant, crime might increase as the result of broad social processes that expand opportunities for offenses.

Perhaps the most unfamiliar element in our conception of offending is the *capacity* of offenders, an element that is ordinarily obscured because it is close to the ideas of both motivation and opportunity. If the motivation is strong enough and the opportunity tempting enough, capacity disappears from the analysis. Moreover, given time, strong motivation will always create capacity. Still, one can think of the capacity to commit offenses as a separate factor. It exists in the general population through three different mechanisms. One is individual endowment. Some people are large and strong, others small and weak. Some are accustomed to violence, others are not.[13] Some are capable of conceiving and carrying out a complicated plan; others are uninterested in doing so or unable to. As in the case of character and motivation, traits or endowments are created by many different factors and are more or less permanent.

A second mechanism is personal investment in *general* capacities to commit offenses. This may be the implicit result of experience, or it may be consciously directed. People can learn how to become skilled offenders and develop the necessary abilities. They can learn how to "case" targets, how to buy a gun, how to pick locks, jimmy windows, or cut through glass; they can learn the best way to deploy a "stall" and a "dip" to pick pockets without risk in a crowded bus.

A third mechanism is the availability of criminal equipment. Many offenses require little equipment and others require equipment that is so valuable in legitimate uses that it is always available to anyone. Cars, butcher knives, and screwdrivers all fit into this category. But some equipment has so few legitimate uses and is so devastating in criminal use that it may be restricted or unavailable legally. Clear examples include machineguns and explosives. A controversial example is the handgun.[14]

Thus a conception of offending as the result of motivations, capacities, and opportunities leaves room for many different ideas about the causes of crime and effective social responses. Those who see crime as the result of social processes can point to the long-term factors that shape character and opportunity. Those who see crime as the product of individual will can find their preferred variables not only in offenders' intentions, but also in the preparations they make to commit crimes, and even in the ways that offenders use their own experience to strengthen their commitment to crime and weaken their inhibitions against it. Those who believe that crime can be attacked by changing the environment or by limiting the supply of criminogenic commodities such as guns, drugs, and alcohol can also find satisfaction in our conception. In any given criminal offense one can see the traces of many different causes.

IMPLICATIONS FOR CRIME CONTROL POLICIES

Viewing crime in these terms has important implications for ideas of just and plausibly effective crime control policies. Our conception states that crime is caused by many factors other than bad people. Provocative victims, stimulation by drugs, disinhibition from alcohol, easy opportunities, even broad social processes all may help create criminal offenses. This perspective suggests attacking crime on a very broad front. The criminal justice system can play an important role by restricting opportunities for offending, incapacitating people who commit offenses, and shaping character through forceful reminders of people's obligations to society. But other institutions and approaches can contribute to the solution as well. Improved economic performance, less discrimination in labor markets, better schooling, more effective mental health services, drug treatment, gun control policies, encouragement of private patrolling by community groups, even more streetlights — all may plausibly make a contribution to crime control.

Moreover, our conception suggests that for some offenses, the guilt or blameworthiness of offenders must be qualified. To the extent that circumstance, impulse, provocation, and social injustice help shape offenses, the justice of holding a particular offender morally responsible for the crime is called into doubt. Our conception of crime thus makes us keenly aware of the practical limitations and potential injustice of viewing the problem as primarily one of dangerous offenders who are consciously and determinedly evil.

On the other hand, our conception also leaves room for the notion that policies aimed at dangerous offenders can be both just and effective. In our conception dangerous offenders are unusual in terms of their motivations and capacities to commit offenses. Confronted by similar opportunities, dangerous offenders commit crimes more often than other offenders, to say nothing of ordinary citizens. Because dangerous offenders commit more than their share of crimes, they are especially and obviously important targets of practical crime control policies. But what is slightly less obvious is that an interest in justice might also compel a special focus on these offenders. To see why this is true, it is valuable to step back and consider the concept of guilt in the context of legal traditions and our conception of criminal offending.

In our legal tradition guilt and criminal responsibility are tied not only to acts but also to intentions. *Mens rea* requirements, diminished competence defenses, such as insanity, and the juvenile justice system, in which the concept of guilt has been abolished in deference to the immaturity of the offenders, all testify to the crucial role of intention in our concept of guilt.[15] In criminal law the concept of strict liability is quite rare: to condemn someone as a criminal, we need to know that the person willed a criminal act as well as that the act occurred.

To those accustomed to thinking that acts rather than character constitute the proper basis for punishment, the preoccupation of traditional law with questions of intent seems anomalous. After all, what role can intention play in defining blameworthiness if it is not linked to an interest in moral character? Even more problematic to this school of thought is the fact that traditional and modern laws make an attempt or a conspiracy to commit an offense subject to criminal punishment just as much as a substantive offense.[16] In short, our statutes make criminal *intention* both necessary and sufficient for criminal prosecution, but a harmful *act* is neither necessary nor sufficient for a judgment of guilt.

Of course, an act is always involved in a criminal case. In a substantive case, an act constituting a crime in itself must be shown. In an attempt or conspiracy case, the act is necessary to show that the person's intentions were more than a passing thought or fantasy. But exactly what role do specific acts play in supporting moral judgments of guilt?

One way of looking at the question is that acts are necessary, not to carry the full burden of justifying punishment, but instead to serve as an objective basis for discovering something about people's intentions and character. Further, it is the judgment about intentions, and what intentions reveal about character, that justifies criminal punishment for acts. Acts are important because they reveal character, and it is character that must be understood in judging guilt and innocence.[17]

No doubt, this view goes much too far in emphasizing character. But it suggests that an exclusive concern with acts is too extreme as well. Indeed, it seems clear as we observe the workings of the criminal justice system that determination of intention as a guide to character is central to establishing criminal responsibility. The Vera Institute's study of the disposition of felony arrests in New York City indicated that many technically illegal acts that were formally charged as assaults or robberies were in fact very ambiguous occurrences. The defendant's guilt was in doubt, not because there was any question that he or she had committed the act, but because there was significant doubt about whether the act revealed a criminal intention and character.[18] The robberies sometimes involved the repossession of property in a collapsing marriage. The assault charges emerged from fights in which the only way to decide who had been the offender and who the victim was by observing who was still standing at the end. So in many crimes the intentions of offenders do not justify moral condemnation.

If a clear-cut, sustained evil intention is necessary and sufficient for a judgment of guilt, then our theory of crime causation offers offenders many opportunities to escape such judgments by offering explanations that emphasize causes other than their intentions. The offender may claim that the offense emerged from a temporary rage and that it was not characteristic of him. Or he may claim that the circumstances were so provocative that nearly anyone would have behaved as he did. At the extreme, of course, a person could claim to be a product of his social environment without any intentions of his own and thereby escape judgments of guilt in the same way that insane people and juveniles now do. In short, our view of crime — pushed far enough — allows there to be many offenses without any criminal offenders.

Only the most radical social determinists would go this far toward erasing the concept of individual responsibility. On the other hand, only the strictest retributivists would find all individuals who had committed a given act equally guilty. In adjudicating guilt the criminal justice system must discern exactly what role the intentions of offenders played in shaping a criminal incident and in judging what those intentions suggest about the person's moral character.

In this view of justice dangerous offenders are important not only because they are the most *active* offenders, but also because they are the *guiltiest*. They have committed criminal acts frequently enough to have clearly revealed their character. After a fourth or fifth offense, the argument that the offender has values and character similar to other people in the society and was simply unlucky enough to find himself in tempting or provocative circumstances must yield to the view that the offender is much more willing than others to violate social rules. Such offenders have set themselves outside the moral order and exposed themselves to judgments of guilt.

An interest in justice thus joins the obvious practical interest in making dangerous offenders an important focus of criminal justice policy. The exact importance of this group depends both on how different they are from other offenders and on how large their contribution is to the overall crime problem and the workload of the criminal justice system. These issues can be resolved only by reference to quantitative, empirical evidence.

THE STRUCTURE OF CRIMINAL OFFENDING

Conventional views of crime include different images of criminal offenders. Perhaps the most important distinction is between "honest citizens" who never commit serious offenses and "criminals" who do. But we also make some distinctions among criminals. Even with murderers we distinguish quite easily among an enraged wife who ends her husband's bullying with a desperate thrust of a kitchen knife, a psychopath who murders women who remind him of a lost adolescent love, and an armed robber who kills his victims to avoid being identified. We can also distinguish among offenders who rely on violence, such as robbers and extortionists; those who are willing to use violence if necessary, such as street muggers and some burglars; and those who go to great lengths to avoid violence, such as pickpockets and con men. And we can distinguish between those who persist in criminal offending—becoming "career criminals" or "criminal recidivists"—from those whose involvement in crime seems more accidental and transient.

Although such distinctions are important, in the past our imaginations have far outstripped and therefore confused our real empirical knowledge. Fortunately, in recent years we have learned a great deal about patterns of offending. It is now possible to find out what the different sorts of offenders are and how they are distributed in the general population. The new data describe individual rates and patterns of offending.[19] This characteristic—denoted as λ by those studying patterns of offending—resembles our concept of an individual's willingness to commit offenses because it is a personal and permanent feature of an individual's character.[20] In fact, however, λ is simply an empirical observation of an individual's rate of offending. If our theory is correct, this rate bears the traces of a great many factors besides individual character, including opportunity, provocation, and broad social processes. But character is increasingly visible as λ takes on a distinctive, measurable shape. Since the concept of λ is so important to the empirical work in this area, and since the empirical work is so important to the overall case for a selective focus, it is worth considering some of the conceptual and technical aspects of measuring λ.

MEASURING PATTERNS OF OFFENDING

The observed pattern of offending is a *rate:* its numerator is an estimate of the number of certain kinds of offenses committed, and its denominator is an estimate of the time an offender was both active and not in prison. Conceptual and practical difficulties arise in measuring both elements.

The crucial conceptual problem in finding the numerator of λ is deciding what offenses should be counted. On one hand, one can argue for including all offenses, since we want to measure overall rates of offending. On the other hand, this approach is obviously absurd since it would implicitly equate a murder with a petit larceny. The obvious solution is to develop a weighting scheme that scores offenses according to their contribution to the sense of public danger. The simplest idea is to distinguish violent from property crimes, and felonies from misdemeanors, but these distinctions pick up only a few of the dimensions that make some crimes worse than others. A more complicated idea would be to use a weighting scheme such as the Sellin-Wolfgang index, which incorporates dimensions reflecting the seriousness of victimization in a more sensitive way than the legal categories of offenses.[21] But this approach misses the relationship of the offender to the victim, and the location of the offense —both of which seem to influence the extent to which the sense of danger generalizes from the victim to others in the society. In the end, there is no very satisfactory solution to this question of which offenses to count and how much. Even if we could solve the analytic problem of deciding which attributes of criminal offenses made them better or worse in aggravating the overall crime problem, we would still face the problem of empirically characterizing actual offenses in these terms. And that is well beyond the capacities of current data bases.[22]

This observation points out the *practical* problems in measuring the numerator of λ. Broadly speaking, one can use convictions, arrests, or self-report data. Each method has strengths and weaknesses, and none is wholly satisfactory. In principle, convictions might seem the most appropriate, for those are the only offenses that one can confidently attribute to particular offenders. This observation has great force when we are concerned with specific individuals, but it has less force in a research enterprise that seeks to develop estimates of individual criminal activity. Since convictions account for only a small part of all crimes committed, and since convictions are influenced by plea bargaining and exclusion of evidence, one can argue that convictions give quite a distorted view of individual offending.

Arrests come closer to accounting for all crimes, though they actually account for only a tiny fraction of all reported crimes.[23] They have the disadvantage of offering fewer assurances that a specific offender actually committed a given act, though legally the police must have some basis for thinking that the arrested person committed the crime.[24]

Self-reports come closest to accounting for all the crimes committed. Moreover, since the offender claims the offenses for himself, there is less difficulty in knowing whether crimes have been accurately attributed. The problem with self-reports is that offenders may not remember or report accurately.[25] One can check their validity many different ways, but one can never completely exclude the possibility that offenders are telling the truth about crimes that can be checked, and either lying or forgetting about crimes for which there are no records.[26]

While the numerator of λ presents obvious measurement problems, the challenge in measuring the denominator is a little more subtle. Obviously, we need to have a sense of the time available to an offender to commit the offenses. Equally obviously, some parts of the offender's life should be excluded from this calculation. It would be foolish to include periods of imprisonment or the times when an offender was either too young or too old to commit offenses. As a practical matter, one must measure this rate of offending for some population, and it seems foolish to measure rates of offending in the general population when what really interests us is the criminal population. By a series of quite natural and sensible steps, then, we arrive at a concept of an active criminal population with a well-defined rate of offending that waxes and wanes over the course of a given criminal career.

This image may be correct for an important subset of offenders. But many offenses occur because of provocative circumstances or temporary aberrations in the offender's character rather than from the durable intentions of a practiced offender; in such cases the image of a criminal career seems quite inappropriate. For example, a fairly ordinary person, enraged by his long period of unemployment and desperate to clothe his family, starts stealing from stores, but he carries a gun and winds up threatening a storekeeper who confronts him as he leaves the store with a sweater tucked under his coat. When did this accidental or temporarily deranged offender become a criminal? How long was his career? What rates of offending characterized his career while it existed?

These are not idle questions. We can imagine a continuous distribution of motivations and capabilities to commit offenses in the general population ranging from very low (but never zero) among the decent citizens to very high among the criminal recidivists, and we can imagine that these motivations and capabilities change over time as a function of age and experience in committing offenses. The aggregate pattern of offending resulting from this sort of distribution would include many offenses committed by people who are criminal offenders in anyone's definition of the word and who are so active that their rates of offending and their careers are well defined. But many other offenses will be caused by people whose motivations are quite ordinary. Moreover, some of these ordinary people with very low propensities to offend will show what appear to be short careers and very high rates of offending, while others with identical underlying propensities to offend will have very long careers with very low rates of offending.

One can demonstrate this with a very simple simulation. We imagined five offenders, each with a 2 percent probability of committing a crime in any given month over a twenty-year period. We then simulated their crime careers with a table of random numbers and got the following results. One offender committed his first crime six years into his "career" and his last with nine years still to run, thus concentrating four offenses in five years. He apparently had a career of five years and a rate of offending of about 0.8. A second offender committed only two crimes in his twenty-year career — one in his second year, and one in his twentieth, with a gap of over eighteen years. His career seemed eighteen years long, and his rate of offending was about 0.1. A little arithmetic shows that about 40 percent of these very low-rate offenders will commit two or more crimes within a single month at some point in their career. If we keep in mind that many thousands of people have odds like these, then it is clearly possible that low-probability offenders will occasionally look like high-rate offenders even when we have perfectly accurate information about actual rates of offending. The concepts of a rate of offending and of a criminal career are not particularly well defined for low-rate offenders who will nonetheless sometimes appear in the criminal justice system as criminal recidivists.

These observations indicate that in defining and measuring λ, and particularly its denominator, we have a choice: we can estimate it for a *portion* of the offending population for which these parameters can be relatively well defined (leaving open the question of what proportion of all crime and all criminal offenders such offenders represent); or we can estimate it for "all" criminal offenders (understanding that the estimate will be badly defined but confident that we have accounted for all crimes). For both practical and conceptual purposes, it seems best to adopt the first strategy: that is, to estimate λ and career length for a limited portion of the offending population. That allows us to focus attention on recidivist offenders who are likely to appear in the criminal justice system and for whom the terms seem well suited.

EMPIRICAL ESTIMATES

Researchers have resolved the measurement issues in different ways and have applied their techniques to different data sets. Inevitably, they get different results. Here we are concerned with what the research can tell us about the average rate of offending in the criminal population, the distribution of rates of offending, and existing patterns in the rates and types of offending. None of these issues has been resolved by unimpeachable empirical evidence. Indeed, the estimates are currently quite uncertain. We are likely to learn more about what is wrong with current estimates, and what better estimates would be, in the near future. Still, for now, we would like to offer our judgments as clearly and straightforwardly as possible.

Table 2 presents adjusted estimates of average rates of offending for two overlapping segments of the criminal population: the general population of offenders (everyone who has been arrested at least once) and the criminal recidivists (those who have been arrested twice or more).[27] Our best estimate is that the average rates of offending for the recidivists is nine to fourteen Part I crimes per year (auto theft, larceny, burglary, assault, robbery, rape, or murder). This is about three times our estimate of the rate for the general population of offenders. The recidivists commit about two or three violent offenses per year and about four times that many property offenses. The general population of offenders commits less than one violent offense per year and from one to five property offenses.

From one vantage point, the estimates seem high. The conclusion that, on average, criminal offenders commit offenses at the rate of several per year seems to support the common view that criminal offenders are frequent recidivists and are likely to continue committing offenses well beyond any ordinary standards of tolerable conduct. From a different perspective, however, the estimates seem quite low. If one imagines, for example, that an offender makes his living from crime, the rate of offending appears too low. After all, even twenty property crimes a year, each yielding several hundred dollars, falls far short of generating a living wage.[28] The estimates also seem low when used to justify the cost of prison. A prison cell is now estimated to cost roughly $36,000 to construct and $9,000 per year to operate.[29] If our estimates are correct, this amount buys for society about six fewer crimes per year (assuming a full incapacitation effect and no effect from deterrence or rehabilitation). This might be worth the price if we were talking about robberies in which people were seriously injured. But in fact, we are talking primarily about

Table 2. Consistent estimates of rates of offending.

Estimate[a]	Index offenses	Property offenses	Violent offenses
Mean annual offense rates for offenders arrested once or more			
Wolfgang, Figlio, and Sellin, 1972	4.2	3.6	0.6
	5.6	4.8	0.8
Greenberg, 1975	4.0	—	—
	5.4		
Shinnar and Shinnar, 1975	5.0	—	—
	11.0		
Williams, 1979	3.0	1.0	0.4
	4.4	3.4	1.0
Approx. range	3–6	1–5	0.5–1.0
Mean annual offense rates for offenders arrested twice or more			
Boland and Wilson, 1978	9.2	—	—
	12.2		
Collins, 1977	12.6	—	—
Blumstein and Cohen, 1979	10.2	7.9	2.4
	13.6	10.5	3.2
Peterson, Braiker, and Polich, 1980	~13	~11	2.1
Approx. range	9–14	8–11	2–3

a. The studies listed here are cited in full in note 27 to this chapter.

minor property offenses such as larceny and car theft. With respect to violent crimes, an additional year of imprisonment for the general criminal population buys a reduction of less than one offense per year. And it is important to keep in mind that this includes drunken fights in which bruises are the most serious injuries.[30]

These numbers have cooled the enthusiasm of those who advocated *general* incapacitation as a crime control strategy.[31] Although our estimates of average rates of offending seem shocking when held against ordinary standards of conduct, they seem much less compelling when considered against the image of violent criminals who are so active that it is worth spending tens of thousands of dollars a year to keep them away from us.

The fact that the estimates of offending for the criminal recidivist population are so much higher than for the general population of offenders indicates that rates of offending may be quite unevenly distributed. Presumably the rates of offending for many people in the general population of offenders must be much lower than one per year. And it is this population of offenders that disappears from the accounting when we look only at criminal recidivists. But because estimated rates of offending are so much higher for criminal recidivists, we are forced to conclude either that there are a great many low-rate offenders or that the high-rate offenders commit offenses at very high rates, or some combination of the two. Otherwise the differences between the two different segments would not be as great.

Fortunately, we do not have to rely on this indirect method to find out about the distribution of rates of offending. Direct evidence backs up what criminal justice officials have long suspected: that a vastly disproportionate number of crimes are committed by a relatively small number of very active offenders. Put in more technical language, the distribution of rates of offending has a very large variance, and the distribution is skewed in a way that produces a very long right tail, representing some unusually active offenders.

The shape of this distribution should not be unexpected. As early as the 1930s social psychologists were noting that many forms of human behavior, ranging from speeding to the depth of genuflection in Catholic churches, approximated this distribution.[32] More recently, investigators have discovered that this distribution describes drinking practices in the general population of most countries and drug use patterns among adolescents.[33] So it is not particularly surprising that the distribution of rates of offending assumes this general shape. What is surprising is how skewed the distribution of offending is, how concentrated criminal offending turns out to be and how active the high-rate offenders are.

Empirical information from two different sources lends support to the hypothesis of a very uneven and very skewed distribution of offense rates. One is some studies of cohorts of young men born in Philadelphia, conducted by Marvin Wolfgang and his colleagues.[34] In the first pioneering study, tracing the criminal records of those born in 1945 until their eighteenth year, the researchers found that 6 percent of this cohort had five or more criminal offenses and that these offenders accounted for 52 percent of all offenses committed by the cohort.[35] Moreover, after controlling for the seriousness of specific offenses, the chronic recidivists became even more significant: they accounted for 82 percent of the robberies, 71 percent of the murders, 73 percent of the rapes, 70 percent of the aggravated assaults, and 63 percent of all index offenses.[36] A similar concentration of offending was observed for a second cohort, born in 1958. Of those youths, 8 percent were arrested five or more times and accounted for 61 percent of the cohort's total offenses.[37] Looking only at serious offenses, these chronic redicivists accounted for 73 percent of the robberies, 61 percent of the murders, 76 percent of the rapes, 65 percent of aggravated assaults, and 68 percent of the index offenses.[38]

The second source of information is surveys of prisoners in California, Michigan, and Texas, conducted by the Rand Corporation.[39] The prison surveys complement the cohort studies in two important ways. First, they rely on self-reports rather than arrest records. The resulting estimates should be closer to actual levels of criminality because of the elimination of the systematic downward bias introduced by the inability of the police to make arrests for most crimes. Second, by focusing on an imprisoned population, the prison surveys allow a closer look at the behavior of those at the extreme end of the distribution in the cohort studies (the chronic recidivists), for it is they who are most likely to be in prison. After we have satisfied ourselves that rates of offending are quite unevenly distributed in the general population, the prison surveys operate like a magnifying lens to look very closely at the worst offenders in the overall offending population.

Close examination of the recidivist population reveals an unexpected result: the distribution of rates of offending seems to be remarkably skewed *even among those who commit offenses serious enough and frequently enough to put them in prison.* Figure 2 shows the distribution of rates of robbery for the California prison sample. Table 3 presents information on the difference between the median and the mean rates of offending for about a dozen different crimes, indicating that skewed distributions are not limited to robbery. The larger the difference between the median (meaning that half of the sample commit crimes at a lower rate and half at a higher rate) and the mean (the average of rates of offending in the sample), the more skewed the distribution, and, in turn, the more concentrated the rate of offending. As one might expect, Table 3 indicates that drug dealing and burglary are more concentrated than attempted murder or use of violence, such as cutting or shooting a victim.

Equally impressive is how active the high-rate offenders seem to be. According to these surveys, some offenders are committing not ten or twenty robberies a year, but more than fifty.[40] These rates are so high that the benefits to society just from incapacitating these criminals, not to mention the practical interests in deterrence or rehabilitation or a moral

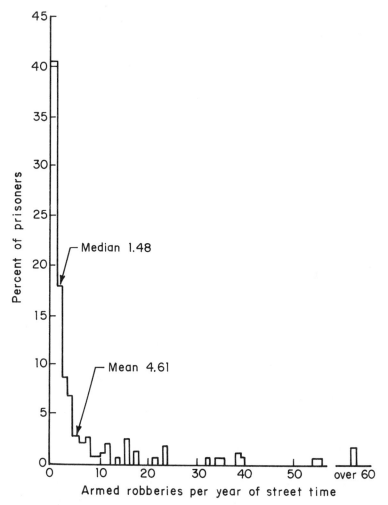

Figure 2   The distribution of rates of armed robbery. (From Mark A. Peterson, Harriet B. Braiker, and Suzanne M. Polich, *Who Commits Crimes: A Survey of Prison Inmates,* Oelgeschlager, Gunn, and Hain, 1981.)

interest in retribution, would justify their imprisonment. Their absolute level of offending, as well as their share in the total volume of offenses, is remarkable. In sum, the prison surveys indicate that there is a very active right tail of the distribution of offenders, even when we are looking at the most serious and persistent right tail of the distribution of the general population. Also, those in the right tail of the distribution commit crimes at very high rates indeed.

Table 3. Median and mean annual offense rates among California prisoners committing the offense.

Offense	Median	Mean
Armed robbery	1.46	5.16
Cons	2.83	11.44
Burglary	2.74	14.15
Forgery	1.54	4.87
Auto theft	1.07	3.90
Drug sales	19.00	115.00
Shot/cut	0.86	2.04
Threat	1.37	3.19
Aggravated assault	0.84	2.81
Attempted murder	0.86	1.60
Forcible rape	0.72	2.89

Source: Mark A. Peterson, Harriet B. Braiker, and Suzanne M. Polich, *Who Commits Crimes* (Cambridge, Mass.: Oelgeschlager, Gunn, and Hain, 1981), p. 24.

This empirical evidence strongly supports the justice and efficacy of policies that focus on unusually dangerous offenders. So far we have neglected a key part of this argument, however: the relationship between high *rates* and dangerous *patterns* of offending. To many, the two are synonymous precisely because high rates of offending reveal that the offenders are dangerous and wicked; no further consideration is needed to make the judgment. Others reserve the idea of dangerousness for those who commit violent offenses but assume that anyone callous enough to commit a single violent offense or repeated property offenses is also callous enough to commit violence repeatedly. From this point of view, once it is established that a person is a repeat offender, it is also established that he is capable of violence, and therefore dangerous.

Other people, however, want to reserve the designation of dangerous for those who commit violent crimes repeatedly, without assuming that repeated property offenses or a single instance of violent crime necessarily indicate violent tendencies. They imagine that there are many types of offenders, some involved in more or less accidental violence, some involved in repeated property or nonviolent offenses, and some involved in repeated acts of violence. It is only the last category that they would describe as dangerous.

The empirical evidence on individual patterns of offending is again drawn from two different sources. One involves the examination of arrest records to determine whether offenders tend to specialize in one kind of crime.[41] The method relies on the construction of "crime switch matrices" showing the probability that an arrest for one type of offense will be followed by a second arrest for the same offense. If those who are originally arrested for robbery, for example, are rearrested for robbery rather than burglary, car theft, or pickpocketing, crime specialization is demonstrated: violent offenders remain violent offenders, and property offenders remain property offenders.

These analyses have consistently shown little relationship between first and subsequent arrests.[42] Table 4 presents a typical crime switch matrix. If criminals always specialized in specific offenses, then each cell on the diagonal would read 1.000, indicating that the probability of a second arrest being for the same offense as the first arrest was 100 percent. The table indicates only weak support for the crime specialization hypothesis. The likelihood of offenders being arrested the second time for the exact offense charged in their first arrest is very low, rising above 0.500 only with the broad category of "other" offenses. If we group together robbery and aggravated assault as violent offenses, and burglary and larceny as property offenses, there is a weak tendency for property offenders to specialize in nonviolent offenses, but no tendency for violent offenders to restrict themselves to violence. More then three-quarters of the subsequent arrests of property offenders are for property crimes, but less than half of the second arrests for violent offenders are for violence. Of course, this method is very crude, but it does suggest that

Table 4. Transition matrix of crime type switches between consecutive arrests (all cohorts combined).

	Probability that next arrest is for:					
Last arrest	Robbery	Aggravated assault	Burglary	Larceny	Auto theft	All others
Robbery	.301	.132	.098	.098	.037	.334
Aggravated assault	.131	.211	.080	.084	.038	.456
Burglary	.090	.082	.333	.149	.039	.305
Larceny	.080	.083	.100	.286	.037	.415
Auto theft	.112	.119	.052	.104	.261	.351
Others	.109	.078	.081	.103	.035	.591

Source: Alfred Blumstein and Jacqueline Cohen, "Estimation of Individual Crime Rates from Arrest Records," *Journal of Criminal Law and Criminology* 70 (1979), 582.

the underlying individual patterns of offending are more complicated than a simple specialization hypothesis would indicate.

Recently the Rand prison surveys have provided a new opportunity to explore individual patterns of offending. Ironically, this research provides evidence both of greater specialization than was suggested by previous studies of arrest records and of a general tendency for some of the highest-rate offenders to commit many crimes and the most violent crimes. The Rand conclusions are based on both an empirical result and a theory of criminal development. The empirical result is that the careers of prison inmates do not represent all possible combinations of offense types. The survey investigated eight different offenses — assault, robbery, burglary, drug dealing, theft, auto theft, fraud, and forgery or credit card swindles. If patterns of offending were truly random, the prisoners would have been distributed widely over the 256 possible combinations of offenses.[43] In fact, however, 61 percent of the offenders could be classified in only ten distinct patterns, so their patterns of offending showed some structure; their present activity bore traces of their past.[44]

The theory of criminal offending advanced by the Rand researchers is that criminals develop their skills and progress through different degrees of deviance. This hypothesis was suggested by the observation that offenders who committed the worst offenses had also commonly committed the less serious ones, while those offenders who committed the less serious offenses had not usually committed the most serious ones. The offenses seemed to be ordered hierarchically, with offenders advancing through minor offenses to reach serious crimes. These results were similar to empirical observations of patterns of drug use and other forms of social deviance.[45]

The authors were motivated to determine whether they could describe unique patterns of offending in the prison population they observed. They began by defining the ten patterns that accounted for most offenders. Figure 3 presents these categories and their defining elements. They then calculated rates of offending for the different types of offenders, as shown in Table 5. They also checked the stability of these patterns by examining the probability that an offender in a given pattern in one period would remain in that pattern (or move to a more dangerous pattern) in the next period. Table 6 presents these results.

Taken together, the results reported in these tables lend substantial support to the notions that distinct types of offenders exist and that some offenders develop as criminals over time. The patterns of development tend to be stable, and if they change, they tend to escalate rather than

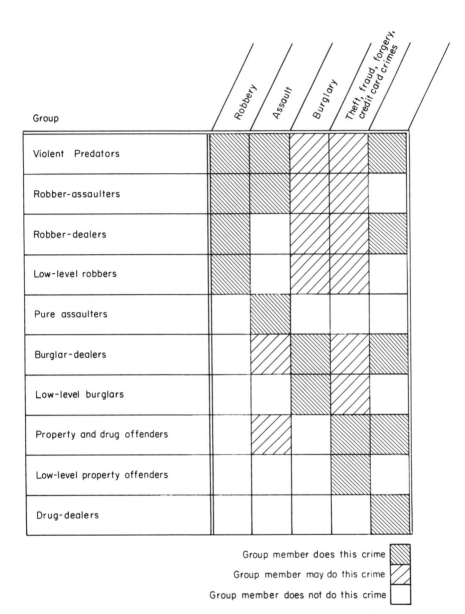

Figure 3   The definition of hierarchical subgroups of offenders. (From Jan M. Chaiken and Marcia R. Chaiken, *Varieties of Criminal Behavior*, Rand, 1982.)

Table 5. Comparison of high-rate offenders among crime complexes, annualized crime rate, 90th percentile.[a]

Variety of criminal behavior	Robbery			Assault	Burglary	Theft	Forgery, credit cards	Fraud	Drug dealing
	All[b]	Business	Person						
Violent predators	135	96	82	18	516	517	200	278	4088
Robber-assaulters	65	46	38	14	315	726	27	293	—
Robber-dealers	41	60	32	—	377	407	255	106	2931
Low-level robbers	10	15	9	3.5	206	189	78	811	—
Pure assaulters	—	—	—	6	—	—	—	—	—
Burglar-dealers	—	—	—	—	113	406	274	64	2890
Low-level burglars	—	—	—	—	105	97	62	36	—
Property and drug offenders	—	—	—	9	—	663	283	264	3302
Low-level property offenders	—	—	—	—	—	560	486	1160	—
Drug dealers	—	—	—	—	—	—	—	—	3035
Significant difference across varieties? (all crime rates considered)[c]	Yes	Yes	Yes	Yes	Yes	Yes	No	No	Yes

Source: Jan Chaiken and Marcia Chaiken, *Varieties of Criminal Behavior* (Santa Monica, Calif.: Rand, 1982), 56.

a. Ten percent of the respondents in the crime variety commit the crime at or above the rate indicated in the table (a different 10 percent for each crime).

b. "All" robbery includes, along with business and person robbery, robberies reported as outgrowths of burglary that could not be classified as either business or person.

c. Significance test is by grouped χ^2 at the .01 level. The test does not refer to the 90th percentiles. Respondents who did not commit the crime are excluded in the test.

Table 6. Forward transition matrix: percentages of offenders in various categories whose criminal behavior changed over a four-year period.[a]

Variety of criminal behavior three and four years prior to measurement period	Variety of criminal behavior during two years preceding measurement period											
	Violent predators	Robber-assaulters	Robber-dealers	Low-level robbers	Pure assaulters	Burglar-dealers	Low-level burglars	Property and drug offenders	Low-level property offenders	Drug dealers	Locked up	Not doing these crimes
Violent predators	68	2	7	2	0	3	0	0	0	0	5	13
Robber-assaulters	20	49	0	13	2	2	0	2	4	0	0	7
Robber-dealers	13	2	53	2	0	3	0	8	5	5	0	10
Low-level robbers	12	8	11	49	0	3	4	0	1	1	0	11
Pure assaulters	0	0	0	6	56	6	6	0	0	6	0	22
Burglar-dealers	14	2	7	0	0	64	2	2	1	3	0	4
Low-level burglars	3	1	3	5	1	16	55	1	3	1	0	14
Property and drug offenders	8	2	12	0	0	16	0	45	2	8	0	6
Low-level property offenders	3	2	1	4	1	6	15	4	49	1	0	15
Drug dealers	1	0	7	0	0	12	1	6	3	68	0	4
Locked up	0	0	0	0	0	1	0	17	0	33	17	17
Not doing these crimes	1	1	2	5	2	4	9	2	8	6	0	61

Source: Jan Chaiken and Marcia Chaiken, *Varieties of Criminal Behavior* (Santa Monica, Calif.: Rand, 1982), p. 38.
a. Percentages add to 100 percent across rows.

decline (at least until aging takes over). More importantly, they suggest there is a hard core of offenders, the "violent predators," who commit *all* offenses at much higher rates than other offenders and who loom particularly large among all violent offenders.

The existence of the violent predator category may explain why the patterns observed in arrest reports seem so random. Since these offenders are very active, they account for a large number of arrests for both violent crimes and property crimes. If we look at patterns of arrest, we will see that they are strongly influenced by the violent predators, who are sometimes arrested for one sort of offense and sometimes for another. As long as violent predators remain in the analysis, the picture of offending is quite confused. Once they are set aside as a special group that commits all offenses at high rates, however, one begins to see specialists. There are occasional robbers, pure assaulters, burglars, and property offenders, as well as violent predators. Interestingly, none of these specialists seem to commit offenses with anything like the frequency of violent predators. So there is a quantitative aspect to the increasing deviance as well as qualitative aspect.

The developmental hypothesis is an intriguing explanation of the patterns of offending and is quite consistent with the conception of criminal offending we have presented. Another explanation of the observed patterns, however, puts more empasis on the special capacity for violence. In this view some offenders have a propensity for violence (whether expressive or instrumental) and some have a propensity for property offenses (largely instrumental, though occasionally expressive, particularly in juvenile offenses). Some have a propensity for both, and for them there is a potentiating effect: both propensities become stronger than they otherwise would be. This hypothesis is consistent with the observed data. Moreover, it is slightly more consistent with the reported finding that the violent predators are young, averaging twenty-three years old.[46] If high-rate offending is the result of a developmental process, one would expect the violent predators to be older, although one could argue that twenty-three is certainly old enough to have completed a deviant developmental process.

The structure of offending sketched above, that is, relatively low average rates of offending even within the recidivist population, a large variance in rates of offending within the criminal population, and a group of violent predators who commit all sorts of offenses at much higher rates than other offenders, is not necessarily a social constant. Conceivably, the structure may be affected by criminal justice policies. It is significant that the Texas prison population shows much lower overall rates of offending than the Michigan and California samples and contains fewer very high-rate offenders.[47]

In sum, what seems constant is a skewed distribution of deviance: a small minority generally accounts for a substantial majority of deviant conduct. The average level of deviance and the level of deviance by the most deviant members of the community seem less constant.

DANGEROUS OFFENDERS AND
THE CRIMINAL JUSTICE SYSTEM

Not all offenses are swept into the criminal justice system. The portion that is included depends on the vagaries of citizen reporting and the operations of police and prosecutors. With the offenses comes offenders —some active, dangerous, and determined, and others intermittent and accidental. How well the criminal justice system catches and holds in its nets the unusually dangerous offenders, and how large a portion of their work concerns dangerous offenders are our next subjects.

Our starting assumption is that all chronic recidivists and violent predators are eventually caught. It is possible that some active and remarkably skilled offenders escape capture, but this seems exceedingly unlikely. One researcher, who interviewed dozens of offenders, both free and imprisoned, reported that none knew or had even heard of active offenders who had escaped imprisonment, much less arrest.[48] Even if such offenders did exist, their contribution to the overall crime problem would be relatively small, for much of the observed crime is accounted for by their less skilled colleagues.[49]

We can also assume that dangerous offenders appear in the system repeatedly. Anyone as active as the Rand study's violent predators provide many opportunities for arrest and prosecution. Moreover, as they become known, they are increasingly vulnerable to detection. Finally, we can assume that such offenders are dealt with rather harshly, for the arguments in favor of concentrating attention on dangerous offenders are far more obvious to those who operate the system than to those outside. In fact, all studies of prosecutorial and judicial decision making indicate that offenders' prior records influence the officials' discretionary choices.[50]

It seems reasonable to assume that dangerous offenders contribute a great deal to the workload of the criminal justice system and that they are given special attention. An apparent implication, then, is that the system is already well focused on dangerous offenders, and little more can be done to enhance selectivity. But even if all of our assumptions are true, this conclusion is not necessarily warranted. For the issue is not simply whether the system snares dangerous offenders, gives them extra attention, and deals with them harshly. Instead, *the issue is whether the system deals with them as often and as harshly as their conduct warrants*. And here one might reasonably have some doubts. What kindles doubts are the findings noted above, which show that these offenders are very active, and much more active than others. Consequently, it is not enough that they get a *little* more attention from the criminal justice system; in a just system their absolute and relative rates of offending would warrant much greater prominence. Anything less indicates that they are getting away with offenses more often than their less active colleagues and that the system is biased in the wrong direction.

The uncertainty about whether the system is now biased against or in favor of dangerous offenders has a great deal to do with confusion about two different probabilities. One probability is whether dangerous offenders will be caught and imprisoned within a given period of time. That probability is very high, which encourages those who believe that the system is already sharply focused on dangerous offenders. But that probability is high partly because the dangerous offenders give the system many opportunities to arrest them. A different probability is whether an offender will be arrested, prosecuted, and convicted *for a given offense*. Arguably, it is *this* probability that is relevant in deciding how the system is biased, for offenses, with some evidence of bad motivations, provide the justification for social punishment. And this probability could conceivably be considerably lower for high-rate offenders than for their less active fellows, and still result in the high-rate offenders turning up very frequently in the criminal justice system.

Indeed, three apparently inconsistent statements could all be true: 1) that dangerous offenders show up in the criminal justice system far more frequently than anyone else; 2) that nonetheless they constitute but a small fraction of the workload of the criminal justice system; and 3) that they are less likely to be arrested for any given offense than much less active offenders. The hypothesis that could make these propositions true is that the rate of offending is remarkably skewed and that the probability of arrest, prosecution, and conviction decreases as a function of an individual's rate of offending. In effect, the operations of the system dampen, but do not entirely obscure, the great differences among offenders. Those who wish to argue that the system needs no greater selectivity can point to the fact that the differences among offenders are not entirely blotted out and that the active offenders are caught and punished. Those who argue for greater selectivity can point to the fact that the system dampens the differences among offenders when it should at least be neutral or more hostile to the dangerous offenders.

The hypothesis that the criminal justice system is biased in favor of high-rate offenders can be supported by describing how the criminal justice system operates, by reasoning from the fact that records of arrests and convictions are less skewed than estimates of underlying rates of offending, and by presenting evidence of the probability of arrest among different types of offenders taken from the Rand surveys.

The account of a systematic bias in favor of high-rate offenders is essentially an account of people who commit offenses more frequently than the system can handle. It begins, however, by noting that the sorts of offenses committed by the dangerous offenders — robbery, burglary, and larceny from the person — are among the most difficult to solve.[51] They happen so quickly or so secretly that the police are unlikely to see them and intervene. And since they are most often committed by strangers, the victims often cannot give much information to investigating policemen. Finally, although dangerous offenders probably become more vulnerable to arrest as they become better known to police agencies, they also may become better at concealing their crimes as they become more experienced. The style of offending, then, may give dangerous offenders an advantage.

The overburdening of the criminal justice system becomes an issue when the system deals with offenders who seem to have committed a great many offenses in a short period of time. Imagine the system's response to a dangerous offender who has committed ten robberies in three months — a rate that would place him in the top 10 percent of offenders. Assume that the police make a good arrest on one of these robberies by arriving on the scene just as the victim is knocked to the ground and the robber is making his escape. The victim is willing to testify. Moreover, the robber fits the description of the offender in several other street robberies in the same location. It is conceivable, then, that the police could conduct investigations linking the offender to at least some of his other crimes, that prosecutors would indict on these other charges, and that judges would take them into account in sentencing.

In all likelihood, however, this will not happen. Neither police nor prosecutors nor judges will see much use in taking the other potential charges seriously. From the police point of view, they have a good case now in hand, and only speculative cases out in the bushes. Even if they managed to compile evidence that the offender was involved in other robberies, chances are that the prosecutor would decide not to prosecute, because his interest is in winning cases and assuring that the robber does some prison time. He has a solid case that would only be weakened if it were confused with additional and weaker charges. Besides, even if the prosecutor did manage to secure convictions on the other charges, the judge would probably sentence the man to concurrent rather than consecutive sentences, simply because it is common practice. Again, the judge's primary interest is in giving some prison time, not guaranteeing that the offender gets exactly what he deserves. Thus the whole system might ignore the robber's other offenses on the grounds that it would make little difference to the ultimate outcome of the case.

The implications of this account are quite important to the issue of whether the system is biased in favor of or against high-rate offenders. Imagine a second robber, arrested for an identical crime, who is committing robberies at the rate of only one or two a year. This person will be treated in the same way as the first robber, ending up with a prison sentence of several years even though he is committing many fewer robberies. To make matters worse, when both these offenders show up in court several years later on new charges, their records make them look similar in terms of rate and persistence in offending, despite the fact that their underlying rates of offending are quite different.

One way to understand this effect is to imagine the criminal justice system as a machine moving at a certain rate in making cases against individuals. Those committing crimes at or below this rate get the punishment they deserve, but those who commit crimes at a faster rate than the machine can handle get away with crimes simply by overloading the system. The effect, obviously, is to decrease the conditional probability of arrest, prosecution, and conviction for high-rate offenders relative to the others.

This explanation gains some credibility if one examines records of arrests, prosecutions, and convictions. In general, these records show less skewness in their distributions than the underlying rates of offending.[52] Part of this result comes from the fact that high-rate offenders have less time to accumulate records because they spend more time in jail. But even if one controls for this possibility, the distributions of arrests, prosecutions, and convictions are less skewed than the distribution of offense rates; if the system were unbiased, they would be *more* skewed. Apparently the criminal justice system tends to dampen rather than exaggerate differences among offenders. Appendix B spells out this argument in more detail.

This indirect evidence on the reverse bias of the system is also supported by a small amount of direct evidence, drawn again from the Rand surveys. Table 7 presents some data on the probability of arrest for armed robbery among offenders of different ages, different records, and different levels of activity. The table reveals that as levels of criminal activity increase, the probability of arrest per offense decreases. Moreover, although the effects are small, they are observed for only a few broad categories of the level of criminal activity. At the tail of the distribution of prior record or level of offending, for example, the differences might be much greater. It seems quite possible, then, that the criminal justice system is biased in favor of high-rate offenders, and that if we want it to be unbiased, the system will have to make additional efforts to ensure that dangerous offenders get what they deserve.

Table 7. Probability of armed robbery arrest, given offense, by age, prior record, criminal identity, and offense rate.

Variable	p (arrest)
Age	
under 21	.25
21–25	.19
25–30	.17
over 30	.24
Prior record	
No felony arrrest	.28
Felony arrests, but never incarcerated	.16
Incarcerated	.22
Criminal identity (self-described)	
Noncriminal or quasi-criminal	.23
Single criminal identity	.21
Several criminal identities	.17
Armed robberies per year (est.)	
1.5	.24
2.0	.21
2.5	.18

Source: Mark A. Peterson, Harriet B. Braiker, and Suzanne M. Polich, *Who Commits Crimes: A Survey of Prison Inmates* (Cambridge, Mass.: Oelgeschlager, Gunn, and Hain, 1981), 56, 59, 79.

One further point concerns the role of the juvenile system in facilitating or hindering a focused response from the adult system. Current evidence on criminal career patterns indicates that criminal offending is most prevalent in late adolescence.[53] Far more people commit crimes during adolescence than they do later, but most adolescents who commit crimes do not continue.[54] A few, typically those who started early and gradually escalated both the level and seriousness of their crimes, will continue.[55] For these offenders, both the level and the seriousness will peak in the late twenties and early thirties, then slowly decline.[56] The juvenile justice system was created to accommodate society's reluctance to treat offenses committed by teenagers as indicative of bad moral character that would justify punishment.[57] Part of the motivation was to avoid labeling a teenager as a criminal, which might prevent or retard the natural tendency to abandon criminal activity. A formal finding of guilt might restrict a teenager's opportunities and shape his self-image in ways that would hurt rather than help his prospects of rehabilitation.[58] Another part of the motivation, however, is more closely tied to conceptions of justice and blameworthiness. Because we think of juveniles as less responsible, more vulnerable to outside influences, and more likely to change in the future, their acts are not treated as the result of considered intentions indicative of character. The juvenile justice system provides no findings guilt or innocence for specific offenses, and juvenile records are sealed from any outside examination.

While there is both logic and justice in this design, it creates an important practical problem in identifying dangerous offenders, particularly in the context of their underlying career trajectories and of the system's general failure to solve crimes. While he is a juvenile, a dangerous offender cannot be considered dangerous. Then, when he graduates from the juvenile system, even though he continues committing offenses he generally escapes punishment because the system fails to solve violent crimes among strangers. Even if arrested as an adult, he is not identified as a dangerous offender because his juvenile record has been sealed. By the time the offender is in his midtwenties, he may have accumulated a criminal justice record that points to his being unusually dangerous. But at this stage, according to the evidence on career trajectories, only a few of his most active years of offending remain.[59] In effect, we make it impossible for the criminal justice system to identify dangerous offenders on the basis of their criminal records while they are most active. When we are finally convinced that they are dangerous offenders, they tend to be in the process of becoming less dangerous.

In sum, although dangerous offenders have a prominent place in the criminal justice system as well as in patterns of offending, they are less prominent than they should be. They show up often and are dealt with harshly, but not as often and not as harshly as their rates of offending warrant. Moreover, during part of their active careers they are protected by their status as juveniles, and during another part they are protected by the difficulty of solving crimes and the system's unwillingness to use juvenile records as evidence of bad character.

It is also important to remember, however, that the vast majority of offenders are not dangerous. Minor property offenders, drunks who get into serious fights, tenants who strike against impatient landlords are also drawn into the system, and unlike the dangerous offenders, they may be there for virtually every crime they commit. And although such people do not commit offenses often, there are so many of them that these incidents account for a large portion of the system's workload. The wash of offenses sweeping through the criminal justice system thus carries many kinds of offenders. Both practical concerns for crime control and a sense of justice motivate us to construct a net that catches the truly dangerous offenders and to develop more effective responses to the others than currently exist. The mesh of this net is woven by the definition of dangerous offenders who deserve special treatment.

A JUST AND USEFUL DEFINITION
OF DANGEROUS OFFENDERS

The theoretical perspective and empirical evidence presented in this chapter accentuate the role of dangerous offenders in the overall crime problem. However, the discussion has unearthed unexpected complexities in the commonsense idea of focusing on dangerous offenders. Should all offenses be considered dangerous, or only those that involve violence among strangers? How many offenses are necessary to establish that an offender is unusually dangerous rather than unusually unlucky?

Such questions indicate how difficult it is to define the dangerous offender. Although this may seem like a mere technicality, it is not. It is essential. Indeed, after reviewing a century of British experience in focusing on dangerous offenders, Radzinowicz and Hood concluded that definition was the central problem in the failure of the British policies. "Inherent in all these schemes was a common fault. They were framed as if to apply to any felony, whatever its degree of seriousness, and they ignored altogether the problems posed by persistent minor misdemeanants."[60] Norval Morris found that between 1928 and 1945, only 7 of the 325 prisoners committed to long-term incarceration under a British habitual-offender statute were sentenced for violence, threat of violence, or danger to the person.[61] The remainder were persistent but minor property offenders.

The confusion in defining dangerous offenders is also apparent in the United States. Table 8 offers a sampling of definitions now in use in different parts of the criminal justice system. The confusion should not be surprising. Nor should we expect a quick or final resolution. For in deciding what we mean by dangerous offenders and how we will recognize them, we must resolve a host of questions with exacting normative and practical implications. Is our interest in dangerous offenders primarily backward-looking and retributivist or forward-looking and utilitarian? Is dangerousness indicated by violent offenses, by high rates of offending, by persistence in criminality, or by some combination of these factors? How should we deal with the fact that the criminal justice system solves so few crimes decisively that underlying patterns of offending are not clearly revealed in criminal justice records? And in developing a tolerably just definition, should we err on the side of inclusion or exclusion? Although these questions have some technical aspects, they are not fundamentally technical. They are most importantly questions of justice and value and therefore, they deserve political debate. We can offer conceptual guidance, establish some limits on suitable definitions, and assess current definitions, but we cannot decisively resolve the issues through sheer force of logic and evidence.

Perhaps our most important idea is that it is better to think of the concept of dangerous offenders as primarily backward-looking and retributivist rather than forward-looking and utilitarian. The current debate about selective incapacitation makes this shift in perspective difficult because it emphasizes the practical benefits of predicting which offenders will commit the most crimes in the future. In this context, the central issues are whether tolerably accurate predictions are possible and whether mere incapacitation really does reduce crime. The question of the justice of this approach seems curiously disconnected. To the pragmatic realists who want to get on with business of solving the crime problem as inexpensively as possible, it is merely an academic issue; to those who worry about justice, any notion of selective incapacitation seems unjust.

We believe that selectivity is not necessarily a utilitarian idea. Indeed, we have found that an interest in dangerous offenders is compelled by

Table 8. Definitions of dangerous offenders in different jurisdictions.

Jurisdiction	Definition
Judiciary	
Texas	One prior felony conviction
California	Pending violent felony conviction *and* two prior violent felony convictions
Nebraska	Two prior felony convictions *and* jail or prison sentence of one year or longer
Prosecutors	
San Diego County, Calif.	One prior robbery conviction *or* one prior personal felony conviction and one other felony conviction *or* three pending robbery arrests *or* high score on points system of subjective assessments and unofficial information
Orleans Parish, La.	Two prior felony convictions *or* five prior felony arrests
Kalamazoo County, Mich.	*Either* 2 prior convictions *or* five prior felony arrests *or* bail status *or* one prior armed robbery, rape, or drug sales arrest *And* high score on points system of prior felony and misdemeanor arrests and convictions Sellin-Wolfgang seriousness of pending offense bail or parole status other pending cases
Police	
New York City	One prior robbery arrest *and* one other violent prior arrest in last three years *and* between sixteen and thirty-five years old
Memphis, Tenn.	Five prior felony arrests *and* high score on a points system of: prior adult and juvenile convictions years since last arrest seriousness of present offense
Stockton, Calif.	Three pending felony arrests *or* one pending felony arrest and two prior felony convictions

justice as well as by utilitarian concerns. Moreover, policies guided by backward-looking retributivist ideas are in many respects more tolerable to common notions of justice than policies guided by utilitarian interests. And further, the practical effects of retributivists and utilitarian policies directed at dangerous offenders may be surprisingly alike. If people continue to do what they have done in the past, a policy focused on past offenses will focus on those who are likely to commit offenses in the future.

Justice compels a special interest in dangerous offenders because those who have committed crimes repeatedly have clearly revealed their guilt through a pattern of criminal activity that merits special attention. If we look at dangerous offenders this way, many of the obvious objections to selective incapacitation disappear. We are back in the commonsense world of punishing people who have inflicted losses on others in the past, rather than in the futuristic world in which social science predictions determine one's destiny. In short, familiar principles of justice support a special focus on those who have committed many violent offenses, and these principles are to be preferred to less traditional, more utilitarian, and technological notions.

There are real differences between retributivists and utilitarians. We know that aging eventually slows down the rate of criminal offending. And it is at this point that retributivist and utilitarian justifications for imprisonment divide; the retributivists argue for continued imprisonment on the grounds that justice requires it, and the utilitarians argue for release on the grounds that no practical purpose is served. Again, if we restrict our attention to records of prior offending, as retributivist principles require, and if juvenile records are sealed and the police, prosecutors, and courts fail to solve most crimes, then it will be very difficult to distinguish dangerous offenders from others. At that point we might be tempted to include other characteristics, such as drug-abuse history and unemployment. Utilitarian principles would warrant the use of such characteristics, but retributivist priciples would not.

So there clearly are some important differences between retributivist and utilitarian policies. But they are identical in one crucial respect: their interest in *prior* criminal offending in distinguishing dangerous offenders from others. Indeed, if the criminal justice system improved in its ability to solve crimes, then retributivist and utilitarian concepts of appropriate policies might move even closer together. Criminal justice records would more accurately reflect underlying rates of offending, and therefore would more accurately distinguish those who had committed many crimes in the past (and were therefore likely to commit more offenses in the future) from those whose commitment to crime was less intensive (and therefore more likely to be abandoned).

If the quality of justice can be enhanced and little practical value is lost in conceiving of a focus on dangerous offenders as a retributivist idea, then it is desirable to shift from a utilitarian to a retributivist perspective. That is what we recommend. In designing selective policies and defining dangerous offenders, the goal should be to distinguish the guiltiest offenders based on past activity and to punish them for their blameworthy conduct rather than to predict which offenders will be most active in the future on the basis of any characteristics which aid in prediction, and incapacitate those predicted to be offenders for as long as they appear dangerous.

The retributivist perspective clarifies our philosophy and purposes and introduces some important restrictions on the characteristics we can use to identify dangerous offenders. But it does not go far enough in determining what acts or patterns of conduct should qualify offenders for the special designation. One might reasonably consider those acts that contribute most significantly to victimization and fear. As Chapter 1 indicated, the narrowest definition of such acts would involve violence among strangers. But cases could also be made for including violence among intimates, property crimes that create significant risks of violence, and perhaps even the minor incivilities that arouse fears in the general population. One can imagine a narrow definition that required evidence of both high rates and persistence in offending, or a much broader definition that simply required willfulness in the commission of the offenses, because willfulness by itself reveals enough about character to be probative as to dangerousness.

Obviously, if we took the broadest definitions on each dimension — acts and patterns of activity — we would end up with a very broad definition of dangerous offenders. Indeed, if we include all conduct that stimulates fear (and is covered by a statute) and if we require nothing more than willfulness in a single act, then the definition of dangerousness is virtually identical with the broad notion of criminal offending and would include virtually all offenders — vandals as well as robbers, disorderly persons as well as rapists. That one could define "dangerousness" so broadly is not too surprising, for minimizing danger to the community is what the criminal law is all about. In today's overburdened system, however, such a formulation is clearly inappropriate. The purpose of focusing on dangerous offenders is to define a subpopulation that represents unusually great risks to society.

One way to narrow the definition is to place restrictions on qualifying offenses. Felonies should be taken more seriously than misdemeanors, violent felonies more seriously than ordinary felonies, and gratuitous or sex-related violence more seriously than instrumental or accidental violence. In effect, we look for dangerousness in the character of the acts committed. Again, however, the concept remains very broad. Moreover, the criminal justice system is already organized to act on precisely this distinction. Courts are commonly divided between those that deal with felonies and those that deal with misdemeanors. Judges, prosecutors, and police quite naturally give much greater attention to crimes involving violence among strangers than to property offenses or disorderly conduct.[62]

What seems new and distinctive in the concept of dangerous offenders is an interest in the offender as well as the offenses. For a person to be identified as a dangerous offender it is not enough that he has willfully committed a violent offense: there must be some additional evidence to indicate that he has committed offenses often, persistently, or both. Indeed, the notions of "high rate" and "persistence" are so closely linked to ideas of blameworthiness that we sometimes use them alone to define dangerous offenders and ignore entirely the nature of the offenses. Conceptions of "habitual offenders," "career criminals," or "criminal recidivists," for example, emphasize the *persistence* of criminal conduct. There is some justice in this concern with persistence and rate because such patterns of offending indicate determination, even defiance, in rejecting social obligations. But focusing on persistence or rates of offending alone could lead to unjust results. For example, under many habitual-offender statutes, a fifty-year-old man, convicted of three widely separated instances of check forging, could be given life imprisonment. Although the man is clearly persistent, he seems far from dangerous, and it would be hard to find either a utilitarian or retributivist justification for lengthy imprisonment. Similarly, an exclusive focus on the *rate* of offending could lead to a person charged with crimes stemming from a single incident or from a relatively short-lived period of anger and desperation being considered a dangerous offender, even though he would soon stop committing crimes, and his current offenses could be better understood as the product of unusual circumstances.

These observations suggest that a proper definition must incorporate three distinct characteristics: *violence* in offending, a high *rate* of offending, and *persistence*. The combination of these characteristics, rather than any one alone, justifies a special focus on dangerous offenders.

This discussion leaves unanswered the question of what specific

record of criminality would be sufficient to identify someone as a dangerous offender, since criminal justice records are poor reflections of the
underlying rate of offending. We think a just and useful operational
definition of dangerous offenders would involve the following elements.
First, the person must have at least two convictions for violent offenses
within a relatively short period of street time, say, three years. This
element is crucial to make sure that the offender is persistently involved
in violence. Because we need to be sure, there must be convictions;
because we need to establish persistence, there must be at least two; and
because the rate of offending must be high, the convictions must be
within a relatively short period. Otherwise, many low-rate offenders
might be included.

Second, to establish both high rates of offending and persistence, some
additional evidence of criminal offending, beyond convictions, is required. The data from the Rand prison surveys indicated that high-rate
violent offenders were very likely to show high rates in all categories of
crime, and to be persistent as well.[63] But the definition could include
some low-rate offenders as well, so it would be valuable to look at other
parts of the criminal record. Perhaps two additional indictments for
violent offenses, or two convictions for risk-creating property crimes,
such as burglaries or muggings, should be required in addition to the two
convictions for violence.

Some will object to including property offenses in the definition of
dangerous offenders; others will object to using arrests and indictments
rather than convictions. But these factors are being proposed as additional requirements, not as a sufficient basis in themselves for defining
dangerousness. Also, property crimes are included only partly because
they carry the threat of violence; the more important reason is that the
combination of repeated violent and property offending seems to be
correlated with very high rates of both kinds of offending. Because property crimes occur more often, they provide a more sensitive indicator of
who is a dangerous offender than a definition restricted to violent offenses. Similarly, arrests and indictments are brought in to distinguish
the most active and persistent offenders from the less active. For an
indictment to be issued, a court must be persuaded that an offense was
probably committed and that a particular person more than likely committed it. In our view, relying on arrests and indictments is surely superior
to relying on information that is not linked to criminal conduct at all,
which is now the norm in criminal justice proceedings.

In reviewing an offender's criminal record, we think that violent offenses and serious property crimes committed as a juvenile should be included. Part of the motivation here is admittedly prudential. Because it is important to find the dangerous offenders when they are in the most active stage of their careers, it is useful to include juvenile offenses. Otherwise, we may identify the offenders too late to have much practical value. But consideration of juvenile offenses in the cases of adults who continue to commit offenses is also arguably just, as well as practically valuable. The juvenile offenses of someone who continues committing crimes as an adult have a different status than if he had stopped. They look like early evidence of a blameworthy character rather than youthful indiscretions.

Characteristics that do not involve criminal conduct should not be included in definitions of dangerous offenders. Employment history, heavy alcohol use, age, and family status may improve our ability to distinguish those who are likely to be dangerous offenders from those who are not, but if we rely on these charcteristics we shift from a retributivist notion to a utilitarian concept. The use of drug abuse history as an indicator is less clear because the law has made many forms of drug use a criminal act. Consequently, this characteristic might be included under a retributivist idea. The problem is that the statutes making drug use a crime seem to be motivated by utilitarian rather than retributivist ideas. The law condemns drug use not because that in itself is bad, but because society believes it leads to bad behavior. Is drug use really criminal in the sense that it clearly indicates criminal intent and bad character? We remain undecided about this issue.

In sum, we think a useful and just operational definition of dangerous offenders would require: 1) two convictions for violent offenses in three years of street time; 2) two additional indictments for violent offenses or two additional convictions for serious property crimes within the same period; 3) inclusion of violent and serious property offenses committed while a juvenile; and 4) exclusion of characteristics unrelated to prior criminal conduct.

No doubt this definition will seem too stringent to some and too inclusive to others. From the point of view of individual justice, our definition may be considered too tight or too lenient in terms of identifying people who are guilty enough to deserve some special treatment. Our view, however, is that we have constructed a proper conceptual definition of dangerous offenders as well as an operational definition that copes with the deficiencies of the existing system.

Another consideration is the aggregate implications of adopting this definition. How many people, or what fraction of the existing caseload of the criminal justice system, will be dragged into this net? In thinking about how broad the definition of dangerous offenders should be, it may be tempting to include nearly everyone convicted of a serious crime. But we are trying to single out a few criminal offenders for stiffer punishment. The broader the definition, the less distictive the population included, and the smaller the practical and moral value of creating the distinction in the first place. Our proposed definition is designed to pick out a small fraction of the criminal justice caseload — probably less than 5 or 10 percent.[64] Any definition much broader than that would risk the very gains that justified the narrow focus.

CONCLUSIONS

To a great extent, this chapter presents a powerful justification for sharpening the focus on dangerous offenders. The concept can be given a theoretical basis, empirical support, and a practical, operational definition. Moreover, one can argue that a sharpened focus on dangerous offenders would be both just and effective. By increasing punishment for those offenders who have clearly shown themselves to be dangerous, and mitigating it for those whose continued commitment to violent offending is in doubt, we can enhance the justice of the system. To the extent that imprisonment reduces crime by incapacitating offenders, and to the extent that scarce prison capacity should be reserved for those who commit violent offenses at the highest rates, the system would be more effective in controlling crime: we could have less crime *and* fewer people in jail.

At the same time, our discussion makes clear exactly what is left out of the concepts of dangerous offenders and selective incapacitation. Not only is a great deal of crime (including violence) committed by nondangerous offenders, but also some of those who commit offenses in patterns that indicate dangerousness are quite ordinary people. Chance alone guarantees that some ordinary people will end up committing a number of offenses. The aggregate and individual patterns of offending bear the traces of broad social trends and short-term effects on motivation and opportunities, as well as the prevalence of blameworthiness in the society.

Our discussion also indicates a wide variety of policies other than incapacitation through imprisonment that can influence rates of offending. Macroeconomic policies, welfare programs, mental health and drug abuse programs, schools, creation of short-term jobs, recreational programs for youth, private security investments, and public expenditures to deter and apprehend criminal offenders — all represent plausible alternative approaches to controlling crime. In fact, many of these approaches might be considered broadly preventive approaches because they reduce the chance that individuals in the society will accumulate experiences as criminal offenders and thus develop a commitment to criminal activities. But these approaches might also be broadly rehabilitative by making it easier for criminal offenders to develop a commitment to legitimate activities and harder to continue in these dangerous pursuits. So the attack on crime can be organized on a broad front. Given the evidence about the distribution of the rates of offending, a policy of selective incapacitation has appeal as one element of a crime policy. It is in the interests of the economical and just use of punishment.

3

Threshold Objections to Selective Policies

POLICIES DESIGNED to focus punishment on dangerous offenders carry risks as well as potential benefits. There is the risk of injustice to individuals. An offender might be inappropriately labeled as dangerous and be exposed to special and undeserved liabilities in the criminal justice system. Or the selective policies may fail in their intended effect. The dangerous offenders might account for fewer crimes than we now believe. They might escape capture or identification. Or they might be replaced by other, equally dangerous characters. There is also the risk of the corruption of criminal justice institutions and the coarsening of our ideology of crime and punishment. Policeman and prosecutors, encouraged to fasten on known dangerous offenders, may become less solicitous of the offenders' due process rights than a free society demands. Over time the society as a whole may become less generous and more suspicious as it accepts the notion that it contains a small group of truly dangerous offenders.

Obviously, any considered conclusion about the desirability of such policies requires a sober reckoning of these risks along with the benefits. Some of the major objections attack the fundamental concept of selective punishment. These can be discussed without having a detailed plan for a selective focus on dangerous offenders. Other objections depend on the details of the proposals for particular stages of the criminal justice system. We will discuss the objections to specific proposals in later chapters. The task of this chapter is to consider the most general and fundamental objections to focusing the attention of the criminal justice system on dangerous offenders.

We have identified nine threshold objections. Two raise doubts about the justice of selective policies, four others are skeptical of their practical value, and the last three concern their corrosive effects on the institutions and ideologies of our society. The objections are powerful — so powerful that they may lead some readers to oppose any further efforts to enhance selectivity. Others will agree that the objections mark out areas of uncertainty, risk, and concern. These areas must be weighed in deciding the merits of selective policies and closely attended as such policies evolve.

THE JUSTICE OF A SELECTIVE FOCUS

The most fundamental objection to policies of selective incapacitation is that they are unjust because of two distinct features. Selective policies depend on establishing differences among offenders on the basis of characteristics other than criminal acts, and they make the risks of arrest and the severity of punishment contingent on those characteristics. This is obnoxious to our sense of justice because people are penalized for characteristics unrelated to their blameworthiness. Moreover, the distinctions are based to some degree on predictions of future conduct rather than observations of past acts. Both features are unjust in a world in which justice is defined as deliberate punishment for past acts.[1]

The second obnoxious feature is that the techniques used to distinguish dangerous offenders from others are inadequate.[2] First, because the discriminating tests are imperfect, errors will inevitably be made: ordinary offenders will be mistakenly designated as dangerous offenders and punished accordingly. Such mistakes, commonly called "false positives," are fundamentally unjust. Second, many of the tests rely on individual characteristics that are not in themselves blameworthy and over which the individual has only limited or no control. To the extent that the tests rely on such characteristics, the justice of the tests is in doubt. These two arguments are powerful, perhaps even decisive. But counterarguments can be made.

THE JUSTICE OF DIFFERENTIAL PUNISHMENT

The most straightforward defense of selective policies is that punishment has appropriate purposes beyond doing justice to individual offenders, such as controlling crime through deterrence, incapacitation, and rehabilitation.[3] If crime can be reduced by focusing the attention of police, prosecutors, and judges toward dangerous offenders, and if this results in their more frequent incarceration, then the policies can be justified in pragmatic terms.

Obviously, there are limits to the proper scope of such utilitarian considerations.[4] It would be wrong to increase the risks of punishment for people who have never been convicted of a crime,[5] but none of the proposals for selective policies urge this. It would also be wrong to radically increase (say, double or triple) an offender's risk of punishment on the grounds of pragmatism alone. But it does not offend justice to allow some utilitarian considerations to determine who will bear the brunt of the criminal justice system. Since most selective policies urge nothing more than this limited role, the policy is tolerably just.

A second justification adds to these practical concerns the legitimacy of both tradition and current practice. Indeed, it is startling but nonetheless accurate to observe that current rehabilitative sentencing policies are identical in operation to proposals for selective incapacitation. The basic philosophy of rehabilitative sentencing is that the primary goal is rehabilitation of offenders.[6] Those prisoners who appear rehabilitated should be released to the community, because no practical purpose is served by keeping them in expensive cells. The institution that decides whether prisoners have been rehabilitated is the parole board. Parole boards consider many factors in making their judgments, including testimony from psychologists and reports of prison conduct, but they are increasingly guided by an assessment of characteristics that seem to predict recidivism,[7] including, typically, current offense, prior criminal record, drug use, and employment history.[8]

As long as one holds in mind the philosophy of rehabilitative sentencing, keeps an eye on those prisoners released rather than on those held by parole boards, and ignores the details of parole decision making, rehabilitative sentencing seems quite different from selective incapacitation — much more merciful and hopeful. But if one thinks about how this system looks to those who are denied parole and if one examines the mechanics of the decision making, the policy is quite indistinguishable from selective incapacitation. In both cases individual offenders are examined with respect to the issue of future criminality, and the time they serve in prison is adjusted to reflect predicted differences. The parole system is concerned with identifying those who are unlikely to recidivate. Selective incapacitation is concerned with keeping those who are likely to commit crimes in prison. But these goals are analytically the same, and most of the characteristics under examination are the same. So except for the rhetoric, and the ideologies invoked by the rhetoric, the concepts are identical. To the extent that current practices are tolerable, then, selective incapacitation is also tolerable.

So far, the justifications for selective policies have sidestepped the challenge that comes from a principled, retributivist view of criminal justice.[9] The first justification denies that retribution should be the sole basis for criminal punishment. The second makes a virtue of current practices and thereby finds room for the closely related idea of selective incapacitation. But neither of these arguments is convincing to those who adhere to a strict retributivist perspective. The third justification puts proposals for selective policies in a retributivist context.

The key to this justification is to shift the goal of selective policies from efforts to predict future criminal conduct toward efforts to distinguish, on the basis of past criminal acts, the most blameworthy criminal offenders among all offenders. Some offenders have been observed to be more blameworthy than others. In this sense, selective proposals rely on the same conception of justice that animates and sustains habitual-offender statutes, which also expose repeat offenders to punishment beyond what is justified by their current offense. While some retributivists object even to habitual-offender laws, others find such statutes quite consistent with retributivist ideals.[10]

If selective policies were designed from this retributivist perspective, however, more than the rhetoric would change. Two important constraints would be introduced, both of which would reduce the policies' practical value. One constraint is that any discrimination among offenders would have to be based *exclusively* on information about prior criminal conduct. Anything else would be inconsistent with the retributivist spirit. To the extent that predictive or discriminating accuracy was eroded as a result, some practical benefits would be lost. The second constraint is that offenders would have to be punished for their offenses even if age or some other characteristic made it unlikely they would commit offenses in the future. To the extent that offenders ended their criminal careers as they became older, and to the extent that selective policies resembled habitual-offender statutes in being based on an *absolute number* of prior offenses (rather than a *rate* of prior offending), the policies would utilize limited prison capacity to incapacitate aging offenders who are not likely to be dangerous in the future.[11] This, of course, represents a further erosion of the practical justifications for the policy.

A fourth justification is that far from biasing the operations of the system against dangerous offenders and risking injustice to them, selective policies actually enhance the fairness of the criminal justice system by compensating to some degree for inequities created by the differential solvability of crimes. A criminal justice system that makes punishment proportional to acts without adding any additional punishment for unusually high rates or sustained periods of offending, if operating fairly, naturally would punish high-rate, persistent offenders more than others. In this case, the distribution of arrest, prosecution, and punishment would exactly mirror the distribution of rates of offending, and dangerous offenders would be spending very large portions of their lives in confinement.

But the criminal justice system does not solve most crimes.[12] Who gets arrested and punished depends on idiosyncratic features of the offenses and vagaries of criminal justice system processing, as well as on actual criminal conduct. For the most part, we assume that the bias introduced by these idiosyncratic elements is not too great or, if significant, that it runs against high-rate offenders. But as we noted in Chapter 2, the question is not simply whether high-rate offenders are more likely to be punished, but whether they are more likely to be punished for each offense than low-rate offenders. Given the enormous differences between high and low rates of offending (forty versus two robberies per year, for example), the high-rate offenders would have to be punished twenty times more frequently in order for the system to be "fair" in terms of acts!

Given the magnitude of the punishment "deserved" by high-rate offenders, one can reasonably be skeptical that the high-rate offenders get their "just deserts" relative to low-rate offenders. To the extent that high-rate offenders get less than they deserve, an important inequity is introduced into the system. The guiltiest, most blameworthy offenders are being punished less than they deserve on the basis of their acts. One way to compensate for this natural bias in favor of high-rate offenders is to introduce selective policies. If these policies result in high-rate offenders being arrested, prosecuted, and sentenced for more of their crimes, justice is enhanced. And if punishments for given offenses are increased for persistent high-rate offenders, justice might be enhanced because the distribution of punishment would more closely fit the distribution of rates of offending.

Admittedly, this argument is more speculative and more dubious on its merits than the others. It is clearly unjust to smuggle additional punishment into the system for high-rate offenders on the basis of speculations about bias in the system's operations when we have failed to show that a specific offender is in fact a high-rate offender. But that is not what is being proposed. Instead, we are proposing that special investigative and prosecutorial efforts be made to solve crimes committed by people who have shown themselves to be dangerous offenders and that some extra punishment be considered for the repeated offending. These proposals may be just in themselves, and they have the additional virtue of reducing a possible inequity in the system's current operations. Whatever the merits of this particular argument, however, it does remind us that one question of justice worth considering is that of fairness across offenders and, further, that some offenders may deserve less leniency than others, even if their current offenses are the same.

In sum, a policy of selective incapacitation can be just. Since practical interests are countenanced in the design of the criminal justice system and since current policies include a great many utilitarian justifications, the mere fact that selective policies are often justified on utilitarian grounds does not exclude them from consideration or use. Moreover, one can argue that a selective policy designed to distinguish the most blameworthy offenders on the basis of past criminal conduct is consistent with all but the most stringent retributivist principles.[13] One can argue more speculatively that selective incapacitation enhances fairness by compensating for the bias in favor of very active offenders. Indeed, selective policies might be the only means to equalize the probabilities of arrest, prosecution and imprisonment among offenders. Obviously, none of these points is conclusive. A great deal depends on the details of the proposed policy. But there is room in our concepts of justice for a policy that seeks to enhance punishment for dangerous offenders.

THE JUSTICE OF DISCRIMINATING TECHNIQUES

Equally prominent in criticisms of selective policies are objections to the techniques used to distinguish dangerous offenders from others. From the justice perspective, the most fundamental objection is that the techniques are inaccurate, so some individuals will be mistakenly classified as dangerous and unjustly exposed to special liabilities.[14] A second concern is that to achieve greater accuracy and discriminating power, the tests will be unjustly based on noncriminal characteristics or characteristics that are not under the individual's control or are inaccurately measured.

In the past the discriminating tests have been discussed in a relatively simple context. It was assumed that a fixed technology of testing existed, that the test's purpose was to predict future criminal offending, and that the crucial characteristic was its predictive accuracy.[15] In the context of our discussion, the matter is a little more complicated. The tests are not seen primarily as predictors of future criminality but as discriminators of dangerousness on the basis of past acts. Moreover, the tests are viewed not as a fixed technology, not even as a technology that changes with the inexorable advance of science, but instead as a flexible instrument. The tests can be given different properties that make them more or less obnoxious to justice and more or less valuable in directing attention toward unusually dangerous offenders. In discussing the justice of these tests, then, our aims are first, to understand their design features; second, to see how considerations of justice should influence the design; and third, to determine whether current tests are tolerably just.

Design features of discriminating tests. In general, a discriminating test is designed to sort people into groups that differ in terms of some important but unobservable characteristic on the basis of some other characteristic that can be observed. Unfortunately, in the case of selective policies, the observable characteristics, such as prior criminal conduct, juvenile record, drug use and so on, are only imperfectly correlated with the unobserved characteristic of dangerousness. Among high-rate, blameworthy offenders the distribution of observed characteristics overlaps to some degree with the distribution of similar characteristics among lower-rate, less culpable offenders. The discriminating power of the test being used depends crucially on the magnitude of this overlap.

Figure 4 illustrates this point by presenting possible distributions of scores on a given test for high- and low-rate offenders. Figure 4B shows the distribution of scores for a good discriminating test: the scores of high-rate offenders overlap hardly at all with those of low-rate offenders. Figure 4C shows the distribution of scores for a poor discriminating test: the scores for both high- and low-rate offenders overlap considerably. Figure 4D shows the typical case of a moderately powerful discriminating test: the scores vary a great deal within the groups, and they overlap with one another, but there is still an important difference between the two groups.

The shapes of these distributions depend not only on the underlying empirical realities, but also on two crucial decisions that the test designer makes. First, what group size and character does the test seek to distinguish? Is the goal to find a small group of people, say the worst 5 percent of offenders, or a much larger group, such as the worst third? Is it designed to find people whose rates of offending are on average ten times greater than other offenders, or only slightly greater? Obviously, the justice and practical value of the tests increase as they identify smaller

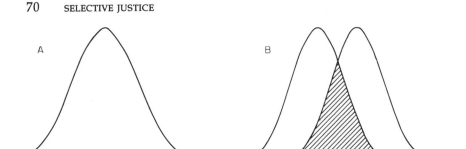

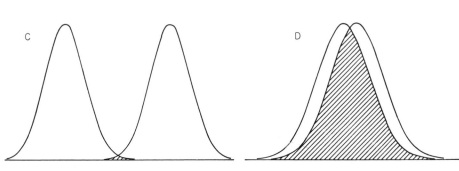

Figure 4   The discriminating power of different test variables.

and more distinctive populations. But in general, the more ambitious the tests become in trying to distinguish a small, distinctive group, the more errors it will make. In statistics as elsewhere, it is harder to hit a small target than a large one. Thus there must be a trade-off between the ambition to home in on a particular group and the aspiration to make no errors in assigning people to the dangerous offender category.

Second, which observable characteristics should be used in defining the test? Should one use prior adult convictions, juvenile arrest history, or history of family stability and community ties? If our only interest is to maximize the test's predictive or discriminating power, any characteristic that helps distinguish among offenders is acceptable. Indeed, we can include many variables, because the discriminating power of the tests generally increases with the number of variables. However, considerations other than predictive or discriminating power come into play. It is preferable to use characteristics that are under the control of the individual, that constitute criminal conduct in themselves, and that are accurately measured. Otherwise, the tests are unjust to individuals, though they might be valuable to the system as a whole.

Once the test designer has decided which groups are worth distinguishing and which variables to use, a third decision must be made: where to fix the criterion that places people in one category or another. This criterion is defined in terms of the observed, not the underlying, characteristic, making it an *operational* rather than a true definition of dangerous offenders. The location of the criterion determines not only the total number of classification errors that will be made in relying on a given set of test variables and a given criterion, but also the distribution of errors of two different types: mistakenly classifying a low-rate offender as a high-rate offender, commonly called a "false positive"; and mistakenly classifying a high-rate offender as a low-rate offender, often called a "false negative." In general, given overlapping distributions of scores, one can reduce the number of false negatives only by increasing the number of false positives. In less technical terms, the more determined one is to find all the high-rate offenders, the more likely one is to mistakenly include some low-rate offenders. This effect is illustrated in Figure 5, showing the consequences of locating the criterion for high- and low-rate offenders in different positions.

The general discussion suggests that many different discriminating tests exist. They can be distinguished from one another in terms of how discriminating they set out to be on the important but unobserved characteristic of dangerousness; what observable characteristics are chosen, such as current offense, prior record, or drug abuse; and the specific criterion or cutoff point of dangerousness. Because many different tests are conceivable, it is hard to come up with a general answer to the question of whether we can justly and usefully distinguish among criminal offenders in terms of dangerousness.[16] What can be discussed is how considerations of justice and practical value should guide those who design the tests and which features make some tests more just and valuable than others.

Toward just and useful discriminating tests. Concerns with justice and practical value push in the direction of identifying a small group of exceptionally dangerous offenders — a group whose average rate of offending is high enough to justify the costs of incapacitation for utilitarian purposes and high enough to eliminate doubt about the offender's determined criminality for retributivist purposes. Given estimates of the distribution of rates of offending, this implies that we are looking for the worst 5 to 10 percent of the offending population.[17]

In terms of choosing variables to be included in the test, interests in justice and in utilitarian benefits push in different directions. Practicality

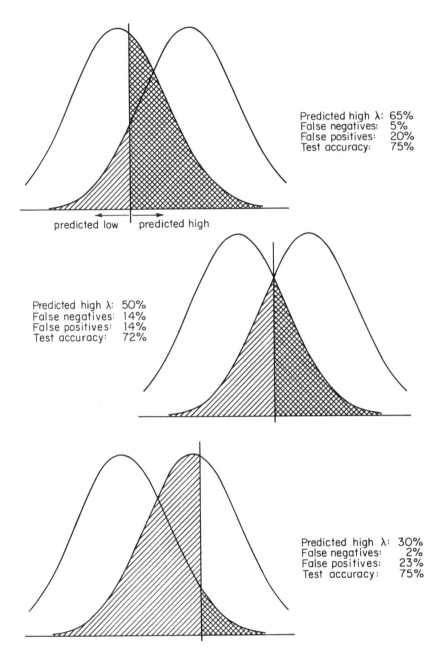

Predicted high λ: 65%
False negatives: 5%
False positives: 20%
Test accuracy: 75%

predicted low | predicted high

Predicted high λ: 50%
False negatives: 14%
False positives: 14%
Test accuracy: 72%

Predicted high λ: 30%
False negatives: 2%
False positives: 23%
Test accuracy: 75%

Figure 5 The effect of moving the criterion in discriminating tests.

counsels the inclusion of *any* variable that helps in distinguishing high-rate offenders, regardless of its standing in our conceptions of individual justice. Interest in justice, however, counsels restraint in the use of variables over which the individual has limited or no control, such as age, sex, or IQ; variables associated with class and ethnic background, including wealth, religion, race, and national origin; variables that are not directly related to criminal conduct and only partly under an individual's control, such as unemployment, or alcohol and drug use; and variables that cannot be reliably measured for individuals.

The wide latitude in the practical choice of variables seems to contrast sharply with the restrictions imposed by concerns for justice. But there may be a substantial overlap. If prior criminal conduct is in fact closely correlated with future criminal conduct, then concerns with justice and with practical benefits will converge on variables measuring prior criminal activity. Indeed, most discriminations between high- and low-rate offenders do rest on variables describing the level and seriousness of prior criminal activity: age at first arrest, number of prior arrests and convictions, fraction of time spent in jail, and so on.[18] The fact that these are the best discriminating variables, even though the records of the criminal justice system tend to understate rather than exaggerate differences among offenders, suggests that if the system could solve more crimes and produce records that more accurately reflect criminal conduct, the interests of justice and practical value could be reconciled. We could restrict our attention to prior criminal activity and lose very little, perhaps nothing, in terms of discriminating capacity. Indeed, the only reason for the present tension between utilitarian and justice interests in the choice of test variables may be that we solve so few crimes and keep such inadequate records.

It is slightly utopian to imagine that the criminal justice system could solve enough crimes to allow us to rely *exclusively* on evidence of prior criminal activity, but the realization that utilitarian and justice concerns could both be satisfied if this were so adds urgency to this task. We need to solve crimes not only because that is desirable in itself, but also because it gives us a just basis for distinguishing the truly dangerous offenders from others.

At present, however, we must resolve the tension between using variables that are just to individuals and using variables that have practical benefit. This means making two difficult decisions: which indicators of prior criminal activity may properly be considered, and whether it is appropriate to go beyond those indicators to other forms of conduct or even social status.

Some people would object to the use of any criminal justice records because those records are far from a neutral indicator of criminal conduct. A criminal record (whether arrest or conviction) is produced by a social process in which the individual's conduct may be only a small part.[19] This social process includes the definition of some conduct as criminal, the circumstances that expose a specific incident to public view, and perhaps even the malicious intent of government agents. Since the observed record reflects these factors as well as the offender's criminal conduct, these people say, there is too much potential for unjust biases to enter.

A less extreme but still quite restrictive view holds that only records of adult convictions should be allowed, since convictions are the only reliably accurate criminal records, and only when a person becomes an adult can we be sure his activities reflect his intentions rather than temporary impulses. A slightly less restrictive view recommends considering both adult and juvenile convictions for serious offenses only if a person is convicted of a serious crime shortly after he leaves the juvenile jurisdiction, since the original reason for protecting the juvenile record has already disappeared.[20] A still less restrictive view could allow the system to examine arrests (particularly those in which a charge or indictment was issued), as well as convictions.

Because fewer variables lead to less discriminatory power, the more restrictions on discriminating variables that are established, the less accurate the tests become and the less practical value they have. There is very little power or practical value in tests limited to adult convictions. There is more power in including juvenile convictions for serious offenses, and there seem to be good reasons for doing so. We are tempted to go still further and allow the use of indictments as an indicator, once an offender has been convicted of some serious crime.

Our reason here is the largely practical one that indictments help distinguish high-rate offenders from others, so inclusion of this information would increase both the accuracy and the practical value of the tests. Moreover, indictments are a direct measure of criminal conduct, unlike other proposed variables. At least in principle, an indictment can be secured only if the government meets a fairly high evidentiary standard. Consequently, indictments measure criminal conduct fairly accurately, not enough to justify punishment by themselves, but conceivably enough to justify enhanced attention. Indictments may be a better indicator than information about drug use or employment. Finally, "rap sheets," which are nothing more than records of previous arrests, are now consulted routinely throughout the criminal justice system. If we limited our attention to indictments, the system might be more just. Views differ on the proper trade-offs between enhanced discriminating power and the use of specific variables whose justice is in doubt. We suspect that most people would end up somewhere between relying on adult and juvenile convictions on the one hand, and using convictions plus serious adult and juvenile indictments on the other, depending on the purpose of the discriminating test.

In terms of variables other than criminal conduct, many are clearly intolerable even to the most devoted utilitarian. Demographic characteristics, including age, race, religion, and so on, should certainly be excluded from consideration. We consider employment status suspect and urge that it be excluded. On drug use, we are ambivalent. On the one hand, the characteristic is under the control of the individual, easy to measure, and illegal.[21] It seems to have significant discriminating power and is now routinely used in the criminal justice system. On the other hand, it is not dangerous criminal conduct. Indeed, the link between drug use and criminal conduct is arguably an artifact of our current social policies.[22] And for some people, drug use may be beyond their control.

In terms of setting the criterion for the test, utilitarianism and justice strike slightly different balances between false negatives and false positives. The utilitarian position weighs the benefits (reduced crime through incapacitation) of including additional high-rate offenders against the cost (wasted imprisonment) of putting relatively low-rate offenders in prison. Ordinarily this position pushes in the direction of inclusiveness rather than exclusiveness. The justice position regards a false positive (unjust treatment of a relatively innocent person) as a much greater problem than a false negative (lenient treatment of a blameworthy offender). Hence, it pushes in the direction of exclusiveness. The most extreme justice position is that any false positives at all, even if based on indicators of prior criminal activity, make the policy so unjust as to be intolerable. We are inclined to weigh false positives very heavily against false negatives and therefore to set a demanding and stringent threshold. This, combined with our earlier position of looking only for very high-rate offenders, puts a great deal of strain on our discriminating tests.

The justice of current tests. To weigh the justice of tests currently proposed or used, it is first necessary to fix a conception of justice. As in the discussion of different treatment for similar offenses, one can argue that it is just for utilitarian interests to come into play even when they seem to create injustices for individuals. Moreover, if we use current practices as the standard of justice, we discover that many changes will improve the overall justice of the system. Against that standard, testing procedures that establish clear criteria based on prior criminal conduct, drug abuse history, and previous employment all seem quite tolerable. All have routinely been used in making sentencing decisions under the philosophy of rehabilitative sentencing. The heavy but not exclusive emphasis on criminal conduct and the firm rejection of demographic characteristics reveal substantial concern for individual justice. Compared with unfettered judicial discretion guided by ad hoc psychiatric judgments, use of the proposed tests would add much clarity and consistency to the present system of criminal justice decision making. In the awkward practical world we live in, the standard of current practices is fairly low, and proposed discriminating tests offer clear opportunities to improve the standard of justice. They are more accurate, more decent, and more useful than many current procedures.

When one holds these tests up to a more exacting standard emphasizing individual justice, however, the proposed tests have greater difficulties: inaccuracy, resulting in false positives, and the inclusion of variables that are not entirely under the control of individuals and are not in themselves dangerous criminal conduct.

Table 9 describes the predictive accuracy of discriminating tests as they have been reported in the literature.[23] As one reviews the table, it seems that over time the tests have become more accurate. But much of this change results from a change in the contexts in which the tests were used. In the first evaluations, the tests evaluated were those used in civil commitment proceedings to determine whether a person was dangerous enough to be confined even though he had not yet committed a crime. In this context, the tests produced vast numbers of false positives for every true positive. More recent tests have relied more heavily on conduct variables and have been used to distinguish the most active and persistent offenders among convicted populations. In this context, many fewer false positives have been produced for each true positive. This gain in accuracy is impressive. But from the point of view of individual justice, the gains are not enough because false positives still occur at far too high a rate. And from a strict point of view, even one false positive is a problem.

The tests now being proposed and used have also improved in terms of their construction. In the past a great debate raged about the relative value of clinical as opposed to statistical approaches to distinguishing

Table 9. Success at predicting dangerous activity.

Author/year[a]	Population studied	Percent identified as dangerous	Percent of all positives that were true	Ratio of false positives/true	Fraction of positives missed (%)
Wenk and Emrich, 1973	4,000 youth wards, 1964–1965, Calif.	6.8; violent parole violators	9.8	10.1	46
Wenk, Robinson, and Smith, 1972	Calif. Dept. Correction	3 (violent recidivists)	14.0	7.1	92
Wenk, Robinson, and Smith, 1972	7,712 parolees, Calif. prisons	21	0.3	325.6	77
Wenk, Robinson, and Smith, 1972	4,146 youth wards, Calif.	10	12.5	8.0	50
Kozol, Boucher, and Garofalo, 1972	592 offenders (primarily sex offenders)	11	34.7	3.1	65
Murphy, 1980	2,000 parolees, Mich. prisons, 1971	4.9 12	40.0 20.0	2.5 3.5	81 68
Murphy, 1980	1,200 parolees, Mich. prisons, 1974	4.2 11.5	32.0 29.0	3.1 3.4	91 71
Peterson and Braiker, 1980	Convicted offenders, Calif.	4 (high-rate robbers) 7 (high-rate robbers) 14 (high-rate robbers)	71.0 72.0 53.0	.40 .30 .85	80 68 52
Williams and Miller, 1977	Recidivists from arrested population, Washington, D.C.	10 15 25	41.0 64.0 92.0	2.4 1.6 1.1	71 61 52
Greenwood, 1982	Imprisoned offenders, Calif.	25, highest-rate offenders (7-factor scale)	50.0	1.0	67
Hoffman et al., 1978	Federal parolees	25 most likely to recidivate	50.0	1.0	62

a. The studies listed here are cited in full in note 23 to this chapter.

among offenders.[24] Clinical approaches accommodated a great many particular features of an individual's condition and made effective use of the diagnostic capacities of trained professionals.[25] Their great liabilities were that the judgments rendered were rooted in psychological diagnoses rather than in the relative blameworthiness of criminal acts and were therefore mysterious to ordinary citizens.[26] The statistical approach, on the other hand, used straightforward, consistent tests that could be empirically verified.[27] But the statistical approach seemed indifferent to important differences in individual circumstances that the models could not accommodate, and the models relied on status variables, such as age, family status, and economic class, as well as conduct variables.[28]

The approaches now being used seem quite different from either of these. While the idea of dangerousness can be thought of as a psychological status, and while some interests in clinical prediction survive, the context has shifted. The tests are now applied to people who have been convicted of serious crimes, not to people who are mentally ill or juvenile delinquents. So a core issue of conduct must be resolved before the tests are applied. In addition, the tests depend much more heavily on conduct variables than either the clinical or statistical approaches did. Finally, like the statistical tests, the current tests are simple, straightforward, and empirically based rather than mysterious and discretionary as the clinical tests used to be. All of these features make them superior to previous testing procedures in terms of individual justice.

Nonetheless, even if we exclude the problem of inaccuracy, the proposed tests still have a fundamental weakness: they still rely on conduct variables that are only partly under the individual's control, only marginally related to criminal conduct, and only imperfectly measured for given individuals. From the point of view of justice, it would be better to base them exclusively on accurate measures of prior criminal offending, renouncing all attempts to predict future criminal conduct in favor of distinguishing the most dangerous and wicked offenders on the basis of past acts. Indeed, only this position can overcome the objections associated with the fundamental injustice of false positives. If selective policies are seen as retribution for past acts, if the discriminating tests are limited to information about criminal conduct, and if the past acts have been attributed through appropriate criminal justice procedures, then having some mistaken assignments to the category of dangerous offenders is no worse (though also no better) than some mistaken convictions for current offenses. In this context a few false positives are tolerable. In short, backward-looking discriminating tests based on prior records are arguably just even if one adheres to the strictest principles of individual justice.

We think that the justice and practical value of these tests depend on improved measurements of criminal activity. In practice this includes five factors:

1. Solving more crimes and attributing them properly to individuals.
2. Developing accurate and comprehensive criminal records in both the adult and juvenile systems.[29]
3. Providing access to juvenile records of serious offending if a person commits a serious offense shortly after "aging out" of the juvenile system.
4. Developing weighting schemes that give greater emphasis to violent than to nonviolent offenses and greater weight to convictions than to indictments or arrests.
5. Analyzing prior criminal activity not as an absolute number of offenses but as an estimated *rate* of serious offending over a given period of time.

THE PRACTICAL VALUE OF SELECTIVE INCAPACITATION

Some critics argue that selective policies would do little to reduce crime and would not be worth the risks of injustice. Four specific arguments are made. *4 criti*

Since discriminating tests are inaccurate, becoming accurate only when high-rate offenders are about to decrease their level of activity, reliance on the tests will produce only small effects on levels of crime.[30] Because opportunities to commit crime remain and attract offenders even though the most likely offenders are already in jail, any incapacitation *in art. too* policy will be less effective than expected.[31] Because the current system already focuses selectively on dangerous offenders, there is little room for greater selectivity and little potential practical value to be gained. By focusing on the most dangerous offenders, selective incapacitation proposals decrease the threat of punishment—and perhaps its deterrent power—to the vast majority of offenders who are less dangerous. Thus a selective focus is seriously deficient as an overall response to crime.[32]

THE PRACTICAL VALUE OF DISCRIMINATING TESTS

Obviously, the accuracy of the tests used to distinguish high-rate offenders from others affects the practical value of selective policies, as well as their justice. If the tests mistakenly assign many low-rate offenders to the high-rate group, then the costs per crime avoided will be greater than if the tests discriminate perfectly. If the tests mistakenly assign many high-rate offenders to low-rate groups, then policies based on the tests will cut less deeply into current levels of crime than they would if the tests were perfectly accurate.

To decide whether discriminating tests are accurate enough to reduce crime significantly, we should consider two questions. First, how much reduction in crime can we expect if no restrictions are placed on the variables used in discriminating tests? Second, how much of this benefit would be lost if the variable used were restricted, to ensure justice?

The Rand researchers have offered some estimates of the potential crime reduction benefits of the tests they propose, based on a simulation model of the criminal justice system that includes four crucial assumptions. First, it is assumed that the underlying distribution of offending in the criminal population approximates the distribution they observed in their California prison sample. Their estimate is adjusted to accommodate the fact that many low-rate or accidental offenders also contribute to the crime problem.[33] But crimes by such offenders do not account for much of the problem of robbery and burglary, which are the focus of their study. Second, the probability of arrest, prosecution, and conviction is estimated at the average rates for California and is assumed to be independent of the rates of offending. In effect, the Rand researchers assume the system is biased neither in favor of nor against high-rate offenders.

Third, the effect of imprisonment is considered solely in terms of eliminating the crimes that an offender would have committed if he had been on the streets rather than in jail. In their model imprisonment neither deters nor rehabilitates offenders. Nor does it accelerate rates of offending on release. All the effects on crime reduction are captured perfectly by the incapacitation of offenders in jail. Fourth, the value of selective policies is estimated by comparing a policy in which every person convicted of a given offense gets the same punishment, with policies that extend sentences for those who are considered dangerous on the basis of different discriminating tests. The estimates of the practical value are given in terms of levels of crime and sizes of prison populations produced by selective policies, compared with the levels and sizes without selective policies. The comparison is useful because the basic question to be answered is whether selective policies would allow us to control crime more effectively with the same prison capacity.

Figure 6 presents the results of these simulations. Each line represents the combinations of crime level and prison population that could be produced by a particular policy. The policies differ in terms of which tests are used to distinguish the high-rate offenders and how much disparity is introduced into sentencing on the basis of the tests. In effect, the policies are more or less selective in terms the precision of the distinctions and the length of time in jail determined by the distinctions. The resulting estimates appear as lines rather than as points to indicate that any given discriminating test and any given sentencing increment for high-rate offenders can result in more or less crime and more or less imprisonment, depending on how much total imprisonment is used. In general, the more

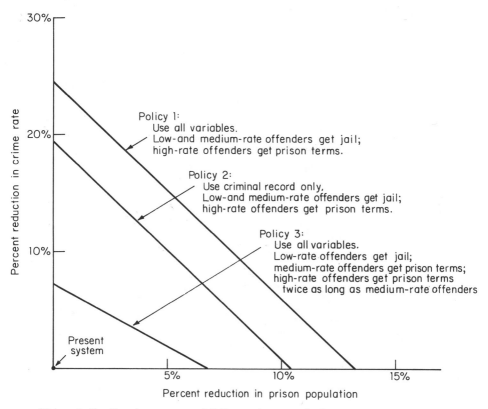

Figure 6   Predicted outcomes of different degrees of selectivity in sentencing.

imprisonment, the less crime because it is assumed that imprisonment lessens crime through incapacitation.

The interpretation of Figure 6 is easier if we assume that society would prefer to have both less crime and fewer people in prison. Then the policies whose lines are farthest from the origin of this graph are preferable to policies that are closer to it. Thus Figure 6 indicates that policies using maximum selectivity, such as Policy 3, are preferable to those that rely on less accurate test procedures, such as Policy 2, or that respond to the estimated differences among offenders with smaller differences in sentences, such as Policy 1.

Figure 7 shows how large the benefits of introducing maximum selectivity into sentencing decisions could be. The diagonal line in this figure represents the combinations of decreases in crime and imprisonment that could be produced with the most selective systems compared with unselective systems. Any point above the origin represents an improvement, in that the society will have either fewer people in prison or less crime, or some combination of the two. Figure 7 indicates that the potential reductions are not small. If we rely on discriminating policies and use all of the potential to control crime rather than to reduce prison populations, the model suggests we could produce more than a 20 percent reduction in crime. If, on the other hand, we use all of the potential to reduce prison populations while keeping crime rates constant, we could reduce prison populations by nearly 15 percent. Selectivity seems to offer some noticeable practical advantages to a beleaguered criminal justice system.

There is so much technical rigamarole involved even in representing these estimates, to say nothing of making them, that it is easy to think that something very powerful and precise has been determined once the exercise is completed. But one must keep two important points in mind while looking at the graphs. First, the estimates are the result of an elaborate back-of-the-envelope calculation rather than a representation of real empirical experience. Moreover, while the mechanics of the calculations are quite complicated, the basic concept is quite simple. It is essentially an account of what would happen if judges started to lengthen sentences for those who seemed dangerous rather than giving average sentences to everyone. Given a very skewed distribution of rates of offending, tests that have some modest discriminating power, and a model that assumes an incapacitative effect of imprisonment, the inevitable result of this calculation is that selective policies produce less crime and fewer people in prison than nonselective policies. So there is nothing particularly mysterious about the conclusion.

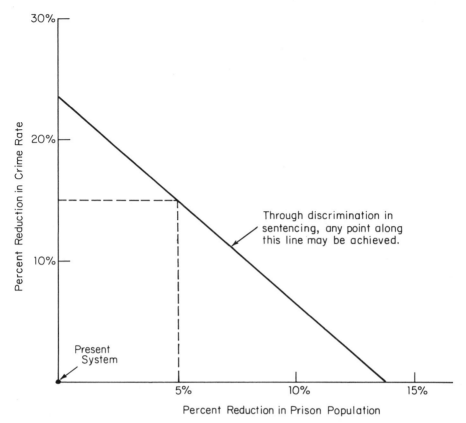

Figure 7   Achievable gains from maximally selective policies.

Indeed, the conceptual simplicity of the calculation makes the second point also easy to see. The potential gains revealed by the calculation are produced by two quite distinct features, the skewness of the underlying distribution of rates of offending and the discriminating power of the tests. Which of these is more important to the result is unclear from the calculation alone. There is evidence to suggest that the skewness in the distribution of offending is the more important factor.[34] The potential benefits are great not because the tests have great discriminating power, for many errors in classification are still made. Instead, it is because the estimated differences among offenders are so great that even weak discriminating tests can produce important practical results.

The next question, however, is whether the practical gains remain large if we restrict the tests to variables that are more just. Figure 8 reveals

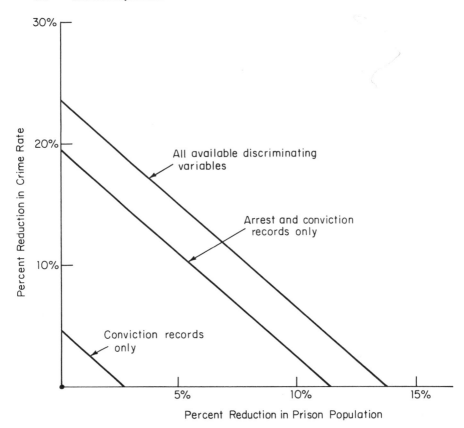

Figure 8   The impact on achievable gains of introducing constraints on test variables.

the effects of introducing constraints on the variables. It indicates that significant practical value is lost if one moves from a test using all discriminating variables (including employment history and drug abuse) to one that relies solely on convictions. In fact, the maximum crime reduction potential moves from slightly more than 20 percent to about 5 percent, and the maximum reduction in imprisonment from about 14 percent to about 3 percent. Much less is lost if one uses a test that includes arrests as well as convictions; the maximum crime reduction potential moves from a little bit more than 20 percent to slightly under 20 percent, and the maximum reduction in prison population from about 14 percent to about 12 percent. This fact leads us to the conclusion that even in the short run it is probably best to rely only on criminal conduct variables, and it makes us optimistic that if we could improve the measurement of criminal conduct variables, the discriminating power of the tests would increase dramatically.

With all these favorable assumptions, however, the maximum reduction in crime seems to be about 20 percent. Viewed from some perspectives, this may seem like a mimimal impact. And if we had to pay a substantial price in the quality of justice for this effect, it would seem to be a bad bargain. But viewed from another perspective, an effect of this size would be worth trying to achieve. After all, a 20 percent reduction in the number of robberies would be 150,000 fewer robberies each year.[35] This is a high number. No other currently available policies offer equally significant reductions in crime, particularly for no additional expenditures of money. So if the policy is tolerably just, if its effects are as large as estimated here, and if it produces no other significant adverse effect on criminal justice system operations, then it might not be a bad idea. But so far we have not shown all that. Indeed, the practical effects may be much lower than the estimates indicate because there are other threats to the practical value of selective policies.

CRIME REDUCTION THROUGH INCAPACITATION

Some people question the practical value of greater selectivity on grounds that increased imprisonment will not necessarily reduce criminal activity. At the extreme, one can argue that focusing on dangerous offenders could *increase* crime as the result of two different mechanisms. First, by labeling people as dangerous offenders and thereby hardening their self-concept and restricting their legitimate opportunities, one might actually accelerate their rate of offending and extend their careers.[36] Second, to the extent that crimes are committed by groups, which will compensate for the loss of a member by recruiting additional people and training them in criminal skills, incapacitation may expand the population of skilled offenders. This last effect may be particularly important for juvenile offenders.[37]

Slightly less extreme is the view that enhanced imprisonment of dangerous offenders, while not increasing crime, will nonetheless fail to reduce crimes committed by dangerous offenders. This "no-effect" hypothesis is also supported by three different arguments. One is that offenders store up crimes while in prison and, once released, commit them at an accelerated rate. Second is that many criminal groups or on-going conspiracies continue to commit crimes despite the loss of group members. The third argument is that opportunities left unexploited by incarcerated dangerous offenders may tempt nondangerous offenders into committing crimes.

Standing against these pessimistic views is a simple incapacitation hypothesis: if a dangerous offender is supervised in a way that makes it impossible for him to commit offenses, then crime will be reduced by the number of crimes he would have committed if he had been free in that period.[38] In effect, putting offenders out of commission for a period of time has no long-term effect, either positive or negative, on underlying rates of offending. On balance, we think that incapacitation of dangerous offenders *will* reduce crime, but also that the effect will be smaller than that calculated on the assumption that all the criminal offenses they would have committed will disappear when offenders are under supervision. We come to this conclusion for several reasons.

First, we believe that a great deal of crime is caused by unusually dangerous offenders because of their unusual motivation and capacities, rather than opportunities. It is implausible that people who commit ten to fifty armed robberies per year are simply tempted by unusually attractive opportunities that would attract others if left unexploited. And it is implausible that punishment will either encourage or discourage dangerous offenders from committing crimes in the future. Age may ultimately discourage them, but additional punishment would seem to make little difference to their self-identity, to their noncriminal opportunities, or to their resolve to go straight. Thus we believe that incapacitation can reduce crimes among determined offenders and that it may be the only way to do so.

Second, we think that in aggregate terms the reduction will be small but not insignificant. Dangerous offenders account for more than their share, but by no means all or even a majority, of serious offenses.[39] Moreover, our practical ability to identify dangerous offenders, although tolerably accurate, is limited. So selective policies operate imperfectly on the small piece of the serious crime problem that is produced by dangerous offenders.

Third, we think that some of the mechanisms conceived by those who hypothesize increases in crime might operate at least some of the time. Given our imperfect abilities to identify dangerous offenders, we think that some people may be wrongly identified and that the identification may affect their future rates of offending and the length of their careers. We can imagine that incapacitation of a single member may not end the crimes by an ongoing "gang" or "ring." So some crime-increasing effects may offset the smaller than estimated incapacitation effects. Taken together, these observations lead to a judgment that incapacitation will reduce crime, but less than perfectly.

THE MARGINAL EFFECTIVENESS OF GREATER SELECTIVITY

The third argument against selective policies asserts that the criminal justice system is already highly selective in its operations and that there is little to be gained from adding new mechanisms. Although a few operational changes could increase the focus on dangerous offenders, any further adjustments would be too difficult to implement. The argument is that the system is already as selective as it is going to be, and the benefits revealed by the theoretical calculation are exaggerated or illusory.

The best way to address this objection is to examine current practices at each stage of the system's operation, which we will do in Part II. But at this point two general points are worth making. As discussed earlier, it is not at all clear that the system is now very selective with respect to dangerous offenders. In fact, our evidence suggests that high-rate offenders may face lower probabilities of arrest and imprisonment for any given offense than low-rate offenders. Also, even if the system is selective at the back end, where sentencing decisions are made, it seems much less certain that it is discriminating at the front end, where investigation and prosecutorial decisions are made.

The reason for this difference in selectivity is the strong desire to keep the determination of guilt and innocence as free from bias as possible. If investigators and prosecutors knew that an offender had a substantial prior record or had the sort of character that indicated he was unusually dangerous, they might be tempted to gather evidence illegally or even to manufacture evidence that would contaminate the fair, objective determination of guilt or innocence. Once guilt has been convincingly established and the only remaining issue is sentencing, it seems more appropriate to allow broad knowledge of the offender's character to come into play.

It probably also matters that at this stage it is a judge who makes the sentencing decision, while police and prosecutors make the decisions in the investigative and prosecutorial stages. In our system the police, at least, and perhaps prosecutors as well are required to have a somewhat more restricted view than judges of the social values at stake in handling individual cases. They are more interested in crime control than in individual justice. The judge, on the other hand, is supposed to balance these considerations according to the law and the broadest interpretations of the public interest. Thus it is appropriate for judges to exercise discretion on a basis that would be inappropriate for police and prosecutors.

There is a convincing coherence and familiarity to these views. And the strongest part of the argument seems truly unassailable: namely, that in considering questions of guilt and innocence, information about the offender's character should be firmly excluded lest it contaminate this determination, on which so much else depends. But adherence to that principle would require only that all such information be kept out at trial. It is not at all clear that this principle should prevent police and prosecutors from taking evidence of character and prior conduct into account as they make decisions about how to spend their resources to develop cases. As long as constitutional restrictions on investigative procedures are respected, and as long as malicious *ad hominem* motivations are excluded, there may be room for investigators and prosecutors to increase their efforts.[40] An admittedly strong interest in equal protection and due process does not entitle all offenders to an equally sloppy investigation and prosecution.[41] Investigators and prosecutors are entitled to vary their level of effort and could do so on the basis of determinations that particular offenders are dangerous.[42] Since the cases they make must ultimately face the rigors of trial (or in the case of plea bargaining, the anticipation of a trial), the offender's due process and equal protection rights are adequately protected.

Finally, from the perspective of the offender, it is not at all clear that the sentencing decision is less consequential than investigative and prosecutorial decisions. Indeed, the opposite seems more likely. Sentencing decisions determine length of time in prison; investigative and prosecutorial decisions determine only the amount of surveillance and investigation an offender must endure. Sentencing decisions have *certain* consequences for offenders; investigative and prosecutorial decisions have only probabilistic implications. If judgments about dangerousness can properly influence how much time a convicted offender spends in prison, they should also be allowed in making less consequential decisions about investigation and prosecution, particularly if knowledge of character is not allowed to intrude in the determination of guilt or innocence.

In sum, existing criminal justice operations could be sharpened to a more discriminating focus. And the greater and more urgent opportunities for enhanced selectivity are not in sentencing, but in investigation and prosecution, where such opportunities are most likely to be missed. And if they are missed at this stage, they will also be missed at the sentencing stage, not only for current offenses, but also for any subse-

- more selectivity at
investig'd prosec.
Stage too is needed

quent arrests and sentencing decisions, because the information about prior offending will be lost because of the failure to solve the crimes.

THE INSUFFICIENCY OF SELECTIVE POLICIES

A fourth objection to the practical value of selective policies is that they are insufficient. They typically leave unanswered the questions of what should be done with offenders who are not particularly dangerous or with offenses generated by temporary, accidental, or opportunistic offenders. If the answers to those questions are that nothing should be done, that the only intention of selectivity is to include solely the offenses committed by dangerous offenders, then one might reasonably be worried about whether selectivity will reduce crime. Even if selective policies reduced the number of crimes committed by dangerous offenders, they might increase the number and seriousness of crimes committed by others. The less dangerous offenders might feel licensed to commit more serious offenses, or the number of minor offenses might increase, and some might escalate unintentionally to serious crimes. In effect, greater selectivity might implicitly create a broader social license to commit crimes.

On the other hand, if less dangerous offenders got the same treatment they now receive, and dangerous offenders received increased punishment, then crime might decrease, but only because the total quantity of social control had increased. Presumably, if one believes in incapacitation, then more imprisonment will always reduce crime.

What makes selective policies interesting, however, is not that they increase or decrease the total amount of social control, but that they redistribute it across offenders. In addition, a number of lesser forms of punishment, other than imprisonment, might be appropriate for less dangerous offenders. Fines, restitution, house arrest, intensive parole, community service for offenders, the use of police as parole officers—all these offer incapacitation benefits more decently and at lower cost than jails and prisons. Experiments with such alternatives for less dangerous offenders should be an important component of any continued investigation of selective incapacitation policies.[43]

INSTITUTIONAL EFFECTS

So far, our analysis of a heightened focus on dangerous offenders has examined only the direct, first-round effects: those on individual justice and on effectiveness in controlling crime. Arguably, however, the most important effects of such policies are the long-term institutional effects. Three different areas could be adversely affected: the integrity of our criminal justice institutions, the stature of the criminal law, and our general political ideology as it affects the criminal justice system. The facts and assumptions that constitute the case for selective policies necessarily affect these broader concerns.

EFFECTS ON CRIMINAL JUSTICE INSTITUTIONS

One of the most important consequences of encouraging a selective focus on dangerous offenders is that it has the potential for corrupting criminal justice institutions by giving greater license to improper, *ad hominem* motivations.[44] By establishing a proper basis for interest in individuals as individuals where none now exists, we may create a greater license for *improper* motivations to intrude. By identifying a group of incorrigibles, we may unwittingly encourage recklessness among police and prosecutors.

This potential threat is not a *logical* consequence of encouraging a more selective focus, but it may be a natural sociological result. It may be difficult to accord identified dangerous offenders the rights they are guaranteed. We think that the risks can be controlled by creating procedural disciplines at each stage of processing and by maintaining the defendant's strict anonymity at the trial stages. But even with these restrictions we note the potential threat to the fairness and integrity of criminal justice institutions.

THE STATURE OF THE CRIMINAL LAW

A second broad question is whether narrowing the focus of the system weakens the power and stature of the criminal law. After all, encouraging a sharpened focus on those few who often commit violent crimes seems to retreat from a standard of general responsibility for all criminal offenses. It seems to admit that we are neither willing nor able to deliver punishment for all offenses now on the books. The implicit "decriminalization" of the first few offenses may radically weaken the moral authority of the law.

This point is worrisome, but it should focus our attention on the question of new forms of punishment beyond imprisonment. Given the current costs of prison, it is quite conceivable that many offenses are worth punishing, but *not* through the clumsy instruments of imprisonment. If we had available less expensive forms of punishment, such as restitution, voluntary service, house arrest, perhaps even public shaming, we could save prison for dangerous offenders and still not erode the current stature of the criminal law.

IDEOLOGICAL EFFECTS

Perhaps the most important effect of selective policies, is that they may subtly influence our most general views of crime and criminal justice. At the foundation of selective incapacitation is the distinctly illiberal view that people differ in their capacity for evil and that these differences are not the result of broad social processes but of something inherent in the individual. This view assumes that the differences among people are relatively permanent and a just basis for punishment. And finally it assumes that, knowing all this, the criminal justice system will nonetheless be restrained in deciding which people are dangerous offenders and that serious criminal acts will be the basis for assigning people to the category of dangerous offenders, rather than factors such as race, culture, political views, and so on.

In our view, the ideological issues are important not only for explaining the politics of the debate about selective incapacitation, but also as a potentially important result of explicitly adopting such policies. As the ideology moves closer to the assumptions about human nature underlying the conceptions of selective incapacitation, real potential for unleashing atavistic passion is created. Social hostility *can* become focused and more intense. Enthusiasm for attacking evil people can overwhelm due process designed to protect the rights of individuals. We take such possibilities seriously, particularly when a selective focus is introduced in the early stages of the system where guilt or innocence on a current offense is still an issue.

In principle, these worries about a major ideological change spawning a more vicious criminal justice system could be sufficient to overwhelm any arguments in favor of selective incapacitation. Indeed, against these worries, the possible benefits may seem small. Still, we think that selective policies can be introduced without necessarily unleashing all these forces. The keys to keeping the passions in check are: maintaining tight due process constraints on the gathering of evidence of criminal conduct, keeping the discriminating tests closely tied to indicators of criminal conduct, and creating some due process guarantees over the decisions that identify dangerous offenders.

CONCLUSIONS

In our view the threshold objections to selective incapacitation do mark out important areas of vulnerability and uncertainty, but none stands as an absolute barrier to further consideration of the issue. Many of the objections depend a great deal on what is being proposed at each stage of the judicial process, what the purpose is, and what alternatives exist. Whether the policy would be more effective than present policies depends a great deal on what is now being done. In Part II we take a detailed look at how a selective policy would operate at each stage of the criminal justice system.

II

SELECTIVE PROGRAMS

4

Sentencing

OUR REVIEW of selective proposals begins at the end. Sentencing is the last step in the process of determining who will be imprisoned and for how long. By the time someone reaches this stage, many important decisions—investigation and preparation of the case, the decision to arrest, choice of charges, the setting of bail, the negotiation of a plea—have already been made. These decisions limit what can justly and usefully be done to control crime at the sentencing stage.

Of the limitations established by earlier steps in the process, the most obvious are those tied to the offense, or series of offenses, for which an offender has been convicted. The criminal law establishes maximum and minimum levels of punishment that may be imposed by judges and parole boards. This range is very broad under indeterminate sentencing laws and much narrower under determinate or mandatory sentencing laws.[1] In the case of convictions for multiple charges, judges also have the latitude to decide on consecutive or concurrent sentencing. How much latitude judges and parole boards have to impose punishment, then, depends fundamentally on what police and prosecutors have done to gather evidence.

The more important limitations imposed by police and prosecutorial actions, however, are those that select who reaches the sentencing stage and what labels they wear when they arrive. If the police and prosecutors fail to solve a crime, it will never reach sentencing. Moreover, if they have failed in the past to properly attribute crimes committed by dangerous offenders, then the records of those offenders will be indistinguishable from the records of more ordinary offenders. Even if the dangerous offenders get to the sentencing stage, they won't be recognized for what they are.

In fact, it becomes apparent that proposals emphasizing selectivity in sentencing are really attempts to use sentencing discretion to retrieve the failures of the earlier stages. If the system were routinely clearing criminal offenses — that is, properly investigating them, arresting those responsible, adding charges to those already arrested when appropriate, and winning convictions as often as the dangerous offenders are allegedly committing offenses — we would hardly need to be very selective at the sentencing stage. The most dangerous offenders would be convicted more often and would spend much more time in prison than ordinary offenders. Because the system is *not* performing in this way, however, it is tempting to try to salvage the situation by turning sentencing decisions to the purpose of selective incapacitation. As we will see, this places strains on the justice of the system. It might be wiser to increase selectivity at earlier stages of the processing and make sentencing more neutral.

In this chapter, we focus on current proposals to make sentencing decisions more selective, to reserve prison cells for the most dangerous offenders. This chapter and the succeeding chapters are organized around four main questions:

> What would a selective focus require at this stage of the criminal justice system?
>
> Would the shift to a more selective focus be just?
>
> What, in practical terms, can we hope to accomplish by adopting the proposed changes?
>
> On balance, given ambiguities about the justice and practical value of the proposed policies, how much potential do they have, and what experiments could be undertaken to resolve the major uncertainties?

FOCUSING PRISON CAPACITY ON DANGEROUS OFFENDERS

The decisions determining which offenders spend how much time in prison are now commonly made by three different public agencies: legislators, who pass laws setting maximum and minimum penalties for offenses; judges, who decide on appropriate sentences in individual cases; and, in at least forty states, parole boards, which adjust the judicial decisions to reflect each offender's capacities for rehabilitation and to keep the prison population within the system's physical capacities. As traditionally conceived, this system has focused primarily on criminal *acts,* not on the offenders' characteristics. True, the parole system adjusts prison sentences in response to psychological assessments of prisoners, their conduct while in prison, and their prospects for rehabilitation, as estimated from characteristics such as prison record and employment history.[2] But this is seen primarily as a wise bit of mercy in a system that is otherwise committed to punishing people for criminal acts. Recently, however, proposals have been made to make sentencing decisions reflect not only the seriousness of criminal acts, but also some estimates of the dangerousness of the offender himself.[3]

The current interest in selective sentencing can be understood only against the background of the current crisis in criminal sentencing. The crisis is largely one of performance. The prison system simply cannot provide the quantity of punishment mandated by existing criminal codes at the current levels of criminal convictions. Table 10 presents data on the average time served, the average maximum sentence, and the level of prison overcrowding for a little more than half the states. Although this table is crude, it indicates the practical dimensions of the problem: the prisons are stuffed full, and the time served is far less than the maximum sentence. This crisis exists even though fewer than 10 percent of reported crimes result in arrests, and fewer than 15 percent of felony arrests result in felony convictions.[4] In an important sense, the system is bankrupt: our criminal laws establish a commitment to punish offenders at levels well beyond our current capacity to administer it.

Of course, there may be nothing particularly admirable about our criminal codes. Indeed, to many, the levels of punishment written into our current criminal statutes seem truly Draconian. And relative to many other countries in the world, the maximum sentences are extreme.[5] So it might be just and wise to mandate less punishment than our laws now do. Others believe that the problem is not the justice of sentencing laws, but the excessive costs of the forms of punishment we have adopted. In this view, the problem has been created partly by the inadequacy of government accounting systems, which failed to register and provide for the gradual deterioration of our prison capacity, partly by the establishment of standards that raised the costs of prison construction and operation, and partly by the extraordinarily high costs of new construction. To still others, the problem is a failure of imagination and an unwillingness to experiment with forms of punishment such as house arrest and community service, which might lessen the financial burdens and be more appropriate for many offenders now being punished by imprisonment. Whatever the sources and possible solutions, the fact remains that the system promises much more punishment than it can deliver.

Table 10. Prison time served, prison time mandated, and prison overcrowding: violent prisoners in 28 states.

State	Average time served (years)[a]	Average maximum sentence (years)[b]	Percent in overcrowded conditions[c]
Arizona	3.3	10.1	17.6%
Colorado	1.8	9.0	50.3
Connecticut	1.4	9.0	51.3
Georgia	2.4	8.9	61.7
Hawaii	3.2	22.3	43.5
Idaho	2.1	6.4	41.5
Illinois	2.8	10.1	65.2
Kansas	2.4	20.7	42.8
Kentucky	1.8	9.7	32.1
Maine	2.5	5.2	84.1
Maryland	1.3	6.5	76.7
Massachusetts	2.0	10.1	32.9
Minnesota	9.6	8.0	17.8
Mississippi	2.8	7.2	91.9
Missouri	2.1	7.2	56.6
Montana	1.8	10.3	22.7
Nevada	3.3	8.4	52.1
New Hampshire	1.5	6.0	88.7
New Mexico	3.1	10.4	55.3
New York	2.0	5.3	54.3
North Dakota	1.7	4.9	96.3
Ohio	4.1	25.6	69.8
Oklahoma	2.1	6.4	38.0
South Dakota	2.5	4.3	7.8
Tennessee	2.8	10.6	67.4
Utah	3.3	23.8	69.9
Washington	2.6	15.8	56.9
Wyoming	2.1	5.7	94.0

a. U.S. Department of Justice, Bureau of Prisons, *National Prisoner Statistics—State Prisoners: Admissions and Releases 1970* (Washington, D.C.: U.S. Government Printing Office, 1972).

b. U.S. Department of Justice, National Criminal Justice Information and Statistics Service, *Census of Prisoners in State Correctional Facilities: 1973,* NPS Special Report SD-NPS-SR-3 (Washington, D.C.: U.S. Government Printing Office, 1976).

c. U.S. Department of Justice, Bureau of Justice Statistics, *State Correctional Populations and Facilities, 1979—Advance Report* (Washington, D.C.: U.S. Department of Justice, 1981).

The crisis is not only one of performance, however. It is also philosophical and moral. Indeed, the political struggles over the scope of promised punishment reflect sharp disagreements about the philosophy, aims, and assumptions of criminal punishment. One crucial conflict is between retributivist and utilitarian philosophies of punishment.[6] The hallmark of retributivist philosophies is that the purpose of criminal punishment is not to help the individual or the society, but simply to serve justice; a criminal offender deserves punishment, and the society is required to administer it.[7] Utilitarian philosophies consider that the purpose of punishment is to improve the society or the offender. Punishment is justified if it deters others from committing crimes, if it prevents offenders from committing crimes while they are incapacitated, or if it discourages them from committing crimes upon release, through deterrence or rehabilitation.[8]

These purposes are sufficiently distinct to allow sharp debates even within the literal terms of the philosophies. However, the debates often reflect other unstated differences about human nature, the role of reason and passion in punishment, the intended beneficiaries of punishment, and the concept of individualized justice, as well as these different philosophies. Those who see people as basically good and redeemable, for example, are inclined toward utilitarian views that counsel lenient treatment and major efforts to reintegrate offenders into society, while those who see some people as bad and incorrigible are inclined toward retributivist concepts that urge harsh treatment with little effort expended on rehabilitation.

Those who depend on tradition to justify punishment, tolerate moral passion as an important component, reject scientific fads as inconsistent, and view instrumental calculations as insufficiently respectful of either individual rights or community values, are drawn toward retributivist ideas. The utilitarian conceptions are built less on morality and tradition than on the possibilities of science. As science learns more about the crime control benefits that come from rehabilitation, deterrence, and incapacitation, sentencing schemes will have to be adjusted, regardless of prior conceptions of just deserts. Thus, while both retributivists and utilitarians are loyal to reason, people who think that reason should be guided by cultivated moral sentiments and tradition tend to be retributivists, and those who feel comfortable with the discipline and possibilities of science are utilitarians.

A third issue in the background of debates over sentencing policies is the question of who should be the principal beneficiaries of criminal punishment: the victims, the community at large, or the offender? Of course, a strict retributivist might argue that such judgments smack of utilitarianism and thus are irrelevant to a just system of punishment. But the current popularity of retributivist ideas is explained at least partly by the fact that they emphasize interests in keeping community order and satisfying the victim, as against aiding the offender. Although current debates tend to link retributivist philosophies to an emphasis on the interests of victims and community, and utilitarian philosophies to an emphasis on the offender, these ideas are not necessarily connected. Retributivist philosophies establish elaborate procedures to protect the interests of accused offenders from the unbridled hostilities of the victims and the passions of the community. Moreover, although this idea is underemphasized in modern statements, early retributivist conceptions assumed that just punishment was good for the character of the offender and provided his only route back into the community's good graces.[9] Punishment was considered therapeutic as well as just. The utilitarian objectives of deterrence and incapacitation, on the other hand, are primarily directed at controlling crime in the interests of the community.[10] Even rehabilitation was originally justified in terms of crime control rather than consideration for the interests of the offender.[11] For utilitarian purposes, both victim and offender are secondary to the more abstract concern of guaranteeing community order. So competing interests in helping victims, the community, and the offender cut across retributivist and utilitarian justifications in confusing ways.

A fourth issue that confuses debates about sentencing policies is conflicting views of what constitutes individual justice and fairness for the offender. Does individual justice mean treating like cases alike? Or noticing and responding to differences among cases that seem relevant to the justice of a particular sentence? Should the offender's characteristics, as distinct from his acts, be admitted as a relevant difference in sentencing, and if so, what characteristics can properly be used? These differing views could be reconciled if we allowed our laws to become ever more complicated and structured all our exceptions in the form of new general rules, but the desire to keep our laws simple and comprehensible prevents this. In short, the desires to keep laws simple and to treat like cases alike run against the desire to do justice to the individual by recognizing particular differences. Any sentencing system is vulnerable at any given moment to criticism from one or more of these conceptions of individual justice.

So philosophies of criminal sentencing are inherently complicated and confusing, and the recent history of sentencing policies reflects all of these tensions and confusions. For the last generation or so, the society seems to have relied primarily on the philosophy of rehabilitative sentencing. The aim was to give criminal offenders just sentences that would also foster their rehabilitation. The key institutions were indeterminate sentencing laws and parole boards. The time spent in prison for a given offense could be lengthened or shortened, depending on the parole board's judgment about an offender's prospects for rehabilitation. Prisons were encouraged to develop services such as basic education, vocational training, and psychological counseling, as well as to set up halfway houses and work release programs for helping offenders return to the community.[12]

Recently the society has become disenchanted with this philosophy, in part because it seems to have failed in its most fundamental objectives. Rehabilitation programs have not, apparently, made offenders resistant to further offending, although their failure may have been caused by inadequate investment.[13] The philosophy has been attacked also on grounds of justice. Those on the right believe that justice is demeaned by sentences that are too light relative to the gravity of the offenses. Those on the left attack the broad discretion that has resulted in offenders convicted of similar offenses serving vastly different sentences.[14]

In the background of our disenchantment with rehabilitative sentencing is probably an important shift in ideology as well. Many now believe that the policy was far too sentimental about criminal offenders and far too willing to sacrifice the interests of the victim and the broader community to naive hopes for rehabilitation. As reasonable as that criticism may now appear, however, the historical record suggests that it is unfair. The original justifications for rehabilitative sentencing were to achieve greater crime control at low cost by applying new scientific techniques that would allow us to distinguish offenders who were capable of rehabilitation from those who were not. Parole boards were expected to introduce greater consistency by providing a way to review the idiosyncratic sentencing decisions of individual judges.[15] In these respects the original discussions of rehabilitative sentencing have an eerie resemblance to modern-day discussions of selective incapacitation.

The philosophies that have begun to gain favor are based on a retributivist view that the purpose of criminal punishment is to do justice and on a pragmatic interest in using prison space for those who would be likely to commit the most crimes if free. Floating above these conceptions are various notions that seek to integrate retributivist and utilitarian justifications for punishment.[16] But there is probably less agreement now about the philosophy of criminal sentencing than there has been for a generation.

The actual performance of the system reveals the depths of our confusion about the philosophy and practice of criminal sentencing. Table 11 shows the enormous variations among states in terms of the conviction offenses of those in prison because of the state's different philosophies of and physical capacities for punishment. A 1978 national survey found that 47 percent of all those imprisoned in state adult correctional facilities had been convicted of violent crimes; 37 percent had been convicted of

Table 11. Conviction offenses of those in prison, by state.

| State | Total | Offense | | |
		Violent	Property	Public order, other
Northeast	33,117	14,957 (45%)	12,435 (38%)	5,725 (17%)
Maine	834	349	346	139
New Hampshire	236	119	92	25
Vermont	117	50	39	28
Massachusetts	2,297	1,886	231	180
Rhode Island	537	335	144	78
Connecticut[a]	—	—	—	—
New York	16,498	4,749	8,578	3,171
New Jersey	5,701	3,179	1,491	1,031
Pennsylvania	6,877	4,290	1,514	1,073
North Central	52,339	27,734 (53%)	17,386 (33%)	7,219 (14%)
Ohio	11,687	6,349	3,071	2,267
Indiana	3,671	2,343	1,128	200
Illinois	10,289	7,193	2,343	753
Michigan	11,841	5,402	3,094	2,545
Wisconsin	2,937	1,451	1,261	225
Minnesota	1,790	929	720	141
Iowa	1,700	694	982	24
Missouri	5,003	1,933	2,434	636
North Dakota	283	122	104	57
South Dakota[a]	—	—	—	—
Nebraska	1,055	280	560	215
Kansas	2,083	1,038	869	156
South	100,000	44,238 (44%)	41,165 (41%)	14,597 (15%)
Delaware	0	0	0	0

Table 11 (*continued*). Conviction offenses of those in prison, by state.

State	Total	Violent	Property	Public order, other
		Offense		

State	Total	Violent	Property	Public order, other
Maryland	6,845	3,223	1,980	1,642
Dist. Columbia	1,002	551	323	128
Virginia	7,246	4,028	2,222	996
West Virginia	1,238	470	591	168
North Carolina	13,421	3,717	7,627	2,077
South Carolina	5,339	1,954	2,347	1,038
Georgia	8,592	4,666	3,233	693
Florida	16,263	8,244	5,481	2,538
Kentucky	3,441	1,175	1,643	623
Tennessee	4,792	1,938	2,320	534
Alabama[a]	—	—	—	—
Mississippi	1,675	602	753	320
Arkansas	2,274	625	1,521	128
Louisiana	1,832	756	783	293
Oklahoma	3,526	1,659	1,385	482
Texas	22,514	10,621	8,956	2,937
West	32,935	16,147 (49%)	9,232 (25%)	7,556 (23%)
Montana	600	152	288	160
Idaho	769	272	375	122
Wyoming	409	149	158	102
Colorado	2,331	1,304	769	258
New Mexico	1,692	546	549	597
Arizona	2,815	1,378	828	609
Utah	789	232	502	55
Nevada	1,141	617	393	131
Washington	3,694	1,556	1,635	503
Oregon	639	245	358	36
California	17,269	9,360	3,149	4,760
Alaska	394	148	134	112
Hawaii	393	188	94	111
Total states	218,391	103,076 (47%)	80,218 (37%)	35,097 (16%)
Federal	23,916	7,169 (30%)	5,468 (23%)	11,279 (47%)
Total state plus federal[b]	242,307	110,245 (46%)	85,686 (35%)	46,376 (19%)

Source: Kenneth Carlson, *American Prisons and Jails,* vol. 2: *Population Trend and Projections* (Washington, D.C.: U.S. Government Printing Office, 1980), 117–118.

a. Information was not available for these states.

b. Data are missing for 8 percent of prisoners.

property offenses. The allocation of Massachusetts prison spaces, for example, appears to be highly selective: 82 percent of the prison population is serving time for a crime of violence. In Missouri, on the other hand, which is more typical, the equivalent figure is under 40 percent. In the South as a whole the prison population has the lowest percentage of violent criminals of any region: 44 percent.[17] Even within the federal system, treatment is remarkably varied. Table 12 shows the differences in sentences meted out by federal judges in different districts. Indeed, there is great variation even within federal districts. Table 13 shows the differences among sentences that would be given by federal judges within a given circuit.

Considering the practical problems and broad confusion surrounding current sentencing policy, it is not surprising that recent proposals reflect complex blends of principles and justifications. One book has proposed a sentencing scheme that is primarily, but not exclusively, offense oriented.[18] Those who commit murder or rob with a firearm would definitely be imprisoned, with few exceptions for a first offense. For all other offenses, however, some evidence of "bad character" must be offered. For nonrobbery assaults, a showing of aggravated seriousness or repetitiveness must be made to justify imprisonment.[19] For burglary and drug offenses, an argument is made for drawing a line between "professionals" and "amateurs." Incarceration is recommended for professionals, while punitive alternatives to incarceration are recommended for amateurs.[20] Presumably the distinction is based on the rate and persistence of criminal conduct, though exactly how this will be discovered remains unclear. How long should offenders remain in prison? The author answers that since the first year of a prison term means much more than the tenth, a maximum of five years per offense might be appropriate.[21] Exceptions would be allowed for unusually vicious offenses and for serious mental disorder. Implementation of these proposals would probably relieve prison overcrowding in the southern states, but not in the hard-pressed northeastern and western coastal states. In a somewhat disguised way, this proposal makes sentencing decisions contingent on judgments of character as well as the offense. Rate and persistence in offending are important criteria in sentencing assaulters, burglars, drug dealers, and so on, making this proposal selective with respect to offenders.

A second proposal goes much farther in this direction by including some characteristics that do not describe criminal conduct.[22] At the center of this proposal is a scale for distinguishing low-, medium-, and high-rate

Table 12. Average length of sentence, in months, for selected offenses, federal courts.

State	Homicide and assault	Robbery	Burglary	Larceny	Auto theft	Forgery and counterfeiting
Maine	—	—	—	144	21	24
Massachusetts	48	115	40	36	20	32
New York (Northern District)	—	39	—	11	9	12
New York (Southern District)	18	130	2	48	12	49
New Jersey	11	103	27	50	32	29
Pennsylvania (Eastern District)	102	88	—	25	49	30
Maryland	6	146	61	45	49	40
Virginia (Eastern District)	66	135	81	50	41	39
Florida (Middle District)	—	126	34	37	32	41
Texas (Northern District)	62	224	46	42	39	66
Kentucky (Eastern District)	24	124	167	25	32	20
Ohio (Northern District)	28	119	36	29	31	35
Illinois (Northern District)	20	81	30	40	45	38
Indiana (Southern District)	40	101	24	35	29	34
Missouri (Eastern District)	27	180	60	54	46	46
Missouri (Western District)	36	120	—	57	36	33
California (Northern District)	79	115	120	32	42	37
California (Central District)	190	96	24	40	41	43
Kansas	74	115	—	46	47	63
Oklahoma (Western District)	29	85	48	31	36	41
District of Columbia	161	103	84	42	40	67
National average	102	120	63	40	38	42

Source: Pierce O'Donnell, Michael J. Churgin, and Dennis E. Curtis, *Toward a Just and Effective Sentencing System: Agenda for Legislative Reform* (New York: Praeger, 1977), 5.

Table 13. Variability in sentences passed by fifty federal appellate judges.

Sentence	Bank robbery	Sale of heroin	Theft, possession of stolen goods	Possession of unregistered gun
Most severe	18 yrs. prison, $5000	10 yrs. prison, 5 yrs. probation	7.5 yrs. prison	1 yr. prison
6th most severe	15 yrs. prison	6 yrs. prison, 5 yrs. probation	6 yrs. prison	6 mos. prison, 3 yrs. probation
12th most severe	15 yrs. prison	5 yrs. prison, 5 yrs. probation	4 yrs. prison	3 mos. prison, 21 mos. probation
Median	10 yrs. prison	5 yrs. prison, 3 yrs. probation	3 yrs. prison	1 mo. prison, 11 mos. probation
12th least severe	7.5 yrs. prison	3 yrs. prison, 3 yrs. probation	3 yrs. prison	2 yrs. probation
6th least severe	5 yrs. prison	3 yrs. prison, 3 yrs. probation	2 yrs. prison	1 yr. probation
Least severe	5 yrs. prison	1 yr. prison, 5 yrs. probation	4 yrs. probation	6 mos. probation

Source: Anthony Partridge and William B. Eldridge, *The Second Circuit Sentencing Study: A Report to the Judges* (Washington, D.C.: Federal Judicial Center, 1974).

burglars and robbers among all those convicted of those crimes. The seven variables used to distinguish among the groups are:

1. Incarceration for more than half of the two-year period preceding the most recent arrest.
2. A prior conviction for a crime of the type that would justify additional incapacitation.
3. Juvenile conviction prior to age sixteen.
4. Prior commitment to a state or federal juvenile facility.
5. Heroin or barbiturate use in the two-year period preceding the current arrest.
6. Heroin or barbiturate use as a juvenile.
7. Employment for less than half of the two-year period preceding the current arrest.[23]

Those who scored high on the seven-variable test would receive longer sentences, and those who scored low, reduced sentences.

THE JUSTICE OF SELECTIVE SENTENCING

In considering these proposals, it is useful to begin by recognizing that it would be difficult to design a system of sentencing that allowed more injustice than the current system. If a just system requires like cases to be treated alike, punishments properly fitted to offenses and offenders, and a fair determination of all the factual issues that place offenders in one category rather than another, then the current system of rehabilitative sentencing is a disaster.

The system's greatest failures are its inability to ensure that like cases will be treated alike and its carelessness in making the factual determination on which sentences should depend. Constitutional principles and legislation do not spell out what characteristics a judge may consider in sentencing, nor how he should make determinations about these characteristics. The only guidance for judges, which covers a broad philosophy of rehabilitation, is the current interpretation by the courts of sentencing principles, as well as the philosophy expressed in most state criminal laws. In deciding the case of *Williams* v. *New York*, for example, the Supreme Court found that criminal sentences should be based "on the fullest information possible concerning the defendant's life and characteristics."[24] Similarly, in *Pennsylvania* v. *Ashe*, the Court decided that "for the determination of sentences, justice generally requires consideration of more than the particular acts by which the crime was committed and that there be taken into account the circumstances of the offense together with the character and propensities of the offender."[25]

The *Williams* case is particularly instructive. The trial judge overruled a jury recommendation of life imprisonment and imposed the death penalty on the basis not only of the shocking details of the crime, which had been revealed, of course, to the jury, but also on the information in the presentence investigation. According to the Supreme Court's account, the trial judge "referred to the experience appellant 'had had on thirty other burglaries in and about the same vicinity' where the murder had been committed. The appellant had not been convicted of these burglaries although the judge had information that he had confessed to some and had been identified as the perpetrator of some of the others. The judge also referred to certain activities of appellant as shown by the probation report that indicated appellant possessed a 'morbid sexuality' and classified him as a 'menace to society.' "[26] The Supreme Court upheld the imposition of the death penalty on this basis against a due process challenge. Noting that the "New York statutes emphasize a prevalent modern philosophy of penology that the punishment should fit the offender and not merely the crime," the Court reasoned that strict adherence to evidentiary rules limiting the bases for sentencing to tesitmony given in open court by witnesses subject to cross-examination would undermine the ability of judges to individualize sentences on the basis of the best available information.[27]

The result, according to former Judge Marvin Frankel, is a system that "allow(s) sentences to be 'individualized' not so much in terms of defendants, but mainly in terms of the wide spectrum of character, bias, neurosis, and daily vagary encountered among occupants of the trial bench . . . The evidence is conclusive that judges of widely varying attitudes on sentencing, administering statutes that confer huge measures of discretion, mete out widely varying divergent sentences where the divergences are explainable only by the variations among the judges, not by material differences in the defendants or their crimes."[28]

Proposals for selective incapacitation advance justice in at least two ways. First, they impose limits on the factors, and the hearsay, that may be considered in imposing a sentence — something that the due process clause, at least as interpreted by the present Supreme Court, does not do. Second, they enhance horizontal equity among offenders: a uniformly selective system would result in similar sentences for similar offenders who commit comparable offenses, regardless of whose courtroom they find themselves in.

But that is not necessarily enough. A uniform system of selectivity may be less unjust than the current system, but that does not make it just. Indeed, if such proposals formalize an only slightly improved version of an unjust status quo, they may make change more difficult in the future. Moreover, efforts are already under way, in Congress and in numerous state legislatures, to replace the unjust discretionary system with systems that set forth specific sentences (mandatory) or ranges (presumptive) for various offenses, with limited if any judicial discretion. Some states have also moved to eliminate the discretion of the parole commission to determine when an individual is "rehabilitated." In 1979 New Jersey, New Mexico, and North Carolina joined Alaska, Arizona, and California in enacting presumptive sentencing laws. In the same year eighteen states passed one or more mandatory sentencing bills covering violent, drug, or repeat offenses, bringing the total number of states having such laws to twenty-seven.[29]

How, then, do we evaluate justice in sentencing? There is, after all, no abstract formula for a "just" sentence. As Hegel put it, "Reason cannot determine . . . any principle whose application could decide whether justice requires for an offense 40 lashes or 39, or a fine of 5 thalers or 4."[30] Under the Constitution virtually no limits exist on the length of a just sentence. Although the Eighth Amendment's cruel and unusual punishment clause limits the use of the death penalty,[31] it provides virtually no limits on the length of a sentence of incarceration.[32] Nor does the due process clause, which limits the evidence upon which a defendant can constitutionally be convicted, impose any real restriction on the kinds of evidence or information upon which he can be sentenced. What is just, then, depends at least in part on our philosophy of punishment, our degree of hostility toward criminal offenders, and the resources available for punishment. In this, our interests in treating like cases alike and in restricting our attention to "relevant factors" when making selective sentencing decisions operate as constraints, but not as complete defining principles.

Many current proposals for selective sentencing appear to be based on a utilitarian philosophy, and the basic justification for selectivity is usually given in utilitarian terms. The claim that one can have less crime and fewer people in prison by being selective, makes no reference to whether the individual offenders have been treated justly. The arguments are based on utilitarian predictions of future criminal conduct, not on assessments of prior criminal liability. Finally, in constructing tests to distinguish dangerous offenders from others, advocates of selective incapacitation often seem to act as though any variable that increases the discriminating power of the test (with the important exception of race, religion, or political values) is justified. All this gives proposals for selective incapacitation a decidedly utilitarian cast. This utilitarian flavor fails to give clear guidance on the crucial questions: how should we think about the inevitable false positives, those offenders who according to the test predictions ought to commit dangerous crimes at high rates but really do not, and what characteristics are appropriate to consider in making sentencing decisions? These are major problems for selective sentencing even for utilitarians.

Any test of dangerousness is bound to identify a substantial number of false positives. Of course, one can try to erase the problem with a semantic sleight of hand: rather than increasing punishment for some, we say we are reducing it for others. Even so, we are left with the question of why an offender who has been wrongly classified as very dangerous is not entitled to the same reduced punishment as other, nondangerous felons. The wrongly assigned offender may also claim that he has been denied individual justice by being made a member of a large class, and that the evidence that subjects him to additional years in prison meets none of the substantive or procedural tests that evidence must meet in order to convict him at trial. In short, should a sentencing system that exposes some people to more punishment on the basis of a few hard-to-verify characteristics stand beside our elaborate system of adjudicating guilt — with its guarantees of counsel and trial by jury, right to confront witnesses, and requirement of proof beyond a reasonable doubt — based on the premise that it is better for ten guilty men to go free than for one innocent man to be convicted?

Many of these difficulties of the utilitarian concept of selective incapacitation are lessened if we take a more retributivist view, focusing punishment on those whose acts have revealed them to be violent, determined criminals. On balance, we advocate a mixed conception of sentencing. We think the society has obligations to control crime and to do justice to individuals; to use science, but also to be guided by tradition; to count on reason, but also to understand the role of values and passions in administering punishment. On balance, we are slightly more retributivist than utilitarian, but we believe there is less tension between their justifications for selective sentencing than is often supposed. Precisely because past acts reveal character and provide a good basis for predictions about future conduct, we can have a largely retributivist system that offers utilitarian benefits. We think such a system would be just.

THE EFFECTIVENESS OF SELECTIVE SENTENCING

The application of the seven-variable test described above to California robbers and burglars indicated some potential to control crime without expanding prison capacity by introducing formal systems of selectivity in sentencing. But that potential should not be overestimated: when the same test was applied in Texas, it did not produce nearly the results it did in California. Among Texas robbers, a 10 percent reduction in crime required a 30 percent increase in overall incarceration. For burglars, the cost of a 10 percent reduction in crime was a 15 percent increase in incarceration.[33] In short, the test really didn't "work" in Texas — if working is defined as reducing crime at no cost in terms of increased incarceration.

Moreover, while the variables included in the test for selective sentencing could in principle be obtained from official records, the variables actually used in the tests were based on what the offenders reported in a prison survey — not on official records. Efforts to distinguish the high-rate offender by relying only on official records were much less satisfactory.[34]

But perhaps the most important reason for treating the crime reduction estimates based on the California calculations as very optimistic is that the present system may already be determining sentences in precisely the recommended ways. Judges may already be sentencing with an eye to prior adult record, juvenile record, and drug use. And even if they are not, parole boards may be making parole decisions of this basis.[35] It is not certain exactly how sentencing decisions are now being made throughout the country, but the evidence suggests that judges and parole boards are already highly selective.

Indeed, judges have repeatedly cited seriousness of the offense and prior criminal record as the most important factors in determining the sentences they impose. For example, a researcher who studied the Philadelphia Superior Court sentences passed in the mid-1950s found that the number of prior felony convictions was the most important predictor of the sentence, aside from seriousness of the instant offense and the number of counts for which the defendant was convicted.[36] These findings were replicated in a later study of Philadelphia courts, in which it was found that judges were 50 percent more likely to sentence an offender to prison, and to a prison term twice as long, if he had a violent conviction in his record.[37] Other researchers, examining judges' decisions in the state of Washington, found that thieves were sentenced to longer terms if their last prior conviction was for a violent crime, and that the type of the last prior offense was almost as important as the total criminal record in determining the sentence passed.[38] An examination of federal district courts disclosed that the criminal record and prior convictions were most important when the instant offense was less serious.[39] Indeed, many offenders convicted of minor offenses would probably not have been punished at all, but for their prior record. Similarly, whether the defendant had previously served time in a jail or prison was an important predictor of the sentence passed by judges in Los Angeles County and the state of Washington.[40] When the sentence is set by the jury rather than the judge, prior convictions may be even more important. A study aimed at determining what influenced California juries to issue death sentences concluded that "the admission of a defendant's 'priors' into evidence at [the sentencing hearing] is the most significant of all the variables analyzed in the study."[41]

The influence of prior arrests is less clear, particularly since offenders with several prior convictions tend to have long arrest records as well. Some researchers concluded that the arrest record was meaningless once prior convictions had been taken into account.[42] Similarly, researchers who examined sentences in Baltimore, Chicago, and Detroit found that the sentences of convicted offenders with prior arrest records were not significantly longer than those of offenders without records.[43] Other researchers produced contrary evidence. One found that a convicted burglar's chances of incarceration increased by 50 percent if he had been previously arrested more than five times. The researcher suggested that the arrests established a criminal "pattern of conduct" that was often obscured if judges relied only on conviction records.[44] Still others found the number of prior arrests to be the most important characteristic of all, next to the instant offense.[45]

If we shift our attention to the determinants of parole decision making, the hypothesis that the system is already quite selective becomes even stronger. Indeed, the original justifications and current practices of parole decision making are almost identical to those now being offered for selective incapacitation. Although we have become accustomed to thinking of parole as a liberal policy reflecting an unshakable faith in the potential for rehabilitation, its early history suggests that parole boards were established to control idiosyncratic judges.[46] After parole boards were established, the average time served by offenders increased.[47] Part of the justification for parole boards was the hope that they would have time to gather information about prior records and thus prevent habitual offenders from manipulating the system.[48]

As the parole system developed, it moved even closer to the procedures that are urged for selective incapacitation policies. Parole boards tended to see their purpose as making judgments about offenders' prospects for rehabilitation, which operationally was identical to the task of predicting recidivism. A second trend was toward more careful and systematic judgments. Specific procedures were gradually developed for parole hearings, and substantive guidelines focused attention on certain characteristics of the offenders. The more refined guidelines were based on empirical tests of the power of different characteristics to predict recidivism. Figure 9 presents some parole guidelines from the early 1950s. The type of offense and prior record appear in this report form, but many individual and social factors appear as well. Table 14 presents a more recent proposal for parole guidelines based on statistical experience. This form eliminates many factors, such as psychiatric assessments, community ties, and conduct while in prison, and emphasizes prior criminal conduct and drug use. Indeed, one corrections system recently established parole guidelines based on nothing more than the instant offense, adult record, and juvenile record.[49]

In sum, parole decision making looks very much like the process being advocated by those who favor selective incapacitation. The only difference seems to be in the rhetoric, which emphasizes the value of keeping high-risk offenders in jail somewhat longer, instead of the benefits of releasing the safe risks earlier. To the extent that parole decisions currently determine which offenders stay in prison for how long, and to the extent that parole boards now use procedures similar to those advocated for selective incapacitation, the sentencing system may already be highly selective. If so, this lowers our expectations for substantial reductions in crime, because that potential may already have been captured.

Even so, there may be room for substantial improvement in our use of prisons. Could the space used by the large percentages of nonviolent offenders be more selectively allocated to those who pose a danger to the community? Although the data do not tell us whether the more dangerous offenders are either not being imprisoned or are not being held long enough, use of selective techniques could increase the percentage of prison space used for dangerous offenders.

In any event, it is worth asking why petty thieves and public order offenders are occupying as many as one-third or more of the cells in state correctional facilities, as well as almost all of our city and county jails. One important answer seems to be that we don't know what else to do with them. Many of the proposals for selective incapacitation seem to assume that the tools are available to punish and even incapacitate the low-level or repeat petty offender without using precious cell space. The fact is, however, that our ability to punish or incapacitate offenders except by imprisonment is almost nonexistent.[50] The traditional tools—

State of Illinois

Division of Correction

Prediction Report of the Sociologist-Actuary

Illinois State Penitentiary System

Joliet-Stateville Division

Number 00000   Name B_____ J_____ Docket May, 1942

Factor	Item	Score
1. Type of offense_____	Murder	1
2. Sentence_____	Life	1
3. Type of offender_____	First	1
4. Home status_____	Average	0
5. Family interest_____	Very active	1
6. Social type_____	Socially inadequate	1
7. Work record_____	Irregular	0
8. Community___ .	Urban	0
9. Parole job_____	Adequate	0
10. Number of associates_____	Two	0
11. Personality rating_____	Inadequate	0
12. Psychiatric prognosis_____	Problematic	0
	Total Score_____	5

This inmate is in a class in which 3 percent may be expected to violate the parole agreement; 2 percent of the persons in this class may be expected to commit serious or repeated infractions of the parole rules; and 1 percent may be expected to commit new offenses on parole.

Figure 9 Parole guideline form, circa 1950. (From Lloyd E. Ohlin, *Selection for Parole: A Manual of Parole Prediction,* © 1951 by Russell Sage Foundation. Reprinted by permission of Basic Books, Inc., publishers.)

fines and probation—have accomplished neither of these goals for the most critical population: petty recidivists and low-level offenders. These tools are not viewed as real punishment by the community, the offenders, or the judges who impose sentence. As a result, a judge faced with an offender whose acts are serious enough or whose record is long enough to require some punishment has little recourse but to impose a short jail or prison term. And since there are many more low-level of-

Table 14. Federal parole guidelines, 1983.

Variable	Score
A. Prior convictions	
No prior convictions (adult or juvenile)	3
One prior conviction	2
Two or three prior convictions	1
Four or more prior convictions	0
B. Prior incarcerations	
No prior incarcerations (adult or juvenile)	2
One or two prior incarcerations	1
Three or more prior incarcerations	0
C. Age at first commitment (adult or juvenile)	
26 or older	2
18–25	1
17 or younger	0
D. Commitment offense	
Did not involve auto theft or forgery	1
Otherwise	0
E. Parole violation	
Never had parole revoked or been committed for new offense while on parole, and not probation violator this time	1
Otherwise	0
F. Drug use	
No history of heroin or opiate dependence	1
Otherwise	0
G. Employment history	
Verified employment (or full-time school attendance) for at least 6 months during last 2 years in community	1
Otherwise	0
Total (sum items A–G)	

Source: Adapted from Peter B. Hoffman and Barbara Stone-Meierhoefer, "Post Release Arrest Experiences of Federal Prisoners: A Six-Year Follow-up," *Journal of Criminal Justice* 7 (1979), 211.

fenders than serious chronic offenders, the sum total of the sentences imposed on the former imposes a limit on the extent to which our system can incapacitate the latter.

The answer lies in the development of new forms of punishment for the low-level and repeat petty offenders who clog our system. We must design alternatives that impose real and *enforceable* sanctions on them. Community service sentencing, which mandates involuntary servitude in a highly supervised framework, is one promising alternative.[51] To be effective as punishment, however, it must not only demand something of the offender — work — but must also back up that demand with a credible threat of incarceration for noncompliance. That threat is credible only if caseloads are low enough to allow the project staff to quickly identify and apprehend those who do not comply. Incapacitation in a jail "costs" one guard for every two inmates. Punishment (or perhaps even incapacitation) on the outside may be cheaper in terms of bricks and mortar, but not necessarily in terms of staff.

THE POTENTIAL OF SELECTIVE SENTENCING

Introducing greater, and better, selectivity into sentencing requires us to face three challenges. The first is to develop and make available the information that puts selectivity on the least objectionable, most justifiable basis — prior criminal record. The problem is to have such information available at an early enough stage in the offender's career to achieve significant crime control. That problem leads some to suggest that we rely upon other predictive criteria, such as drug abuse or employment, which raise substantial justice concerns.

There may be a better answer — making juvenile records available in any case in which a person commits an offense soon after reaching the age of majority. Even more important, police and prosecutors must become more effective in solving crimes — particularly serious offenses against strangers — so that criminal records become more accurate reflections of criminal activity.

The second challenge is to impose limits on discretion in sentencing that do not also limit fair selectivity. As noted earlier, many jurisdictions are now considering or adopting systems in which the legislature sets forth a specific sentence or sentence range, with limited if any judicial discretion and limited or no option for early parole. Such systems are not necessarily inconsistent with a focus on dangerous offenders: mandatory sentences do select, albeit only on the basis of offense, and presumptive schemes generally take account of prior criminal record in setting a sentence within the specified range. Moreover, most such schemes specify longer sentences for subsequent offenses and include habitual-offender statutes. Such systems, however, have almost as much discretion — and potential for abuse — as the systems they are designed to replace. The charges brought by prosecutors become the critical factor in any mandatory scheme; judicial discretion is replaced by even less reviewable prosecutorial discretion. Many habitual-offender statutes provide for as much as life imprisonment, based on number, rather than rate, of prior convictions, and in many cases include all prior felonies rather than only serious ones. These schemes create the potential for the same charges of unfairness and disparity that have been aimed at the open-ended systems. Efforts to improve our ability to select, if they are to succeed practically and politically, should be accompanied by efforts to limit discretion, so that only serious, repeat offenders receive increased punishment.

The third challenge is to develop alternatives to imprisonment for low-level and petty offenders. Developing means to deliver punishment outside of prison is critical if we are to maximize the incapacitative effects of available jail and prison space.

5

Pretrial Detention

THE PUBLIC RESERVES a special hostility for crimes committed by defendants free on bail. Partly it is the gall of the offenders that is so enraging. What clearer expression of disdain for the criminal law and its moral obligations could there be? But also it is indignation about the futility of a system that, having succeeded against all odds in identifying and arresting a suspect, then releases him to commit additional offenses. This indignation has produced a spate of proposals requiring judges to detain arrested dangerous offenders in jail.

The most radical of these proposals call explicitly for preventive detention, meaning that accused defendants who are found to be dangerous to the community can be detained until trial.[1] Other proposals require or allow judges to take dangerousness into account in setting the offender's bail.[2] Depending on how much latitude is left to judges in setting bail, such proposals may have the same effect as preventive detention, but they leave intact the theoretical right to bail.

Obviously, proposals for pretrial detention have much in common with proposals for selective incapacitation in criminal sentencing. They are motivated and justified by the same utilitarian interest in reducing crime. Their appeal is rooted in the same, simple idea of incapacitation, and they raise the same difficult questions about justice that selective incapacitation does. Much of the analytic framework and discussion of Chapters 3 and 4 can be carried forward to this chapter.

But some special issues arise in preventive detention and risk-adjusted bail. The most crucial involves justice. Confinement of dangerous offenders *before* the adjudication of guilt or innocence for a given offense carries the risk of injustice to the accused defendant in a way that selective incapacitation in sentencing does not. Another issue is the practical value of such proposals. Because the total amount of detention time is less than that for selective sentencing, the potential for reducing crime must be less. Another factor is that there are attractive alternatives for controlling crimes commited on bail, such as speedier trials or making crimes committed on bail a special offense, which involve much lower risks of injustice. Given the risks of injustice and the limited practical value of preventive detention and risk-adjusted bail, these alternatives may be preferable.

The purpose of this chapter is to summarize and assess proposals designed to focus on dangerous offenders in pretrial detention decisions. We will consider the justice of such proposals and their likely impact on crime.

PRETRIAL DETENTION FOR DANGEROUS OFFENDERS

A person who has been accused of a crime with sufficient evidence to cause a neutral magistrate to believe that he did commit the crime, but who has not yet been convicted at trial, poses a major problem for the criminal justice system. On one hand, since he has not been convicted, the state has little legitimate power over him. Arguably, the state should promptly release indicted offenders, not only to give the presumption of innocence a concrete expression, but also to guarantee their right to due process in preparing their defense.[3] On the other hand, the state has an uncontested interest in ensuring that the accused person will appear for trial and reason to believe that the accused person has committed a crime. These factors justify some kind of supervision over the defendant, even if a practical interest in crime control does not.

In the past century these competing interests have been balanced by the system of bail.[4] In current practice the judge decides what amount of money is necessary to assure the defendant's appearance at trial, and that amount is deposited with the court by the defendant, his family, or other surety. The interest in preventing the defendant from committing additional crimes is, in principle at least, excluded from this decision.

There are four major problems with this system as it now operates. First, a substantial proportion of the defendants are detained rather than released on bail. A national survey found that about 15 percent of all arrested defendants were detained until trial; an additional 3 percent were detained for more than thirty days before being released in advance of their trial.[5] One important consequence is that the nation's jails are now so full that many are under court order to improve conditions.[6] Not only are unconvicted defendants being subjected to very harsh conditions, but also less jail and prison space is available for convicted defendants. In effect, our most crowded and congested form of imprisonment is given disproportionately to those who have not yet been convicted of crimes.

Second, the people detained are not necessarily those who have committed the worst crimes or have the strongest cases pending against them or represent the greatest risks of flight or new crimes. Instead, they are the ones who could not raise the required bail. Although the amount of bail is increased as the seriousness of the offense and the chance of flight increase, this correlation is far from perfect. What determines who stays in jail is the defendant's financial capacity to pay the required amount. A national survey of pretrial release found that more than half of those detained were arrested for crimes considered less serious than larceny and auto theft.[7] More than a third were charged with crimes against public morality (prostitution, gambling, public drunkenness, for instance) or public order (weapons, disorderly conduct, vagrancy).[8] Most of these people were not denied bail or had bail set at outrageously high levels; they simply could not meet even minimal bail demands. Twenty-nine percent of the defendants facing less than $1,000 in bail, which requires no more than a $100 cash payment to a bondsman, failed to make bail and stayed in jail until their trial. On the other hand, about one-third of those facing more than $10,000 in bail — typically facing serious charges — were released.[9] So the money bail system has led to the detention of many minor but impoverished offenders and the release of some serious but financially resourceful defendants.

A third problem is that the current system does not guarantee the defendant's appearance at trial, nor does it eliminate crimes committed on bail. About 6 percent of required court appearances are missed by released defendants.[10] About 16 percent of those released are rearrested before their trials, usually on minor charges.[11] To many, these rates of misconduct seem low and testify to the overall success of the bail system. If one expects that these rates could and should be zero, however, the bail system seems to be failing in each of its intended practical effects.

A fourth problem is that although the bail system operates under some explicit guidelines, either legislatively or administratively established, judges retain a great deal of discretion. Leaving room for judicial discretion allows a more tailored response to individual circumstances, but it also creates the potential for abuse and diminishes the apparent fairness of the overall process.

Taken together, these points suggest a lack of focus in pretrial detention decisions. Too many defendants seem to be detained, but also too many flee and commit too many crimes. Moreover, the crucial question of who is detained depends on the vagaries of judicial discretion and the financial capacity of defendants, rather than a principled judgment.

The most radical proposals to sharpen the focus of pretrial detention decisions mandate or allow preventive detention. Despite their radical character, such measures have been advocated by influential groups. The Attorney General's Task Force on Violent Crime, for example, recently recommended that courts be permitted to deny bail to persons "who are found by clear and convincing evidence to present a danger to particular persons or the community"; that the government have the right to appeal release decisions; that penalties for bail jumping be increased; and that "in the case of serious crimes, the current standard presumptively favoring release of convicted persons awaiting imposition or execution of sentence, or appealing their convictions" be abandoned.[12] In a similar spirit, the American Bar Association's Task Force recommended that "judicial officers should be authorized to detain persons without bail pending trial where, after a full hearing it appears that (1) the defendant meets criteria which establish his danger to the community, and (2) there is substantial probability that the defendant committed the offense with which he is charged."[13] Finally, the Judiciary Committee of the U.S. Senate, in the Criminal Code Reform Act of 1981, proposed holding hearings to determine whether a defendant should be detained on grounds of dangerousness "to any other person or the community."[14]

These proposals all target broad classes of suspects, limited only by the formal procedures for determining dangerousness. No substantive detention guidelines are offered. An alternative approach is to define the categories of defendants who would be selected for preventive detention. In 1982, for example, Illinois voters overwhelmingly approved a referendum that allowed judges to deny bail to defendants facing life imprisonment. At the same time Colorado voters amended their constitution to permit denial of bail to defendants who had previously been convicted of one crime of violence or of two nonviolent, serious felonies.[15] And the Florida and New York state legislatures recently passed legislation that would permit bail to be denied any defendant "charged with a serious felony while free on bail for another."[16]

A more traditional approach is to mandate or allow judges setting bail to consider characteristics that indicate dangerousness or risk to the community. Basically, the more dangerous the offender seems, the higher the bail should be.[17] Such proposals seem unjust because they allow bail to become "excessive" relative to the offense charged. They also leave the question of who is detained to the financial capacities of defendants. And they offend those who think that the only appropriate consideration in setting bail is to guarantee the defendant's appearance at trial.

Despite these difficulties, such proposals have found favor with voters and with judges. In 1982 voters in California supported a change in the state constitution that would require judges making bail decisions to "take into consideration the protection of the public, the seriousness of the offense charged, the previous criminal record of the defendant, and the probability of his or her appearing at the trial or hearing of the case."[18] The new language in the constitution further states that "public safety shall be *the primary consideration*" in bail decision making.[19] Wisconsin voters amended their constitution in 1981 to change bail policy, and the state legislature has since enacted legislation specifying the form and nature of pretrial detention hearings.[20]

Judges in Philadelphia decided to act on their own without public referenda or legislation. Working with John Goldkamp, the judges established guidelines to be used in setting bail in individual cases. The recommended levels of bail range from release on recognizance to cash amounts of hundreds of thousands of dollars, depending on the seriousness of the crime charged and the probability that the defendant will fail to appear or be rearrested following release.[21] The probabilities are based on such characteristics as prior criminal record, current residence, and so on, and are derived from earlier empirical research on bail risk.[22]

This brief review indicates that there is a great deal of interest in reforming pretrial decision making, focused in part on reducing the number of crimes committed on bail. But a spirit of reform also animates these proposals. They aspire to making the process much more explicit, rational, and principled than it is now. Despite these advantages, the proposals have attracted strong opposition, mostly from those who think the proposals are unjust, but also from those who think they are impractical.

THE JUSTICE OF SELECTIVE PRETRIAL DETENTION

To many, the notion of jailing someone not yet convicted of a crime on the basis of uncertain judgments about the danger he presents to the community seems antithetical to our most fundamental legal traditions.

And although pretrial detention is not the explicit goal of guidelines that increase bail for offenders estimated to be dangerous, that is the frequent and unlamented result.

Two objections to both preventive detention and risk-adjusted bail are commonly voiced. It is wrong to jail — and therefore punish — people who have not been convicted of crimes, and it is particularly unjust to detain them on the basis of predictions about future crimes. Stated affirmatively rather than negatively, the argument is that the state's only proper interest is to guarantee that accused individuals appear for trial. The amount of bail should be determined with this purpose in mind, and bail can hardly ever be denied on that basis. It is especially inappropriate to detain people solely to promote community security.

While compelling in principle, this position is undercut by three observations. First, the actual operations of the existing system reveal the bankruptcy of the guiding principles. The defendants who are detained are not those whose appearance at trial is of greatest concern to the state, but those whose financial resources are most limited. Some critics urge the release of more defendants on their own recognizance, others propose substitution of community sureties for money bail on the grounds that these would be more equally available to all defendants.[23] Such reforms might well lead to less pretrial detention without harming the state's interest in guaranteeing appearance at trial. But the most important implication of the present system is that we are apparently willing to detain people without a finding of guilt simply to guarantee their appearance at trial. If the right to be free before trial can be overwhelmed by the state's limited interest in guaranteeing future appearance, then the right cannot be so fundamental, and it occasionally might be overwhelmed by the state's interest in reducing crime.

Second, many deny that the state's interest is limited to guaranteeing appearance at trial. Some legal scholars have argued that bail and sureties were also designed to promote community security.[24] And as a practical matter, both citizens and judges clearly think it is not only appropriate but crucially important that the citizens' interests in security be reflected in pretrial detention decisions.

Finally, the Supreme Court has so far refused to establish an unlimited right to bail, nor has it been willing to limit the state's interest to guaranteeing the defendant's appearance at trial. True, the Court has not yet heard a case on the constitutionality of preventive detention because all such cases have become moot before the court could take them up.[25] And in the leading bail case, *Stack* v. *Boyle*, the Supreme Court did indicate that guaranteeing appearance should be the most important factor.[26] But the constitutional right of an individual to be set free on bail based solely or primarily on the need to guarantee appearance at trial has not been established.

To many, the court's reluctance in this area seems inexplicable, for the constitutional language seems clear and straightforward. The Eighth Amendment to the U.S. Constitution asserts flatly that "excessive bail shall not be required." Unfortunately, this simple assertion can be given at least three different interpretations.[27] One is that defendants have a right to reasonable bail, and the Supreme Court will determine what is reasonable. That interpretation, which would establish a right to be released on reasonable bail, has been supported by a historical analysis of bail in England.[28] A second interpretation restricts the amount of bail to reasonable levels but leaves it to the states to pass laws indicating what is reasonable. No conception of a constitutional right is envisioned in this interpretation. Indeed, the states could decide that it was reasonable in some cases to deny bail. A third interpretation is that "in the absence of constitutional or statutory direction . . . judicial discretion determines the appropriateness of bail within the bounds that it should not be 'excessive.'" This also rejects the notion of any right to bail, but it allows judges to set bail even in cases where statutes do not explicitly authorize it.

The District of Columbia enacted a preventive detention statute in 1970, and the constitutionality of the statute was tested recently in *United States* v. *Edwards*.[29] The District of Columbia Court of Appeals held that the statute was constitutional, narrowly rejecting the interpretation that the Eighth Amendment guarantees a right to bail. The court reviewed the origins of the excessive bail clause and the case law pertaining to it and concluded that the aim of the Eighth Amendment was not to limit the power of Congress to deny pretrial release for specified classes of offenders or offenses, but rather to limit the discretion of the judiciary in bail setting.[30] The court also ruled that the Fifth Amendment due process clause was not violated by the preventive detention statute.[31] Opponents of the statute objected on grounds that it permitted punishment of the defendant prior to full adjudication of the case. The court concluded that pretrial detention is not a form of punishment but rather a regulatory action and hence permissible.

The case was appealed to the Supreme Court, but the Court declined to consider it, perhaps for reasons similar to those justifying its reluctance to consider a previous Nebraska case, *Murphy* v. *Hunt*.[32] That case involved the constitutionality of a Nebraska constitutional amendment requiring "the denial of bail to defendants charged with forcible sex offenses when the proof is evident or the presumption great." The U.S. Court of Appeals for the Eighth Circuit found the amendment to be an unconstitutional restriction on the right to bail and asserted that "the constitutional protections involved in the grant of pretrial release by bail are too fundamental to foreclose by arbitrary state decree."[33] The Supreme Court vacated the Eighth Circuit's decision and found that the case was moot because the defendant had already been convicted for rape and sentenced to prison.[34] The *Edwards* case might also have been viewed by the court as not presenting a "live" issue because Edwards entered guilty pleas in both cases in which preventive detention was sought. Such a ruling poses an interesting dilemma since "pretrial detention orders will almost surely not outlive the appellate process."[35] The Court could choose to treat a future case as an exception embodying the principle of being "capable of repetition, yet evading review," and this rule was employed by the District of Columbia Court of Appeals in its review of the case. Although the notion of pretrial detention seems to be contrary to our legal traditions, there is apparently no constitutional principle that bars it.

By far the strongest reason to detain dangerous offenders before trial is not to reduce crime on bail, but to *limit* and *rationalize* the current system. Just as selective incapacitation of convicted offenders could lead to having fewer people in prison, pretrial detention of dangerous offenders might lead to having fewer people detained and to the use of explicit criteria that would be fairer. A system that detained only those few who represented great risks of flight or new crimes, regardless of their financial resources, would be a welcome relief, even if it required making explicit decisions about who was to be detained and who released. Compared with the current system, the only loss to justice would be in the explicit recognition of a community interest in controlling crime committed on bail, a principle that already seems to have some political and legal vitality despite the controversy over whether it is constitutionally recognized.

THE PRACTICAL VALUE OF SELECTIVE PRETRIAL DETENTION

One can construct a moral license for pretrial detention of dangerous offenders, but there are risks in doing so. For the policy to have social value, these risks must be balanced by some practical benefit that the society feels entitled (or even obliged) to pursue. The practical aim of pretrial detention is to reduce crime on bail. Whether this purpose is valuable and can be achieved depends on how much crime is now committed on bail, whether it is serious, and whether it would be possible to focus pretrial detention on those most likely to commit crimes on bail.

Recent research based on eight jurisdictions in the United States found that 16 percent of the released defendants (476 out of 2,956) were rearrested while awaiting trial.[36] There was variation among cities in the rate of rearrest: 7.5 percent in Baltimore, Maryland; 14.6 percent in Santa Clara County (San Jose), California; 17.5 percent in Dade County (Miami), Florida; and 22.2 percent in Washington, D.C. For the most part, these arrests were for minor offenses.[37]

Research conducted in Washington and Philadelphia produced similar findings. In Washington 13 percent of felony defendants released prior to trial were rearrested, and in Philadelphia 16 percent were rearrested.[38] Less than half of released defendants were rearrested for serious crimes, including murder, manslaughter, rape, robbery, burglary, aggravated assault, kidnaping, or drug offenses.[39]

Estimates of the relationship of crime on bail to all crime have been made by compiling data from six jurisdictions on the percentage of defendants with pending cases against them when arrested.[40] Table 15 presents the results, ranging from a high of 17.3 percent for defendants charged with felonies and 14.1 percent for all defendants in Washington, D.C., to a low of 5.6 percent for felony arrests in Miami. These data supported the following conclusion: "Based on the very limited and poor information available, it appears that 'crime on bail' accounts for no more than 10 percent to 15 percent of all crime in most major urban areas."[41]

Although the data are crude, they point in one direction very consistently: a small but noticeable fraction of those released on bail do commit crimes, these crimes account for a small but noticeable fraction of the overall crime in a society, and violent crimes on bail are less common than new property crimes or other minor offenses. There is much less consistency in how these facts are weighed, however. One expert refers to "a *mere* 6 percent of all defendants" rearrested on bail for serious crime.[42] Another states that "the extent of crime on bail seems to be much less than popularly assumed."[43] On the other hand, Chief Justice Warren Burger has used the same statistic to deplore the "high figure" of crimes committed by people on bail,[44] and another expert has noted that the "advocates of pretrial detention appear to have had the better of the argument in recent years."[45] The judges participating in the Philadelphia

Table 15. Estimates of the percentage of defendants with cases pending when arrested.

Site	Sample	Percentage with pending cases
Washington, D.C.	442 defendants randomly selected from arrests made in 1977	11.5[a]
Washington, D.C.	Defendants arraigned in D.C. Superior Court in 1974:	
	felony charges ($n = 4,631$)	17.3[b]
	misdemeanor charges ($n = 6,249$)	11.7[b]
	all charges ($n = 10,880$)	14.1[b]
Tucson, Ariz.	409 defendants, randomly selected from 1977 arrests	7.3[a]
Tucson, Ariz.	2,610 felony defendants interviewed by pretrial release program, Oct. 1974–May 1975	9.2[c]
San Jose, Calif.	370 defendants randomly selected from arrests, Dec. 1977–May 1978	13.9[a]
Louisville, Ky.	435 defendants, randomly selected from 1977 arrests	11.3[a]
Miami, Fla.	427 defendants, randomly selected from felony arrests, Jan.–June 1978	5.6[a]
Philadelphia, Pa.	Approximately 3,600 defendants selected to be representative of about 8,300 defendants appearing at preliminary arraignment, Aug.–Nov. 1975.	7.6[d]

Source: Adapted from Mary A. Toborg, "Potential Value of Increased Selectivity in Pretrial Detention Decisions," in *Dealing with Dangerous Offenders*, vol. 2: *Selected Papers*, ed. Daniel McGillis, Susan M. Estrich, Mark H. Moore, and William Spelman (Cambridge, Mass.: John F. Kennedy School of Government, 1983), 3.

a. Data from National Evaluation of Pretrial Release; percentage shown probably understates true percentage of defendants with pending cases because of inaccuracies in data sources.

b. Jeffrey A. Roth and Paul B. Wice, "Pretrial Release and Misconduct in the District of Columbia," (Washington, D.C.: Institute for Law and Social Research, April 1980).

c. *Annual Report for the Correctional Volunteer Center, Pima County Superior Court, 1975–1976.*

d. John S. Goldkamp, *Bail Decisionmaking and the Role of Pretrial Detention in American Justice*, research report draft, Utilization of Criminal Justice Statistics Project (Albany, N.Y.: Criminal Justice Research Center, 1977).

experiment with bail guidelines also view the rearrest figures as unacceptably high.[46]

Whether one considers the figures high or low, they represent the upper limit of the potential reduction in crime through pretrial detention. How much of that potential would actually be secured depends on how bail policies are changed. Presumably crime committed on bail could be eliminated by detaining everyone, but the price in terms of overcrowded jails, to say nothing of broad injustice, would be far too high. It might be possible to sharply reduce crime on bail if judges adopted more conservative criteria in setting bail. But that, too, would come at a substantial price: many defendants would be unjustly detained for every one whose detention prevented a crime.

As in the case of selective sentencing, the most attractive alternative would be to improve the quality of the tests used to distinguish dangerous offenders from others. By applying the tests systematically it should be possible to reduce the amount of crime committed by defendants free on bail *and* the number of defendants detained. No one has yet constructed the simulation models that would allow us to analyze the consequences of using different tests and thresholds in pretrial decision making, but one estimate, based on 424 cases in Washington, D.C., is available.[47] The court's decisions resulted in 170 of the 424 (about 40 percent) being detained before trial. Of the 254 released (about 9 percent), 22 were rearrested.[48] The researchers show that if their tests (based on current charge, criminal record, and social characteristics such as drug use, employment history, and age) were applied, the system could have improved its performance in both dimensions. Specifically, if the judges had chosen the 170 people to detain on the basis of the tests, they could have decreased the number of rearrests from 22 to 14 — a small absolute number, but an appreciable percentage.[49] If, on the other hand, the judges were willing to tolerate 22 rearrests, they could have released an additional 72 defendants by applying the tests.[50]

Theoretically, it seems there is some potential for improving the selectivity of pretrial decision making. But it seems to be harder to reduce crime through improved discrimination than to release additional people without having to accept more crime. Given that so many are now detained because they cannot meet even minor bail demands, this finding should not be surprising.

In estimating how much of the theoretical crime reduction potential could actually be realized, it is important to keep three points in mind. First, the results are *estimates;* they are not based on actual comparisons of different pretrial decision making procedures. Second, these results were produced with a test that included variables that would be considered unjust, such as age, race, and employment record. If the test were restricted to a smaller number of more appropriate variables, some discriminating power would probably be lost. Third, the real extent of the potential depends on current practices throughout the country. If other cities are more selective than Washington then the potential is overestimated. If other cities are less selective than Washington, then the potential is underestimated. In gauging the real potential, then, it is important to have some sense of current pretrial practices.

Several empirical studies have been made. As in the case of sentencing, pretrial decisions are often shared by a judge and a pretrial service agency that rates defendants according to the likelihood that they will flee or commit additional crimes. Most studies that have been conducted of judges who set bail without the benefit of explicit guidelines or the advice of an administrative agency using routinized procedures find wide variations in the amounts of bail required from defendants who seemed similar in terms of current charges, prior record, community ties such as job and family, and so on.[51] Of course, these differences in bail may reflect the judges accurate perceptions of real differences in risks, but from the outside the decisions look somewhat unpredictable.

There is more consistency in the decisions of judges who are aided by pretrial service agencies. Typically, these agencies gather otherwise unobtainable facts concerning the defendant's neighborhood ties and offer recommendations to the judges on bail and appropriate referrals to pretrial diversion programs. Not all defendants are interviewed by pretrial service agencies even in those jurisdictions that have them, however. Both the worst offenders and the most minor offenders seem to be excluded from the administrative system and handled directly by the judges. A recent survey of 119 pretrial service agencies found that about a third immediately excluded offenders who had outstanding warrants from other jurisdictions, and about a sixth excluded offenders charged with violent felonies.[52] Presumably, all those excluded went immediately to the judge, who either denied bail or set it very high. At the other end of the spectrum, about a tenth of the programs do not interview those charged with minor misdemeanors and violations of ordinances, most of whom presumably are released on their own recognizance.[53]

Table 16 describes the characteristics that are assessed by pretrial agencies. They emphasize community ties, as shown by local residence and employment, and prior criminal record, as revealed in criminal con-

Table 16. Offender characteristics used in making pretrial release decisions, based on responses from 117 programs.

Criteria	No. of programs	Percentage of programs
Community ties		
Local address	111	94.9
Length of time in community	108	92.3
Length of time at current address	99	84.6
Living arrangements (with whom)	87	74.4
Employment/education/training status	107	91.5
Ownership of property in community	59	50.4
Possession of telephone	31	26.5
Someone expected to accompany defendant at arraignment	23	19.6
Prior record		
Prior arrests	78	66.7
Prior convictions (any type)	101	86.3
Prior convictions (felony only)	66	56.4
Prior failure to appear	7	6.0
Other		
Income level or public assistance status	50	42.7
Excess use of drugs/alcohol	9	7.7
Miscellaneous	7	6.0

Source: Donald E. Pryor, *Program Practices: Release* (Washington, D.C.: Pretrial Services Resource Center, 1982).

victions. Indeed, five-sixths of the programs used at least some of these criteria. Other criteria, used by more than a third of the programs, included living arrangement in the community and prior arrests.

The factors considered by both judges and pretrial service agencies are theoretically linked to the risk of flight. Arguably, defendants are more likely to flee if they face serious charges, have an extensive prior record, and lack community ties. But if the studies of offending patterns are correct, these characteristics are also linked to the likelihood of committing crimes while out on bail: prior record and employment history are both useful in distinguishing the high-rate offenders. So the current procedures may be close to those that would be recommended if we were to design pretrial procedures to reduce crime on bail.

THE POTENTIAL OF PRETRIAL SELECTIVITY

On balance, we think that the potential advantages of introducing more selective guidelines into pretrial decision making are relatively small. This judgment is not based on minimizing the importance of the problem of crime committed on bail. We think that the 5 percent to 15 percent of all crime in a city committed by people out on bail is significant. But we are pessimistic about the potential for improving, at the margin, the system's current discriminating capacity; we are concerned about the implications of putting possible future crimes at the center in pretrial decisions; and we believe there are more satisfactory ways to deal with the problem of crime on bail.

We are pessimistic about improving discriminating capacity largely because the tests currently utilized rely on variables that should be reasonably selective. Some improvements could be made in the consistency of bail decisions, and it is *conceivable* that tests could be designed to make better, more accurate distinctions among defendants in terms of their risk of flight and danger to the community. Indeed, we urge that such research be conducted. But if we had to bet now, we would bet that the discriminating power of the tests would go up only a little and that the major problem would continue to be the detention of too many people in crowded jails rather than the release of too many obvious risks. As awful as crime on bail is, we accept it because we value being able to release people who have not been convicted of crimes, and it is hard to distinguish those who will flee or commit crimes from those who will do neither. We can cut down the amount of crime on bail but apparently only at the price of increased detentions. And that seems too high a price to pay, given our philosophy and our current institutional capacities.

The prospect of basing pretrial detention on tests designed to predict future crimes, in addition to predicting flight, raises our second major worry. In principle we are not opposed to including considerations of dangerousness in bail decisions. We think such considerations are appropriate, but they should count *less* than our interests in releasing defendants, because justice requires a very strong interest in not detaining people before trial. Hence we should accept much greater risks of future crimes than if the defendant has already been convicted of a crime. Put another way, it is much more costly to our social values to detain one unconvicted defendant for an additional month or so than to detain a convicted offender. Moreover, in pretrial detention decisions, discriminating tests are obviously and inevitably predicting future conduct rather than judging past blameworthiness. This makes pretrial decisions different from decisions to increase sentences, which can be seen as retributivist. Unless the potential practical gains are found to be enormous, the pretrial stage should be considered less appropriate for the introduction of selective concepts than other stages.

Finally, if the problem of crime on bail is considered very urgent, alternative methods are available for reducing it that are superior in terms of justice. Specifically, we could reduce the delays between arrest and trial to limit the time the released defendant is at risk;[54] we could impose harsher sentences on those who commit crimes on bail;[55] we could give consecutive rather than concurrent sentences to those who commit crimes on bail so that these crimes are not "free"; or we could increase supervision over defendants considered to be high risks by imposing detailed conditions of release and by closely monitoring their adherence to the conditions while free on bail.[56]

The public debate on an issue such as bail is often dominated by superheated rhetoric, dramatic horror stories of celebrated but highly unrepresentative cases, and promises of a utopian future if only some proposed policy is implemented. We are more skeptical about the potential for major improvements in this area. We can easily imagine improvements in the consistency and quality of pretrial decisions, and we can even imagine that this would result in decreased crime on bail and constant or declining jail populations. But we think the more likely result of such innovation will be to reduce the size of the jailed population, which would, of course, be a major social gain. However, the best chances for reducing the amount of crime on bail lie in the alternative approaches described above, which are more just and conceivably as effective.

6

Prosecution

ON A PROSECUTOR'S DECISION hangs great consequences for a defendant.[1] By quashing a charge, he can calm the defendant's fears of ruined reputation and prison. By threatening an aggressive prosecution aimed at proving the worst conceivable charges, he can strike fear in the heart of even the most callous defendant. Indeed he can hound a defendant at every stage from investigation to pretrial detention to sentencing.

What makes the prosecutor's powers even greater is that they are largely unregulated. As a constitutional matter, the courts have been reluctant to impose restrictions on prosecutorial discretion, other than ruling out obvious discrimination and malice.[2] And the courts have also established very high barriers to proving such allegations.[3] Apart from this fundamental restriction, the courts have been silent, leaving prosecutors free to pursue a wide variety of rational law enforcement objectives.

Perhaps the most powerful controls on prosecutors are those imposed by their role in the system. But that role is a complex one with a great deal of latitude.[4] Viewed from one perspective, prosecutors stand between the police and the courts. To the police, prosecutors often seem obstructionist, insisting on due process and equal protection against police ambitions to arrest people whom they know to be guilty despite the lack of hard, legally acceptable evidence. To the courts, on the other hand, prosecutors often seem a little too willing to protect community order rather than the rights of individuals.

Viewed from a slightly different perspective, the prosecutors stand between the victims of crime and the apparatus established to defend the interests of accused defendants, through public defenders overseen by the courts. One of the prosecutor's jobs is to make that apparatus intelligible to the victim of a crime, partly because he needs the victim's cooperation to win his case.[5] Indeed, his position with respect to victims seems broadly analogous to the defense attorney's with respect to the defendant. But this appearance is deceptive, for unlike the defense attorney, who can be a fairly pure advocate, the prosecutor is obliged to serve the broad purposes of the state, which embrace protection of the defendant's rights as well as of community order. Still, if anyone in the court system is to represent the interests of the victims, and also remind the court of its interest in maintaining community order and administering just punishment as well as protecting defendants' rights, it is the prosecutor.

The task of this chapter is to discover how much room exists in the prosecutor's role for giving special attention to dangerous offenders. At the outset it seems that there is much to be done. If a focus on dangerous offenders is seen as a just and effective way of reducing crime and lessening the sense of public danger, prosecutors are duty-bound to be interested. Such a focus would advance the values for which they must be the strongest advocates. Also, like every other agency in the system, prosecutors are overwhelmed by their current caseloads. To cope with them and ensure that at least the most important cases are dealt with effectively, the prosecutors need some principle for rationing their efforts. The concept of dangerous offenders offers such a principle. On the other hand, there is the risk that prosecutors may go to excess if licensed to focus attention on dangerous offenders. They may become more zealous and strident than justice would allow and sacrifice defendants' rights to due process and equal protection.

One might think that the risks of injustice at the hand of prosecutors are less than those associated with the sentencing and pretrial decisions of judges. A prosecutor can threaten only an intensive prosecution, and even that is ultimately limited by the requirements of a trial. Judges, on the other hand, have the discretionary power to set the magnitude of the punishment to be imposed and directly to deny a person's freedom. But if one thinks of the crucial power of the criminal justice system as the power to determine guilt — in Andrew von Hirsch's elegant phrase, to conduct a "ceremony of condemnation" — then one might reasonably conclude that prosecutors' powers are greater than judges', for their role is both influential and discretionary with respect to the issue of guilt.[6] Consequently, any threat of injustice by prosecutors is grave, indeed.

What can prosecutors do to sharpen their focus on dangerous offenders? And can the risks to justice and to the long-run health of the criminal justice system be controlled in introducing a selective focus? We begin by examining the current practices of prosecutors and the modifications that have been introduced by special units focusing on "major offenses" or "career criminals."

A SELECTIVE FOCUS BY PROSECUTORS

Prosecutors have long been forced by both legal and administrative responsibilities to have some principle for screening cases. Legally they must abandon cases that do not warrant prosecution, to save defendants the costs and anxieties of a frivolous court proceeding.[7] Administratively they must save their resources for the cases that are significant to the overall justice and security of the community.[8]

The most commonly adopted principles are those that weigh cases in terms of the seriousness of the offense charged and the strength of the supporting evidence.[9] Prosecutors' offices have separate units for felonies and misdemeanors and provide far greater resources per case to the felony unit.[10] Specialized screening units examine the quality of the evidence at an early stage of the proceedings, eliminate many weak cases, and move the strong cases to priority attention.[11] Murder cases for which there is solid evidence receive the greatest attention; minor property crimes based on circumstantial evidence get the least. These principles reflect the act-based orientation of prosecutors' offices. The defendant's character is largely ignored. As one empirical study of prosecutors' offices concluded: "The prior record of the defendants appeared to have no independent influence on actual case processing decisions, which were moderately influenced by the seriousness of the crime, and heavily determined by the strength of the evidence.[12]

The heavy emphasis on the strength of the evidence as well as the seriousness of the offense charged can be understood as a proper effort to protect citizens from unwarranted prosecutions. It can also be understood as a kind of triage to preserve prosecutorial resources for cases that could be won. But a third explanation, less favorable to prosecutors, is that the prosecutors are overly influenced by political and bureaucratic incentives to maintain a high rate of convictions, that they have become too conservative in accepting cases for prosecution, and that they concentrate too much of their attention on already strong cases rather than trying to strengthen weak cases. The statistics on conviction rates lend some credibility to this hypothesis, since 90 percent of the cases that reach some disposition result in convictions.[13] If the prosecutors were following a conservative policy of prosecuting only those cases that were 80 percent likely to win at trial (a standard that many would view as being far too conservative and leaving far too many cases with prosecutorial merit unprosecuted), then their conviction rate would probably be much lower than 90 percent. So there is a worry that prosecutors are not taking large enough risks with their cases and that consequently too many defendants are being treated too leniently.

This suspicion is underscored by documentation of what appear to be shocking levels of case attrition following felony arrests. Typically, fewer than 15 percent of felony arrests result in felony convictions, and even fewer result in prison sentences.[14] Most felony arrests become misdemeanor convictions, and a noticeable fraction drop out of the system altogether. Of course, much of this attrition is justified. Although many cases are quite properly charged as felonies, they lack the vicious and malevolent quality we ordinarily associate with that term. For example, a husband who reclaimed a television set from his wife, who had forced him to leave their house, may have threatened to hit her if she tried to stop him. In other cases the charge might be dropped because the victim decided not to prosecute. For example, a man might drop charges against a friend in an incident that stemmed from a barroom brawl. Such fact patterns as these are by no means rare. In a recent New York City sample, 36 percent of robbery arrests, 69 percent of assault arrests, and 83 percent of rape arrests involved an offender who was known to the victim before the crime was committed, most often as a friend or family member. In 58 percent of these cases, the victim refused to cooperate with the prosecutor in pursuing the case.[15] In other cases the evidence may have been insufficient to support the charge or may have deteriorated as a result of endless delays. These explanations of case attrition, although correct and compelling, do not quite erase the suspicion that prosecutors are not doing enough to control crime.

Moreover, dangerous offenders may have been most likely to benefit from case attrition, partly because they commit crimes such as robbery and burglary in which it is notoriously difficult to gather strong evidence, compared with homicides, rapes, and assaults among people who know one another. Consequently, these cases might be screened out early by conservative prosecutors accepting lenient guilty pleas. Even worse, a dangerous offender facing a strong case might have the knowledge and sophistication to delay it until the case drops through the cracks of an already porous system. Indeed, the data indicate that the chances of conviction are cut in half as the number of continuances rises from four to more than seventeen.[16]

The mechanisms are not hard to imagine. As the defendant asks for one continuance after another, and the case drags into its eighth or ninth month, the evidence gradually falls apart. Victims become frustrated by the indifferent treatment they receive and the frequent court appearances, which produce nothing but more continuances. Eventually they stop coming, but long before they give up, the memories are fading. And even if the victims and witnesses hold together long enough to see a case through to the end, the short tenure of a young prosecutor often ends before the case is over.[17] It is even conceivable that some crucial physical evidence will be lost. So it is always in the defendant's interests to delay, and he has ample opportunities to do so.[18]

These observations and concerns led many to think that prosecutors could make stronger efforts to win convictions in meritorious cases. One line of attack was to assign the most important cases, involving the most important offenders, to special units, variously called "major offense bureaus" or "career criminal units." These units sprang up in prosecutors' offices throughout the country. From 1974 to 1978 the U.S. Department of Justice funded more than fifty special prosecutorial units with broadly comparable goals and operating procedures.[19]

The goals of these programs included a reduction in the proportion of targeted offenders released prior to trial, a reduction in the time taken to process cases, increased overall conviction rates, increased conviction rates for the most serious charge, reduced plea bargaining, increased probabilities of incarceration, and increased average sentence lengths.[20] Additional goals claimed by some projects included reduced crime through longer incapacitation of career criminals and deterrence of potential criminals because of heightened risks of prosecution, improved public attitudes because of successful prosecution of repeat offenders, and improved morale.[21]

The programs also shared certain operating procedures. One was the establishment of new formal procedures and criteria for screening cases. The criteria usually included the seriousness of the offense (typically measured in terms of the charge, the use of violence or weapons, and the magnitude of the financial losses, but not the relationship among offenders or the location of the offense); the strength of the evidence (number of witnesses, their relationship to the offender, and existence of physical evidence); and the defendant's prior criminal record (total number of prior arrests and convictions with different weights for felonies and misdemeanors and for convictions and arrests).[22] There was much local variation in the emphasis on these elements and their definition. Dallas focused on violence among strangers, San Diego emphasized robbery, and New Orleans concentrated on all those with a prior record.[23]

A second important procedure was called "vertical prosecution," meaning that a single attorney would be assigned to a case and would stay with it from arraignment through bail hearings, pretrial motions, and plea bargaining, all the way to trial and sentencing. In this way the prosecutor would get to know the case more closely, have a better relationship with the victims, witnesses, and police involved in the case, and be more accountable. It was a sharp break from the former practice of horizontal prosecution, in which different prosecutors specialized in different stages, such as indictments or trials, and individual cases moved through many different hands en route to final resolution.

A third important change called for both expedited case processing and restrictions on plea bargaining. To a degree, faster processing depended on innovations such as "open discovery," in which prosecutors fully disclosed their cases to defense attorneys to avoid lengthy pretrial discovery motions,[24] and the creation of special units in the courts to expedite the cases. But probably the most important factor was the prosecutors' determination to move cases to a conclusion. This spirit was maintained not only by the enthusiasm of the prosecutors, who were invigorated by their special mission, but also by their administrative accountability to their supervisors because of the combination of vertical prosecution and new information systems that kept track of case processing times. Somewhat unexpectedly, it was possible to restrict plea bargaining despite the pressure to move cases quickly. Apparently the strong pressures supporting the restrictions did not cause more defendants to risk trial; instead they accepted pleas within the tougher guidelines.[25]

These units also made special efforts to develop and protect evidence in the cases that came to them. By establishing close working relationships with police departments, prosecutors could become involved in a case early enough to influence the collection of evidence. Some offices went so far as to give their attorneys radio-controlled beepers that sounded when an arrest was made, so that the attorneys could work at the crime scene with police investigators.[26] Also they maintained close, supportive relations with victims and witnesses to assure that they would be available to give testimony if needed.[27] Since these activities were above and beyond the prosecutor's ordinary tasks of filling out forms, preparing for trial, and so on, the special units were often given lighter workloads than other attorneys, which also enhanced the quality of the case that was developed.[28] But perhaps the most important method used to protect the evidence in the case was simply moving it quickly.

Prosecutors in the special units also participated more closely in judicial decisions on custody for the defendant. They often gathered information about his prior record and argued against pretrial release and in favor of high bail.[29] They recommended maximum sentences and pressed for whatever sentencing enhancements were relevant to a given case. In some programs, they even monitored the parole hearings of serious, repeat offenders and recommended continued incarceration.

These innovations in prosecutorial procedures certainly seemed designed to alleviate the problems of case attrition. But from our vantage point, what is noticeable is that these innovations are not particularly focused on dangerous offenders. One might think that increased convictions, reduced plea bargaining, expedited case handling, enhanced case development, and protection of evidence would already be the goals of a well-run prosecutor's office across the entire caseload. It is somewhat unsettling to find that these goals and procedures apply only to special units that deal with a small fraction of the cases.

Whether these procedures were focused on dangerous offenders depended entirely on the screening procedures, for these determined which offenders faced the special prosecutors. Given that the special units were often called career criminal units and that the screening procedures often included information about the accused person's prior record, one might assume that these units did focus on dangerous offenders. But that was not necessarily the case. In order to focus on dangerous offenders rather than on well-supported serious offenses, the prior record would have to be weighed heavily relative to all other characteristics. It is not entirely clear how much the prior record counted even in the announced policies, let alone the actual practices of the specialized units, but there are reasons to suspect that it counted less heavily than the current offense and the strength of the evidence.[30] In all likelihood many career criminal units remained primarily offense-oriented rather than offender-oriented.

It is easy to imagine other procedures that would focus on dangerous offenders, especially screening procedures giving a very heavy weight to characteristics that indicate dangerousness and deemphasizing the current offense and the strength of the evidence. A person who met the dangerous-offender criteria would be very carefully prosecuted even if he was arrested on a less serious charge with relatively weak evidence.

Obviously, at the extreme, this policy would be ridiculous and unjust. It would be unwise and unfair to prosecute dangerous offenders aggressively for minor misdemeanors, and it would be useless and unjust to prosecute a case that had little chance of winning at trial simply because the defendant happened to be classified as dangerous. Such actions clearly verge on harassment. But prosecutors may be justified in taking more aggressive stances in cases involving offenders whose prior record shows that they are dangerous.

Probably the most important procedures in dangerous-offender cases are those that lead to stronger and more durable cases, such as working closely with police, developing more supportive relationships with victims and witnesses, and speeding up prosecutions. In crimes committed by dangerous offenders, the evidence tends to be particularly hard to come by and fragile. Almost as important is a commitment to avoid plea bargaining. Part of the reason for this emphasis is admittedly to deal more harshly with dangerous offenders. But also it is in the interests of justice that the cases involving dangerous offenders should meet high evidentiary standards. If the dangerous offenders are exposed to special prosecutorial efforts, they should have the benefit of the special protections afforded by trial. If it were possible, we would recommend that all cases involving dangerous offenders be taken to trial.

Should these procedures be implemented within a special unit focused on dangerous offenders, or should they be utilized generally in prosecutors' offices whenever an appropriate case appears? We think there is a strong argument against the special units and in favor of the general procedure. A special unit has a fixed size, and it creates a certain élan, features that are often taken as virtues. The fixed size guarantees that enough resources will be available to implement the special procedures; the élan enhances the motivation of the attorneys. To our mind, in focusing on dangerous offenders, both seem like liabilities. We cannot be sure how many cases will meet the criteria for dangerous offenders; in all likelihood, the number will be small. (Indeed, if it becomes large, it means we have defined the population incorrectly.) But if the workload is small and unpredictable, an aggressive, elite unit will seek additional work to do. A great deal of pressure will be created to broaden the definition of dangerous offenders, which will threaten the gains in justice and enhanced security that originally motivated the introduction of selective policies.

Broadly speaking, then, there are two approaches to creating a more selective focus among prosecutors. One is to follow the model pioneered in the 1970s — using special units for cases referred through a special screening procedure and dealing with these cases through vertical prosecution, expedited processing, limitations on plea bargaining, close working relations with the police, supportive relations with victims and witnesses, and appearances by prosecutors when continued custody of certain offenders is being considered. The second approach is to adjust that model in two important respects, leaving the rest of it largely intact. The first adjustment is to create a special procedure for handling dangerous offenders throughout the office rather than relying on a special unit. The second is to emphasize those characteristics that reveal the defendant to be dangerous — a criminal record that shows violence, persistence, and high rates of offending.

THE JUSTICE OF SELECTIVE PROSECUTION

By singling out a distinct group of offenders through procedures designed to give prosecutors the upper hand, selective prosecution threatens the rights of defendants to due process and equal protection on two levels. At the most general level, selective prosecution seems to attack the principle of equal protection. If some defendants, identified as dangerous offenders, are prosecuted more vigorously than others accused of similar offenses, then arguably, they have not been equally protected. Indeed, it seems even worse if dangerous offenders are prosecuted more determinedly for relatively minor offenses or for charges in which the evidence is relatively weak. As noted above, if prosecutors organized an overwhelming, high-pressure onslaught against a dangerous offender charged with a serious crime, or if they kept prosecuting dangerous offenders for vagrancy or disorderly conduct, or if they kept bringing robbery cases on the basis of trumped-up evidence, they would have crossed an important line that makes our system of justice fair and restrained.

The interesting question, however, is not at the extremes, but in the middle range. Should prosecutors give a slightly more vigorous and determined prosecution to cases involving dangerous offenders? A vigorous prosecution could mean enhanced effort in cases of serious crime in which the evidence was very strong — refusing to accept plea bargains, conducting extensive collateral investigations, or moving very quickly in a case in which there were strong physical evidence and eyewitnesses. It could also mean a greater willingness to prosecute less serious offenses where the evidence was strong — for example, holding out for a felony conviction in a case of gun possession where the testimony of two police officers is corroborated by a witness. Or it could mean being willing to risk failure in prosecuting a serious crime in which the evidence was well above the constitutional standard but much less than the usual prosecutorial standard of 90 percent certainty to win at trial—for example, a robbery case in which there is no physical evidence and the eyewitness testimony is shaky. It is in these areas that a selective focus among prosecutors would operate, and it is the justice of these actions that must be considered.

Prosecutors have a great deal of discretion in the level of effort they can make in prosecuting an accused person. The courts have tolerated this variability as long as outright malice or discrimination could be ruled out by the existence of an articulable and reasonable law enforcement purpose.[31] Prosecution focused on unusually visible, active, or culpable defendants has been tolerated as long as the methods used in the prosecution were not extreme.[32] Apparently, then, there is no constitutional right to a particular level of prosecution, and certainly no right to the relatively superficial prosecutions typical of today's overwhelmed criminal justice system. As a practical matter, the level of prosecution has always varied within a broad range. Some cases were assigned to vigorous and competent attorneys, others went to those who were more indifferent or inexperienced. Some cases attracted publicity or the interest of attorneys in the office, others did not. Indeed, prosecutors deliberately created such variations by establishing organizational units with very different caseloads. Those who committed felonies received much closer attention than those who committed misdemeanors, murderers got stiffer prosecutions than armed robbers. So variability in prosecution is not an issue. To the extent that there is an issue, it must be the appropriateness of focusing on characteristics of the defendant rather than his crime.

At this point, we return to the basic question at the core of all selective proposals: is it just to distinguish dangerous offenders from all others? And our answer here is the same: to the extent that we think an individual's bad intentions are revealed by a pattern of criminal conduct, it seems just that offenders who reveal themselves to be dangerous should be subject to greater risks and liabilities than they now are.

The special context of prosecution does raise an important due process issue, however. The justice of selective prosecutions would be enhanced if those subjected to it knew, before they committed an additional offense, that they would be vulnerable to such special procedures, and if they had a chance to contest their status. Both ideas seem wise to us. We would recommend that, as part of his sentencing process, the defendant be formally apprised of his change in status when he is convicted of an offense that establishes him as an unusually dangerous offender. Moreover, he should be informed that for a limited time he will be vulnerable to special prosecution if he appears again in the criminal justice system. Such warnings would not only enhance the justice of the policies, but also conceivably would increase their effectiveness through deterrence as well as through incapacitation of offenders. If the defendant ignores the warning and shows up in the system again, he should still have the opportunity to contest his status, since the records on which the decision is based are far from perfectly accurate.

Such features may seem to do nothing more than give some due process trappings to a policy that is fundamentally unjust. But we think that interests in both justice and crime control justify a special prosecutorial focus on offenders who have revealed themselves to be unusually dangerous. On balance, then, although we see the threat to due process and equal protection, we think that selective prosecution is justifiable.

Some more particular concerns deserve special attention. Perhaps the most important is that aggressive prosecutions might overawe defendants and lead them to accept much less favorable plea bargains than would ordinarily be offered, given the strength of the evidence and the practices of a given court. There are many reasons to be concerned about this. A trial is an uncertain process, whose outcome cannot be reliably predicted simply from looking at the evidence in a case. Since there is uncertainty about the outcome, the natural human tendency is to be overimpressed by small probabilities of very bad results. And that is exactly what a prosecutor threatens when he stretches the evidence. Consequently, a defendant might agree to a more serious plea if the prosecutor threatens uncertain and unlikely, but still very serious, consequences.

Two observations mitigate but do not eliminate this worry. One is that the prosecutor's capacity to intimidate depends at least partly on the defendant's experience. Inexperienced defendants, unable to evaluate the strength of the evidence and uncertain about common court practices, may be frightened more easily than more experienced offenders, who are able to discount the most dire threats of the prosecutor. Since our definition of dangerous offenders singles out those who have had prior experience with the criminal justice system, the worst abuses in this area are unlikely to occur. Dangerous offenders can still be frightened by threats of harsh punishment, but not as easily or as unjustly as less experienced offenders. In order for the dangerous offenders to be frightened, they must see a connection among the case against them, what the prosecutor can prove, and what the system will do to them if the case is made.

Indeed, this observation underscores the importance of our second argument. In plea bargaining the defendant's right to go to trial can never be taken away. Because he has that alternative, there are limits on what an offender will agree to, depending on his expectations of what can be proved at trial and of what punishment will be meted out, both of which are fixed by statute. In effect, the defendant is threatened by nothing more than what the state could justly administer under existing laws. In this sense, all plea bargains represent a concession from the state.

We know, of course, that the punishments threatened by our criminal statutes are severe. We also know that they are rarely carried out. Consequently, equal protection may require that we threaten offenders with no more than the usual punishment in cases like theirs (which is usually much less than would be warranted). But although it might be easy to threaten a defendant with a more than usually severe prosecution, it is very hard to threaten a defendant who has the right to a trial, some experience, and moderately competent counsel with more punishment than current statutes would justify. Thus the biggest problems in plea bargaining may be created by the wide latitude that criminal statutes give manipulative prosecutors.

At any rate, we worry about "coercive" plea bargaining less than we would if selective prosecution policies embraced inexperienced defendants. Moreover, if our laws threatened punishment that the community was prepared to administer, and if defendants had access to competent counsel who could help them weigh the case against them, worries about manipulative plea bargaining would virtually disappear.

The second particular concern for justice is that selective prosecution will introduce inequities in the resources available to prosecution and defense—that the defense will be overwhelmed. This concern seems justified, and we would recommend allowing some added resources on the defense side. We hope that many of the cases involving dangerous offenders would go to trial so that a judge could get a good look at the evidence in the case and control the prosecutor's zeal by reminding him that his responsibility includes protecting defendant's rights as well as defending the victim's interests in retribution and the community's interests in order.

The third concern is that the impartiality of judicial decisions might be threatened. If the judges become aware that a case involves a dangerous offender, they might consciously or unconsciously bias their decision against the defendant. That the judges would notice is almost inevitable, especially if the prosecutions are handled by special units and if the file folders for dangerous-offender cases are distinctive. But even without these obvious cues, the judges will probably notice simply by observing the prosecution's actions. Whether such knowledge would prejudice a judge is unclear. All the usual apparatus of appeal and review is available to defendants who think their right to a fair trial has been abridged, but we do not know whether these are sufficient to control an uncertain potential for abuse. In this area it may be desirable to let some case law develop.

On balance, we do not find the concept of selective prosecution unjust. The differences between dangerous offenders and others, as well as the proposed bases for discovering that difference, provide a just basis for varying levels of prosecutorial effort and risk. Whether it would be worth it to make this effort is our next question.

THE PRACTICAL VALUE OF SELECTIVE PROSECUTION

There is little hard empirical evidence of the practical benefits of focusing prosecutorial attention more sharply on dangerous offenders. Although the experience of the career criminal units has been documented, these programs have not been quite as selective as we would recommend. Their screening procedures do not accord enough importance to the offender's characteristics, and the characteristics utilized are not the most just and useful in distinguishing dangerous offenders. In estimating the potential of selective prosecution, we have only theory to guide us.

The effects of career criminal programs have been recorded by evalua- tors at three different points along the lengthy causal chain that links the adoption of selective prosecution policies to the desired outcome of re- duced crime. The first point is the impact of the programs on the admin- istrative procedures and morale of prosecutors' offices. Here clear suc- cesses have been registered. One study surveyed seventy-five jurisdictions that had adopted career criminal programs. Of these, 83 percent indicated that the programs had improved case intake proce- dures, 69 percent indicated improvements in case tracking and monitor- ing, and 66 percent indicated improved use of internal investigative resources. Fully three-quarters of the chief prosecutors and program directors surveyed reported an improvement in morale among the attor- neys as a result of the targeted prosecution program.[33]

Career criminal units had a less clear-cut impact on the outcomes of the cases. One study of four criminal career programs across the country showed no increase in either conviction rates or incarceration rates, but a small increase in the seriousness of conviction charges.[34] An evaluation of twelve programs in California showed a marginal increase in conviction rates (from 89.5 percent to 91.6 percent), and a larger increase in sentence lengths (from 4.5 years to 5.4 years).[35] Some observers have disputed the generalizability of these results on grounds that the California Criminal Code's unique provisions for sentencing enhancement allow a broader scope for selective policies than would be available elsewhere.

The third point of evaluation was the impact on crime in the community. Here, no effect could be found. Advocates of career criminal programs explained this failure by observing that the units were too small to produce a noticeable effect on the wide, random fluctuations of the reported crime rate.[36] They also observed that the cases selected for prosecution were already the strongest and that little more could be done to strengthen them further.

Such explanations may help us understand why career criminal programs failed to control crime, but they weaken the arguments in favor of selective prosecution. After all, part of the appeal of selective policies is that even small programs should produce noticeable effects on crime. Moreover, unless these policies can add something to current methods, there is no reason to consider their adoption; implicitly, we are already doing what can reasonably be done.

If we had nothing more than the operating experience of the career criminal programs and these explanations to rely on, we would have to be quite pessimistic about the practical benefits of selective policies. But knowledgeable practitioners and academics believe there are substantial benefits to be gained from selective prosecution.[37] Their confidence seems to be based on three observations.

First, the skewed distribution of offending and the very high rates of the most dangerous offenders must establish some potential benefits of concentrating on this group. In short, the general theory of selective incapacitation should apply in the area of prosecution as well as elsewhere. Second, and perhaps more to the point, the career criminal programs were not nearly as selective as we would propose. The seriousness of the offense and the strength of the evidence continued to be counted heavily in determining the cases referred to the special units. Those cases would have been dealt with harshly even under the old system, and little more could be done since the evidence was already strong. Also, cases involving serious charges against dangerous offenders supported by less than ironclad evidence were avoided by the special units. Yet these might be precisely the cases in which extra prosecutorial effort and risk-taking would have produced important benefits. Similarly, cases involving dangerous offenders charged with less serious crimes were also neglected. But if dangerous offenders are active in all sorts of crimes and are hard to catch, then the aggressive prosecution of these cases, too, might have yielded noticeable reductions in crime.

Another part of the problem, however, was that the prosecutors did not use the most effective bases for distinguishing the dangerous offenders from others. Because the programs were conceived as career criminal programs, the screening criteria emphasized the length of the adult criminal record. Few programs included juvenile records, and those that did often found it difficult to obtain them. Some programs established a minimum age of twenty-one to be considered a career criminal, and very few programs took serious note of whether an offender used drugs, and if so, what kind.[38]

Concentrating on the adult criminal record obviously makes sense if the objective is to find people who persist in criminal offending over a long period of time. But it makes less sense if one is trying to focus prosecutorial attention on *dangerous offenders* — people who are violent, active, and persistent. Dangerous offenders are not typically old. One researcher described the most appropriate target of selective prosecution as "a young person in his late teens or early twenties arrested for robbery or burglary or a series of property crimes with a juvenile record and a long criminal history given only a few years on the street who is unemployed, and who uses drugs."[39] The criteria used by many career criminal programs would reject such offenders because their adult record was not long enough. Selective prosecution effectively targeted on dangerous offenders might succeed in controlling crime where programs targeted on career criminals have not.

An improved screening device, developed by the Institute for Law and Social Research, is presented in Table 17. It is based on characteristics that predict high rates of recidivism among federal prisoners, characteristics that could conceivably be known by the prosecutor shortly after arrest. It is offered not as a rigid decision-making machine but as a guideline that would probably help distinguish the dangerous offenders more effectively than current procedures do.[40]

Those who are optimistic about the potential of selective prosecutions see substantial room for improvement through expanded efforts to col-

Table 17. Proposed point scores for selecting career criminals.

Variable	Points
Heavy use of alcohol	5
Heroin use	10
Age at time of instant arrest	
Less than 22	21
23–27	14
28–32	7
38–42	− 7
43+	−14
Length of criminal career	
0–5 years	0
6–10	1
11–15	2
16–20	3
21+	4
Arrests during last five years	4 per arrest
Crimes of violence	3 per arrest
Sale of drugs	4 per arrest
Other offenses	2 per arrest
Longest time served, single term	
1–5 months	4
6–12	9
13–24	18
25–36	27
37–48	36
49+	45
Number probation sentences	1.5 per sentence
Instant offense was crime of violence[a]	7
Instant offense was crime labeled "other"[b]	−18
Critical value to label an offender as a career criminal	47

Source: William Rhodes, Herbert Tyson, James Weekley, Catherine Conly, and Gustave Powell, *Developing Criteria for Identifying Career Criminals* (Washington, D.C.: INSLAW, 1982).

a. Violent crimes include homicide, assault, robbery, sexual assault, and kidnaping.

b. Other crimes include military, probation, parole, weapons, and all others *except* arson, burglary, larceny, auto theft, fraud, forgery, and drug sales or possession.

lect and preserve evidence. Recent research on case attrition has indicated that many cases meriting prosecution are now lost because of insufficient evidence.[41] At the crime scene, potential witnesses sometimes scatter, physical evidence is overlooked or mislabeled, or important legal procedures are ignored. Later, evidence may be misplaced, or testimony becomes doubtful because of inadequate notes and records. The prosecutor may lose contact with victims and witnesses or fail to understand and use the evidence the police have gathered.

Prosecutors have an important opportunity to prevent such problems. If they establish close relations with the police, work the crime scene, make an early and thorough review of the case file, maintain close relations with victims and witnesses, and take risks with cases that merit prosecution, then more convictions can be won.[42] Although these opportunities may exist in all cases, limited resources prevent giving them all such close attention. Consequently, these procedures might be engaged first in cases involving dangerous offenders.

These observations do not guarantee that prosecutions more sharply focused than those carried out by career criminal programs will reduce crime. They simply establish the possibility. Our estimate of the potential benefits of selective prosecution is not a single-point estimate but a distribution of possibilities centered around prospects for minor improvements.[43] The only way to find out if more significant improvements are possible is to try the program.

Our discussion has concentrated on estimating the first-round effects of a sharpened focus on dangerous offenders, but another effect is worth noting. If prosecutions improved in general as a result of introducing selective procedures, we would have more reliable information sooner about the offenders who are unusually dangerous, because it would be apparent in their records. Also, there may be some practical benefit simply in developing some response to dangerous offenders. If part of the broad sense of public danger is generated by the idea of vulnerability, an adequate and visible response might partially allay these fears.

THE POTENTIAL OF SELECTIVE PROSECUTION

Many people feel that selective prosecution would corrupt a powerful institution that is now delicately balanced within the criminal justice system, putting in jeopardy defendants' rights to equal protection and due process. And since career criminal programs have not been able to reduce crime, we would run these risks of injustice for little practical gain.

But no one has a constitutional right to the limited prosecution now typical of our overwhelmed criminal justice system. We have always relied on prosecutorial discretion to focus the wrath of the system on those who are most deserving, and offenders who have been active, violent, and persistent are among the most deserving. One can argue that the career criminal programs were not sharply enough focused to test the selective prosecution idea.

Our deliberations have persuaded us that selective prosecution, to be triggered by the arrest of dangerous offenders charged with felonies or high misdemeanors, and consisting of special efforts to develop and preserve evidence, to expedite processing, to resist plea bargaining, and go to trial are in the interests of both justice and more effective crime control. If these special procedures were used throughout the prosecutor's office rather than by a special unit, we could lessen the risk that the definition of dangerous offenders would broaden unjustly, and we could improve the overall quality of prosecutions. If the general quality improved, we would be able to find the dangerous offenders earlier and more accurately. We also think that creation of a visible response to dangerous offenders might alleviate the public sense of danger.

So we see enough potential in this area to merit experimentation. The risks to equal protection and due process can be controlled by warning defendants when thay have accumulated enough convictions and arrests to be counted as a dangerous offender and by allowing them to contest the factual basis of their designation. The risks can also be controlled by providing special defense resources and by taking cases involving dangerous offenders to trial. The risk that our ideology will become meaner and less forgiving than it is now does exist, but so does the risk that we will fail to establish justice because we are unable to discover and deal with the most dangerous offenders. Our hope is that the prosecutors' responses to dangerous offenders can be what we have always wanted them to be: measured and deliberate but stern in their support of the current laws. That is all that selective prosecution demands.

7
Police Practices

THE ACTIONS TAKEN by the police to intercept and solve crimes focus the criminal justice system through two mechanisms. First, it is the police who initiate criminal proceedings. If the police are unable to solve the crimes committed by dangerous offenders, then it does little good to organize prosecutors and judges to deal with them.

Second, police investigations lay the basis for justly distinguishing dangerous offenders from all others. We recognize those who are dangerous by their acts, which we know largely through the investigative efforts of the police, so they create the potential for just and effective policies focusing on dangerous offenders. If the police fail to solve the crimes they commit, or attribute them to the wrong offenders, we not only fail to prosecute the dangerous offenders, but we also fail to establish the criminal records that reveal them as unusually persistent, active, and violent.

This does not necessarily imply that the police themselves should be selective in their practices. Indeed, one can make exactly the opposite argument. Precisely because so much depends on police investigations, it is crucial that they be scrupulously objective. To grant the police a license to focus on the few who seem to be dangerous offenders would be unfair and would threaten the objectivity that makes criminal records a just basis for distinguishing dangerous offenders. It is easy to believe that the police are already too zealous in their pursuit of seemingly dangerous offenders, and a broader license in this direction would sharply increase the threat to individuals' rights to equal protection and due process. Moreover, overzealous police actions might focus on those whom the police are suspicious of and have prejudices against rather than on the dangerous offenders.

On the other hand, dangerous offenders may have some advantages in confrontations with the police that allow them to get away with more. One can imagine a system in which cases are investigated in the usual ways until an offender accumulates a criminal record indicating that he is dangerous (two convictions for violent offenses within two years of street time plus two additional arrests or convictions). Only then would the special procedures swing into action, primarily as a means for reducing a bias that now operates in favor of dangerous offenders rather than for introducing a bias against them. This system might allow a fair but sharper focus on dangerous offenders than we now have.

Our purpose in this chapter is to explore the desirability and feasibility of introducing special police procedures focusing on dangerous offenders. Our specific aims are to determine whether current police practices make it likely or unlikely that a dangerous offender will be arrested for an offense; to imagine some adjustments that would allow the system to identify dangerous offenders earlier and more reliably and to increase the likelihood that they will be arrested for any new offenses; and to evaluate these proposals in terms of their justice, practical value, and long-run implications.

FOCUSING ATTENTION ON DANGEROUS OFFENDERS

A central tenet of law enforcement in a free society is that criminal investigation should be minimally intrusive and fair. A citizen's privacy should be firmly protected unless there is good reason to intrude. Moreover, the reasons that justify an intrusion should apply equally to all. There is a strong social interest in solving crimes, which often seems to stand in opposition to the individual's right to privacy and fairness. The challenge is to find the proper balance between these competing interests.

A key feature of our traditional enforcement system that helps maintain a proper balance between these interests is the requirement that a criminal act be completed before an investigation can take place.[1] This requirement guarantees that investigative attention will be focused on the relatively small area surrounding a known offense.[2] Government agents are not authorized to range broadly over the social landscape in search of crimes. This allows most of us to go about our business most of the time without worrying too much about police scrutiny.

The focus on acts means not only that the scope of the police interest is narrow, but also that it is justified by social interests in justice and crime control. If an offense has occurred, in all likelihood there is an offender to be identified and captured. Whatever privacy is lost through the investigation of the offense is offset by the public interest in solving the crime. Because there is a good reason for conducting the investigation, the chance that it is being undertaken for improper reasons is lessened, though not eliminated. We cannot rule out personal hostility, racism, or even political antipathy among the investigators, but the fact of an offense gurantees that these motivations are not the sole reasons for the investigation. Thus the focus on acts establishes many useful guarantees to the reasonableness of criminal investigations.

Given the importance of criminal acts, it seems dangerous to allow investigations to be guided by anything else. Organizing investigations around offenders, for example, would create too great a risk to the values of due process and equal protection. Although the police interest might still be relatively narrow, there would be too great an opportunity for improper motivations to be expressed or developed. This risk would seem to end any discussion of police practices focusing explicitly on dangerous offenders.

However, an enforcement system that focuses on acts and is truly unbiased with respect to criminal offenders will quite naturally focus punishment on the dangerous offenders, for it is they who commit most of the crimes. Of course, one could go even further and argue that dangerous offenders should face heightened risks of arrest, given offenses, to reflect their greater blameworthiness. But that goes too far for us. We would be content with a system in which an offender's probability of arrest, given an offense, were unbiased with respect to his rate of offending; in less technical terms, dangerous offenders would be neither more nor less likely to be arrested, given similar offenses, than lower-rate, less persistent offenders.

The problem is that criminal enforcement is probably not unbiased with respect to offenders. Some crimes are solved more easily and reliably than others, exposing some offenders to greater risks of arrest and punishment. How does this bias run? Do dangerous offenders face a higher or lower probability of being arrested than less dangerous offenders? If dangerous offenders face a lower probability of arrest, then the enforcement system can be considered biased in their favor; and it might be fairer if the police focused on dangerous offenders. But if dangerous offenders now face higher probabilities of arrest, focusing the system even more sharply on their activities would risk great injustices.

It is commonly assumed that the bias is strongly against dangerous offenders. This assumption is consistent with a broad sociological theory that views criminal law, the criminal justice system, and each of its agencies as the instruments of class-based social control. In this conception the bias begins with the very definition of criminal offenses: by emphasizing street crimes such as robbery and burglary rather than white collar crimes such as fraud and illegal disposal of toxic wastes, the criminal code reveals a class bias.[3]

The bias is also apparent when one examines patterns of police activity. Sociologists have hypothesized that the likelihood of a crime being solved is determined by the social positions of the victim and the offender.[4] An influential victim commands a great deal of attention from the police for a crime that would be ignored if the victim had lower status. And a wealthy suspect can ward off an investigation that would be insistent if conducted against a poor person. Thus the most likely crimes to be solved are those that involve victims of high social status and offenders of low status — the sort of social relations we imagine to be typical of robberies and burglaries.[5]

Other sociologists have reached a broadly similar conclusion through a somewhat different set of hypotheses, which emphasize the motivations of the police. In this conception the police quite naturally develop strong hostilities toward people they guess to be the criminal element. Over time they develop a list of "usual suspects" who become the focus of virtually all investigations, and as a result, virtually every crime those suspects commit is solved. So vulnerable are the usual suspects that they are often charged with crimes they did not commit. The system is thus biased against active street offenders who have attracted police interest and hostility.[6] These views have helped to shape the conventional wisdom that the dangerous offenders already bear the brunt of the criminal justice system's wrath. If they are accurate, then encouraging the police to become more selective would be unjust and unwise.

Another line of analysis, however, leads to very different conclusions about the bias of the system. That line is less concerned with the latent functions of the criminal justice system, its vulnerability to social influence, or the motivations of the police. Instead, it focuses on the *capacities* of the police to solve crime, specifically, the mechanics of assembling evidence to build a case against a specific suspect.

These analyses show that the most important factor determining whether a crime will be solved is the amount and quality of the evidence that victims and witnesses can supply to the police.[7] If citizens can describe their assailant specifically and accurately, an arrest is very likely, no matter what the social position of the victim or the offender. The second most important factor is the specific character of the police investigative effort.[8] If the police locate multiple witnesses, search the crime scene for physical evidence, and take other investigative steps, the likelihood of a crime being solved increases dramatically.[9]

The importance of these mechanical factors in solving crimes leads to several implications about the bias of the system. One important implication is that crimes involving strangers are much more difficult to solve than those involving people who know one another in some way. There is a great deal of evidence that this is true.[10] So if dangerous offenders are, by definition, those who commit violence among strangers particularly often, then the system is biased not against but in favor of dangerous offenders.

A second, more speculative implication is that crimes committed by inexperienced or impassioned people can be solved more easily than those committed by more practiced and detached offenders. To a degree, of course, this hypothesis overlaps with the one above. An inexperienced or passionate offender is most likely to commit a crime against someone he knows. But holding the relationship between offenders and victims constant, impulsive offenders still might be more vulnerable to arrest if they are more likely to leave useful witnesses and other sorts of evidence in their wake. On the other hand, one can argue that the advantages of experience for practiced offenders may be offset by increased notoriety. What little evidence exists on this point supports the hypothesis that practice and experience tend to reduce rather than increase an offender's chance of arrest. The Rand prison surveys indicated unambiguously that the probability of arrest, given an offense, decreased with the offender's level of activity.[11] The effect of age was a little less clear. The probability of arrest decreased with age until age thirty, but rose thereafter.[12] One possible interpretation is that when an offender turns thirty, the effects of decreasing activity and increasing notoriety finally catch up to him.

If crimes among strangers cannot be easily solved, and if practiced offenders can reduce their risks still further with experience, then dangerous offenders are less vulnerable to arrest than many other street criminals. If we add one additional hypothesis — namely, that the police tend to stop their investigative efforts once they have built a solid case supporting one serious charge — then there is a strong argument that the system is biased in favor of unusually dangerous offenders. The anecdotal information supporting the hypothesis about police conduct is very strong.[13] From the police point of view there is little practical advantage to adding criminal charges if one serious charge has been firmly established, since prosecutors are unwilling to charge additional offenses, and judges are unwilling to adjust their sentences accordingly. Some inexpensive field investigations could clear up the uncertainty about the hypothesis.

It is not necessary to give up the broader sociological view to reach the conclusion that the system is biased in favor of dangerous offenders. The sociological theories are seeking to answer the broad question of whether our system of justice is fair across economic class and racial lines. None of our observations rules out class bias or racial prejudice; indeed, the broad sociological processes might well be reflected in the mechanics of solving crimes. The police may discourage lower-class victims from supplying information but eagerly accept information from upper-class victims. The police may work harder to take the appropriate investigative steps when the victim is important than when he is not. But whatever biases are operating to the disadvantage of the poor and powerless and in favor of the rich and powerful, there is also a bias against the passionate, amateur offenders and in favor of the calculating and practiced offenders. If the system is currently biased in favor of dangerous offenders, then it would be more equitable to focus enforcement strategies on dangerous offenders. Of course, enhanced equity among offenders is not the only aspect of justice at stake. Due process and equal protection are also important. But if concerns for due process can be protected, it might be in the interests of justice to focus attention on dangerous offenders.

It is significant that a focus on dangerous offenders is not wholly alien to existing enforcement procedures. In areas such as organized crime, narcotics trafficking, extortion, and terrorism, the police have long based their investigative activities on known offenders rather than known offenses. One reason for this departure from traditional practices is the difficulty of solving these crimes because victims or witnesses are unwilling or unable to testify. Also there is justice and practical value in focusing on the most culpable offenders rather than those who are easiest to catch. These reasons could apply equally well to dangerous street offenders.

Even the current methods of solving street crimes depend on knowing a great deal about specific offenders. Robberies, rapes, and burglaries are often solved by showing the victims mug books of known offenders.[14] Some street crimes are solved by linking a specific modus operandi to a known offender who happened to be in the area of the crime without an alibi. Obviously, each of these techniques depends on knowing something about offenders, independent of the offense.

Thus dealing fairly and effectively with dangerous street offenders may require giving them more attention than they now receive. Moreover, the present use of offender-based methods to deal with problems similar to those posed by dangerous street offenders, also provides some license to consider offender-based enforcement strategies. We have not yet answered the question of whether specific methods would be just and practically effective. But it is worthwhile to imagine some possible strategies and to evaluate them in terms of their justice and practical value.

We will start by considering enforcement strategies that focus on acts rather than offenders. One strategy would be to focus on the sorts of offenses that dangerous offenders are particularly likely to commit, such as robbery. Preliminary results from an evaluation of a special robbery suppression experiment in Birmingham, Alabama, suggest that focusing on one kind of robbery could produce a discriminating effect on the sort of offender who was arrested: stake-outs of commercial targets were likely to yield arrests of robbers with extensive prior records; decoys sent into parks to attract muggers produced arrests of people with less serious prior records.[15]

A second strategy would be to give special investigative attention to any offense involving a suspect who has previously been designated a dangerous offender on the basis of his criminal activity. That is the basic idea behind New York City's Felony Augmentation Program. Whenever a previously designated dangerous offender appears as a suspect in a criminal case (no matter what the charge), the police make special efforts to gather evidence.[16] The success of this strategy depends on the precision with which dangerous offenders have been identified, the reliability of the link between a particular case and the offender, and the value of additional investigative efforts in establishing a stronger case.

A third strategy involves not only strengthening the evidence for the offense, but also widening the investigation beyond the original charge. In the past the police often "cleared" unrelated offenses by administratively charging them to offenders whom they suspected or who "confessed" to the crimes. Typically, these charges were not carried over into indictments, nor was much effort expended gathering evidence to support them. The goal was to meet an internal administrative requirement of police departments rather than to prosecute offenders more aggressively. But if prosecutors become willing to charge additional counts, and if judges become willing to sentence consecutively rather than concurrently, then it may be worth the time of the police to carry out more careful investigations of offenders whom they suspect of multiple crimes. Even if the investigations do not result in longer prison terms, they might establish the records of offending that would aid in identifying those who are dangerous. Both effects would help the overall selectivity of the system.

There are reasons to believe that wider postarrest investigations could be successful. For one thing, the evidence on rates of offending by dangerous offenders suggest that at least some will in fact commit other crimes during the usual time taken by the criminal justice process. In addition, in principle it should be easier to solve a crime when one has a suspect, who can be interviewed and shown to witnesses to other crimes in line-ups, and whose alibis can be checked.

A fourth strategy would require patrol officers to observe and record their observations of specially designated dangerous offenders. This overt surveillance of dangerous offenders would not require a major change in the deployment of patrol personnel. Such reports might become significant to investigators if they implicated specific dangerous offenders as suspects in a crime or refuted an alibi.[17]

A fifth strategy extends the fourth by relying on intermittent, continuing, covert surveillance of dangerous offenders. This strategy is unlikely to be productive unless the police have additional information about likely times and places of offenses, since even the most active offenders commit crimes relatively rarely. Several days or weeks could easily go by without an observed offense, even if the surveillance was continuous and undetected. Moreover, most offenses happen so quickly that even a continuous surveillance might fail to disclose them.

The limitation of the fifth strategy suggests a sixth possibility, based on identifying a related crime series that the police might be able to interrupt through a proactive operation. The assumption is that dangerous offenders commit a number of crimes using a similar modus operandi and leave behind witnesses who offer similar descriptions of the offender. If the offenses can be linked to one another and to a known offender, and future targets predicted, surveillance of either the suspect *or* the predicted location might allow the police to apprehend the offender in the act of committing a crime. A police researcher offers a plausible scenario for an investigation of this type:

An investigation of offender A is begun because it is suspected that offender A is involved in several commercial robberies. At this point, only a suspicion exists as to A's guilt and A cannot be found. An informant tells a detective that offender A is associating with offenders B and C and that the three have been committing armed robberies of convenience stores. The informant has no direct knowledge of this and would not testify to the fact even if he had direct knowledge. Files on offenders B and C provide addresses of their residences and descriptions of their cars. Surveillance of B and C leads detectives to offender A. Surveillance also shows that none of the three are employed and that they spend most of the day inside, coming out only at night. Photographs of offenders B and C are shown to witnesses of earlier robberies in which A is a suspect, one witness picks the photo of B out of a photo spread. Meanwhile, several convenience stores are staked out in an area the three offenders have been frequenting. Offenders A and C are captured at one of these locations while committing a robbery. The entire robbery is witnessed by the detectives staking out the store. Offender B escapes but is arrested later at his apartment.[18]

A seventh strategy would be to set up intermittent or continuous surveillance of dangerous offenders only while they were on probation or parole.[19] In effect, the police could become useful adjuncts of probation and corrections departments. This strategy avoids civil liberties objections that might be raised against the unequal attention given to dangerous offenders, and it increases the special deterrent and incapacitation effects of probation and parole. It has the disadvantages of requiring some potentially large redeployments of police personnel and, conceivably, of harming offenders' rehabilitative prospects by identifying them to potential employers as convicted offenders. Whether it would be useful to deploy patrol officers for this purpose is a suitable subject for experimentation.

THE JUSTICE OF SELECTIVE POLICE TACTICS

As in every other phase of the criminal justice system, we must address the question of whether it is decent and just to focus police attention on dangerous offenders. To a degree, this discussion mirrors the general discussion of this subject. One can defend the idea by arguing: 1) that the criminal law has always been interested in character as well as acts, that dangerous offenders have revealed their character through their acts, and that it is in the interests of justice to allow accurate information about rates of offending to influence police actions toward individuals; 2) that although there are some objectionable features, a selective focus is sufficiently useful to be adopted anyway; 3) that a selective focus is necessary to compensate for nonselective, unjust biases introduced by the natural functioning of the system; and 4) that explicitly adopting selective policies would codify current practices, and therefore discipline the current system and enhance justice.

But a selective focus by the police also has some significantly different aspects. If we consider the seriousness of the consequences for the offender of decisions made at each stage of the system, selectivity in investigation may be less significant than selectivity in sentencing or pretrial detention, because the consequences are not so direct. The offender exposed to heightened police interest loses some privacy and anonymity and is more vulnerable to arrest and prosecution. But he retains his freedom, and he is protected by constitutional rights in the adjudication of any charges against him. All he has lost is the average citizen's expectation of police indifference and an ordinarily sloppy police investigation. Since this loss seems small relative to imposition of a jail or prison sentence, and since selective sentencing seems to have relatively widespread support, it must be permissible for the police to take a special interest in dangerous offenders.

But if one emphasizes the central role of the adjudication of guilt and innocence, selective police strategies seems more threatening than selective sentencing, because the police supply the evidence on which the adjudication turns. For that decision to be made fairly and accurately, the police must maintain scrupulous objectivity, and that objectivity is threatened by a selective focus. If the police know they are dealing with a dangerous offender, they may develop strong personal animosities toward defendants, which may motivate them to violate due process guarantees.

On balance there are three strong arguments for the justice of a selective focus in police operations. First, people do not become designated as dangerous offenders simply on the basis of police suspicions; they earn this status by committing crimes before they come under special scrutiny. Before they are identified as dangerous offenders, they are treated just like everyone else. Second, none of the strategies described above licenses more intrusive or more coercive investigative methods than are now used. The increased police interest comes only in the form of more resources and attention, not greater reliance on informants, undercover operations, or wiretaps. These strategies are much more benign than those now focused on those suspected of narcotics trafficking, extortion, or other organized crimes. Third, these methods may be necessary simply to equalize the risks among offenders. In sum, the concept of selective police practices seems tolerably just. All that the dangerous offenders have lost is the ordinary citizen's expectation of a somewhat lackadaisical investigation. And just as there is no constitutional right to an average prosecution, there is no constitutional right to an average investigation.

But we can still make some distinctions among the proposed strategies in terms of their protections of important civil liberties. Some strategies seem more just, either because they are more respectful of privacy or because they require greater misdeeds from the criminal offenders before taking effect.

The proposal to focus on specific kinds of offenses seems relatively unobjectionable if the offenses are serious in themselves, such as robbery. The question of justice is less clear if the offense is illegal gun carrying or larcenies from the person. But robbery is clearly the most important offense on which to focus.

The proposals for additional investigative efforts following an arrest also seem fairly unobjectionable. In both case enhancement and widened postarrest investigations the offender must have been previously convicted of and indicted for enough crimes to qualify as dangerous, and also be strongly suspected for a new offense. Only that combination of factors could trigger these strategies.

For different reasons the proposal to use police to strengthen probation and parole supervision also seems unobjectionable. If an offender has been convicted of sufficient crimes to qualify him as dangerous, he is vulnerable to state supervision, even if he has been released on parole for some reason. It may not aid rehabilitation to have the police continually checking on paroled offenders, but it hardly seems unjust.

The only problematic strategies are those involving selective surveillance of dangerous offenders, whether casual and open or focused and covert. Of course, this strategy, which involves nothing other than more intensive surveillance of public places, is wholly within constitutional boundaries. Yet there may be a problem of fairness if some individuals are under more surveillance than others. The fact that dangerous offenders earn this status by their acts might dispel fears of arbitrary police designations, but it is debatable whether it would be sufficient to make us feel that this strategy was tolerably just.

Thus there is scope within the law and our common notions of justice for an explicit police focus on dangerous offenders. The major risks to justice arise from the encouragement of corrupting *ad hominem* motivations among the police, which could lead to important due process violations. One risk is that the police might improperly select those who would be vulnerable to the special procedures. The best way to control this is to establish a clear, narrow definition of dangerous offenders, to establish administrative procedures to ensure that only those who fit this definition are subjected to special strategies, and to warn such offenders, when they are indicted or convicted for the offense that qualifies them as dangerous, that they are subject to these procedures. A second risk is that the police will take liberties in investigating such cases and thus violate important due process guarantees. But all cases must still face the rigors of a trial, and if some evidence has been improperly gathered, that fact will probably come out.

THE EFFECTIVENESS OF SELECTIVE POLICE TACTICS

To see whether selective police efforts could be effective requires an empirical demonstration that these tactics could produce prosecutable cases *and* that the tactics are not already routinely used. Some experiments in patrol and investigative strategies similar to those suggested here have been completed or are sufficiently advanced to have produced useful interim data.

Table 18 indicates which studies have produced information about particular strategies.[20] Although the coverage is neither complete nor precisely linked to the proposed selective strategies, one can draw several important conclusions from the existing studies. First, case preparation seems to matter a great deal in felony cases involving serious offenses among strangers.[21] Simply performing traditional investigative tasks with precision and determination can make important differences in rates of indictment, conviction, and felony-time sentences for important cases. An interim evaluation of an experimental effort to improve the quality of felony case preparation in a New York City precinct showed rather remarkable results on the disposition of robbery arrests.[22] Sentences for more than a year in prison rose from 18.5 percent of all arrests to 24.6 percent in the experimental precinct. The comparison precinct showed a decline from 26.4 to 18.7 percent over the same period. The conviction rate for all robbery arrests (including those for which prosecu-

Table 18. Field experiments containing information about selective investigative and patrol strategies for dangerous offenders.

	Strategy						
Source[a]	1: case preparation quality	2: case augmentation	3: postarrest investigation	4: patrol field intelligence	5: perpetrator-oriented patrol	6: proactive suppression of crime series	7: police as adjuncts to probation, parole
Pate, Bowers, and Parks, 1976				X	X		X
Chelimsky and Dahmann, 1981	X						
Boydstun et al., 1981					X	X	
McElroy, Cosgrove, and Farrell, 1981	X						
Gay, 1983	X			X	X	X	
Eck, 1983	X	X	X				

a. The studies listed here are cited in full in note 20 to this chapter.

tion was refused) rose from 45 to 51 percent in the experimental precinct. The control precinct showed a decline from 54 to 46 percent. The indictment rate for all robbery arrests in the experimental precinct rose from 33.9 to 48.4 percent. The control precinct showed a much smaller increase, from 39.1 to 42.2 percent.

These results complement earlier findings that the quality of a case matters in determining its ultimate judicial disposition. The quality of cases can be improved if the police pay attention to this problem, and if they do so, the dispositions will be much stronger.

A second important finding is that a police focus on dangerous offenders does seem to increase the probability that they will be arrested and that crime will be reduced. The most striking evidence of this point is found in an evaluation of the San Diego Police Department's Career Criminal Program.[23] This program consisted of three elements: improved investigation and case preparation, special attention to crimes in which a dangerous offender was a suspect, and identification and suppression of crime series through proactive investigations. However, it seems clear from the evaluation of the study that only the first and second strategies were in place during the program's "career criminal" period, when it was targeted primarily on robbery and burglary.[24] What is remarkable about the results of this program is that while arrests for robbery actually declined a little in the experimental period, the actual level of robbery in the community declined as well. Figure 10 shows the difference in reported robberies between the baseline period and the experimental period. This is the result one would expect if the robbery arrests were successfully focused on the unusually dangerous offenders. Moreover, at that time the program to identify and focus on dangerous offenders was not fully operational.[25] In later stages the program shifted to a broader focus on all crimes, away from the *reactive investigative* focus and toward a *proactive patrol* focus. In that phase the results were less impressive.[26] But the results of the career criminal stage, focused on robberies and unusually dangerous offenders, suggest some real potential for a selective investigative focus.

An evaluation of proactive patrol in Kansas City found that these methods could increase arrests and convictions, at least when compared with less focused strategies.[27] One part of this program involved distributing to patrol officers information on those designated as dangerous offenders, some of whom were assigned to general random patrol and others to tactical missions that focused on specific locations (location-oriented patrol), or specific people (perpetrator-oriented patrol). Table 19

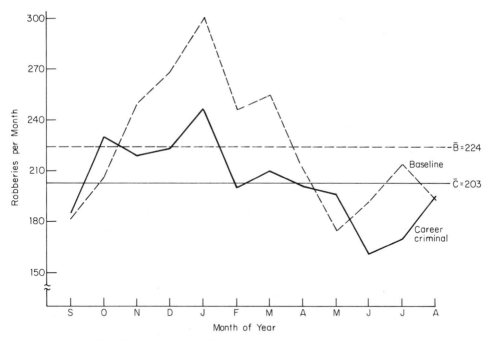

Figure 10 Levels of reported robberies in the baseline period and the career criminal program period, San Diego Career Criminal Program.

presents data on the effectiveness of these units in arresting designated offenders and on the influence of the supply of information and the particular mission (general, location-oriented, or perpetrator-oriented patrol). Review of this table indicates that the tactical units were more successful in arresting designated offenders and that information from crime analysis units did not have much impact on their effectiveness. The authors speculate that the information had no effect because these special units already knew who the dangerous offenders were.[28] The table also indicates, however, that information is more valuable to general patrol units: those that had information doubled their arrests of designated offenders compared with the general patrol units that had no information. Unfortunately, more than half of these arrests were for crimes other than dangerous felonies.[29]

A second part of the Kansas City study involved a comparative analysis of the arrest effectiveness of the different strategies. Table 20 presents data on the arrests, indictments, and convictions for robbery and burglary per man-year expended for each of the three enforcement strate-

Table 19. Effect of information provided to police units on the likelihood of arrest of target subjects.

Information provided to other units		Information provided to tactical unit					
		No	(%)	Yes	(%)	Total	(%)
No	Arrested	8	(30)	15	(56)	23	(43)
	Not arrested	19		12		31	
Yes	Arrested	21	(78)	19	(73)	40	(75)
	Not arrested	6		7		13	
Total	Arrested	29	(54)	34	(64)	63	(59)
	Not arrested	25		19		44	

Analysis of variance

Source	Chi-square	Significance level
Information provided to tactical unit	0.94	$p = .33$
Information provided to other units	11.35	$p < .001$
Interaction effect	2.44	$p = .12$

Source: Tony Pate, Robert A. Bowers, and Ron Parks, *Three Approaches to Criminal Apprehension in Kansas City: An Evaluation Report* (Washington, D.C.: Police Foundation, 1976).

gies. In addition, to determine who was being arrested and convicted, the table shows the median number of felony convictions for those arrested for robbery as a result of each of the strategies. These data suggest that the perpetrator-oriented patrol is more effective than general patrol in producing arrests and convictions and more effective than location-oriented patrol in focusing on unusually dangerous offenders. If the structure of offending is as skewed as it seems to be, the perpetrator-oriented patrol may be more effective in controlling target crimes, even though it produces fewer arrests because it focuses on unusually dangerous offenders.

It is also important and interesting to note, however, that the fraction of arrests for target crimes that resulted in convictions was *higher* for general patrol than for location-oriented or perpetrator-oriented patrol. This suggests that the arrests made in the tactical patrol were weaker than those made in general patrol—an unexpected and troubling result.

Table 20. Arrest effectiveness of alternative patrol strategies.

| Strategies | Outputs of patrol strategies for robbery and burglary per officer-year expended | | | Median prior felony convictions (robbery arrestees) |
	Arrests	Indictments	Convictions	
General preventive patrol	1.04	0.39 (30% of arrests)	0.13 (13% of arrests)	2.34
Location-oriented patrol	12.42	3.77 (30% of arrests)	0.96 (7% of arrests)	3.82
Perpetrator-oriented patrol	6.97	1.90 (27% of arrests)	0.53 (8% of arrests)	5.80

Source: Tony Pate, Robert A. Bowers, and Ron Parks, *Three Approaches to Criminal Apprehension in Kansas City: An Evaluation Report* (Washington, D.C.: Police Foundation, 1976).

These findings suggest that patrol forces focused on dangerous offenders can increase the number of arrests and convictions of dangerous offenders. The price, though, is that the arrests are for less serious charges, and they have a weaker evidentiary basis. The implication of these findings is sobering: we may pay a price in terms of fairness and due process for targeting patrol efforts on dangerous offenders. Whether this is offset by reductions in crime remains unclear because of the lack of outcome data in the evaluation of the patrol strategies.

A third important finding is that police departments do not now have and do not quickly develop the institutional apparatus that would allow a focus on dangerous offenders. At the least, the police must develop, distribute, and update a list of dangerous offenders generated by some combination of analyses of arrest records and discussions with experienced officers. More ambitiously, some analytic capacity, perhaps computer assisted, would be required to link crimes on the basis of similar modus operandi, similar description of offenders, geographic proximity, and so on. This linking would be important in identifying an emergent crime series that could be intercepted, as well as in supporting postarrest investigations designed to add counts to the charges against a suspected dangerous offender.

While one might expect that this rudimentary intelligence is routinely available in police departments, it is not. Moreover, even when special efforts are made to create such capabilities, they develop very slowly. An ongoing evaluation of the Integrated Criminal Apprehension Program (ICAP), in which crime analysis is a central focus, and the development of a serious, habitual-offender program is a minor component, revealed that *few* police departments could create the required capabilities.[30] Only three of the four evaluated cities even attempted to develop and distribute a file of habitual offenders.[31] Moreover, in the three cities that tried, it took from twenty-four to thirty-six months to develop the first version of the file.[32] With respect to crime analysis, equally discouraging results are reported: arrests are not usually based on crime analysis. One major reason for these disappointing results is that the crime analysis units are poorly staffed and not linked directly to operating patrol or investigative units.[33]

So there is substantial room for improvement in the intelligence operations of police departments with respect to dangerous offenders. Whether such improvements could be made and, if so, whether they could enhance the focus and crime control capacity of police departments, remains uncertain. This is a suitable area for experimentation.

THE POTENTIAL OF POLICE SELECTIVITY

We have discussed what is known about selective police strategies. Still unexplored are the possibilities of postarrest investigations leading to multiple-count charges (and therefore more successful identification of unusually dangerous offenders), and the use of police as adjuncts of probation and parole. We think there are opportunities to increase the selectivity of the patrol and investigative efforts, and that such actions could be both just and effective. To guide experimentation in this area we recommend that administrators and evaluators keep in mind five basic principles.

First, it is important to describe procedures in detail, not only to make the experiment effective, but also to allow for political and legal oversight of the program. Second, the procedures for designating dangerous offenders must be defined in detail, and there must be some mechanism for allowing those offenders to know about and challenge the designation. Ideally, this would happen when a person was convicted of the last offense in a series that qualified him as a dangerous offender. In addition, a procedure should be established for removing the designation if a person has been on the street for a certain length of time without convictions or arrests for offenses.

Third, we think reactive programs that are put into practice after a crime has been committed (such as quality case preparation, postarrest investigation of multiple offenses, and proactive suppression of a crime series) contain fewer risks to fairness and due process than those that operate before a criminal act has been committed (field intelligence on dangerous offenders or perpetrator-oriented patrol). The reactive strategies should be tried first.

Fourth, the programs should be evaluated in terms not only of arrests, indictments, convictions, and sentences, but also of the characteristics of those arrested and ultimate outcomes, including observed effects on serious crime. This is particularly important for the evaluation of *selective* arrest strategies because the purpose is to have a greater impact on crime rates through a smaller number of arrests focused on an unusually active group of offenders.

Finally, previously evaluated programs should be reanalyzed. The San Diego, Kansas City, and ICAP programs provide a wealth of evidence that can be mined to improve our judgments about what sorts of selective patrol and investigative strategies are just, feasible, and effective.

8

Criminal Justice Records

A POLICY OF SELECTIVE incapacitation depends crucially on our ability to distinguish dangerous offenders from others. As a practical matter, this capacity depends on the quality of records maintained by and available to the agencies of the criminal justice system. In assessing the potential of selective incapacitation policies, it is important to establish specifications for a record-keeping system and to evaluate current record-keeping capacities against these standards.

SPECIFICATIONS FOR A RECORD-KEEPING SYSTEM

The record-keeping system must meet certain standards of justice and practical value or else the selective policies themselves will fail.[1] As in many other areas of criminal justice, there seems to be a tension between record systems that protect civil liberties and promote individual justice and those that enhance crime control. If records were maintained about many people who had not been convincingly accused of crimes, if the records were used improperly or leaked to unauthorized private agencies, or if they were inaccurate and did not allow for correction, then civil liberties and individual justice would be adversely affected.

But many features can be included in criminal record systems that serve both justice and crime control and that do not involve major risks to important civil liberties. For example, it is in the interests of justice and effectiveness, and is certainly not inimical to civil liberties, to keep accurate, comprehensive records of criminal acts attributed to particular offenders. The records should be readily available to several different agencies when investigative, prosecutorial, or judicial decisions are to be made. This requires that information circulate quickly and easily within the criminal justice system, which might increase the chance that it could leak outside the system. But there is no reason why it should. Some may also find a threat in having information circulate from police to prosecutors to courts. But if each organization is authorized to have information about criminal records, then it makes sense to keep that information centrally and to make it available to all.

Our purpose here is to establish standards for record-keeping systems in four areas: accuracy, completeness, ready availability, and security. Our interests in these features and our judgments about which standards should apply are derived from commitments to justice, civil liberties, and effectiveness.

ACCURACY

By far the most important characteristic of a record-keeping system is accuracy. Ideally for the purposes of effective crime control, criminal records should include a complete account of the criminal activity of every offender. Obviously, some error is introduced into the system by the failure of the police to solve most crimes and perhaps by their mistaken attribution of crimes. So, the best we can hope for is an accurate reflection of the criminal justice system's actions with respect to individual offenders and specific offenses. But even this limited kind of accuracy is difficult to achieve, as is apparent to anyone who has worked with criminal justice records.

The first problem is to accurately identify offenders, since the whole concept of selective focus depends on being able to attribute a series of criminal activities to a specific individual. The files must be *offender*-based as well as *offense*-based, and they must indicate unambiguously that a specific suspect, defendant, or convicted person is the same person who committed the previous offenses recorded in the files. One might think the problem of linking current subjects to past known acts would be simple, but in fact it is quite challenging. The only completely accurate method for doing this is through fingerprints, but fingerprint identification is less widely used and much slower than people imagine.[2] The other identifiers (name, date of birth, mother's maiden name, and so on), although much less reliable, are much more commonly used — particularly at the front end of the system, where investigative, prosecutorial, and bail decisions are made.

A second difficulty is that information about the disposition of specific charges against an offender is not always included in the records. Arrests seem to be reliably entered in either local, state, or national records, and the majority of felony arrests are reflected in national records.[3] But data on charges, convictions (by trial or plea), and sentences are much less comprehensively reported.[4] This implies that existing records lack information concerning the strength of the evidence linking an offender to a crime. We know there was enough evidence to support an arrest, but not whether the evidence is strong "beyond a reasonable doubt." Lacking disposition data, we cannot be confident in attributing an offense to a specific subject.

A third problem concerns the confusing relationship between the legal categories that define offenses and the actual events that occur in the world. When we use words like "robbery" or "assault," certain images come quickly to mind. These images typically do *not* include that of a divorced husband returning to his apartment and seizing a television he claims is his and verbally threatening his former wife. Nor do they include a barroom scuffle in which one person spits at another. Yet these incidents can be defined as robbery and assault, and they often are.[5] In effect, the legal categories do not always correspond closely to our intuitive sense of an offense that would be serious enough to reveal a dangerous person at work. To some extent, differences in the "degrees" of offenses charged and in their disposition signal something about the nature of the offense, and this constitutes another important reason to improve the reporting of information on dispositions. But a troubling gap remains between the actual criminal event and the legal charge. This gap weakens our capacity to discern dangerous offenders by examining criminal records.

Given these difficulties in creating accurate records, given the importance that will be attached to them in a system of selective incapacitation, and given a strong interest in individual justice, it is important for individuals designated as dangerous offenders to have the right to examine the records and correct inaccuracies and misrepresentations. To make this right effective, unambiguous criteria must be established for designating someone a dangerous offender. The person must be notified when he has been so designated and given an opportunity to contest the factual basis of the designation. This procedure could be a normal part of the sentencing process, and the offender could be warned about the consequences of this designation: that he will be subject to increased police interest, that cases against him will be pressed with unusual vigor, that bail decisions may be affected, and so on.

COMPLETENESS

It is in the interest of both equity among offenders and the efficacy of the criminal justice system to have information that is complete as well as accurate. Unevenness in the recording of offenses will produce inequities among offenders in a world where a person's record has an effect on his treatment by the criminal justice system: similar offenders will be treated differently. Effectiveness is also threatened, because the best indicator of dangerousness (both in the past and in the future) is probably the record of accumulated serious offenses.

There is a drawback to comprehensive record keeping. If malicious police, prosecutors, and judges are willing to sacrifice due process and equal protection when dealing with dangerous offenders, better records might increase their capacity to do harm. More comprehensive records might even foster these attitudes. In this sense, sloppy and incomplete records may provide some protection for individuals who would otherwise become targets of malevolent officials.

But this seems like a strange argument in favor of incomplete records. If we are afraid that officials will use information improperly, the solution is to design just policies and procedures governing the use of these records and to insist on compliance. We have worked hard to design just and effective procedures that rely on knowledge of prior criminal offenses, and we think that the risks associated with complete records can be managed.

The two main obstacles to the completeness of criminal records involve crimes committed outside of a given jurisdiction (city, county, or state) and the question of juvenile records.

We believe that serious offenses committed outside of the jurisdiction should be included in an offender's record. If our task is to identify the most dangerous offenders, and our method is to examine criminal histories, then failing to include all offenses will substantially reduce the effectiveness of selective policies. It has been estimated that more than one-third of all offenders commit crimes in more than one state, and it is very likely that the vast majority of offenders commit crimes in more than one city or county.[6]

An incomplete records system is unfair as well as ineffective. Fragmentary records cause us to deal more harshly with offenders who commit all their offenses in one jurisdiction. If anything, those who commit serious crimes in several cities and states may be more deserving of a selective focus than their stable counterparts, for their offenses can more clearly be attributed to evil motivations rather than bad companions or the lure of criminal opportunities in their neighborhoods.[7] By keeping incomplete criminal records, the system shows a bias in favor of the mobile offenders.

The problem in developing comprehensive, interjurisdictional records is that they would have to be maintained by the federal government. Because our political traditions encourage us to think that the power of the government and its indifference to individual rights grows as one moves from the local to the state to the federal level, we assume that the creation of national records poses a greater threat to individuals.[8] But even if we assumed an abusive federal government, the mere fact that it kept the records would not inevitably lead to unjust criminal justice operations, most of which are conducted by local agencies. They would be the consumers of the information, and their policies and procedures would determine the quality of the operations. We could still benefit from the more benign qualities of local government even if records were kept at the federal level.

Because our interest is in identifying dangerous offenders, we could exclude from a national record system the vast majority of offenses for which most people are arrested. Only violent crimes, offenses that carry a substantial risk of violence, and property offenses that indicate frequent and persistent criminal activity would be included. Relatively few people are arrested even once for these offenses, let alone several times in a few years. If the criteria were narrowly defined, there might even be a reduction in the volume of national records now held. On balance, although there is some potential for misuse of national records, we think that potential is outweighed by the interest in fairly and accurately identifying dangerous offenders.[9]

The discussion of juvenile records includes some of the same issues raised by interjurisdictional records. If juvenile records are excluded, offenders with extensive juvenile records will be treated just like offenders with similar adult records but no juvenile records. This raises a question of equity among offenders. But the central issues concern the justice and practical value of sealing the records as against opening them up to the adult courts. Interestingly, there are principled and practical arguments on both sides of this question.

The argument for sealing the records as a matter of justice is rooted in the idea that people's acts as juveniles are not indicative of their character and intentions and therefore should not be used in determining their dangerousness as adults. The practical argument is that by treating the bad actions of juveniles as indicative of character, we may unwittingly guarantee this result by influencing the juvenile's perception of himself and restricting opportunities in ways that make bad conduct seem inevitable.[10] These are the considerations that stimulated the development of a separate juvenile justice system and strong policies guaranteeing the privacy of juvenile records.

On the other hand, the practical argument for opening the records is very strong. Studies of criminal careers indicate that those who become dangerous offenders start their careers relatively early.[11] Not only do they commit minor crimes at very high rates, they also commit fairly serious crimes even while juveniles. Perhaps even more significantly, the peak level of activity for dangerous offenders seems to be the late teens and early twenties. Because juvenile records are sealed, the adult criminal justice system fails to identify the unusually dangerous offenders among the young offenders who come before it. Table 21 shows how different the population that appears before adult felony courts looks when juvenile records are included in the information available to the courts. When juvenile records are excluded, only 16 percent of the population appears to be chronic offenders. When these records are included, the fraction identified as chronic offenders doubles — reaching 33 percent.[12] From this perspective, it seems obviously desirable to have access to juvenile records.

Although these two positions seem completely antithetical, there is a position that stakes out a compromise. If a person is arrested for a dangerous offense shortly after he graduates from juvenile status, then the adult

Table 21. Effect of juvenile records on criminal histories of young defendants.

Age	Percentage chronic[a]		Number of defendants
	Adult record	Adult and juvenile records	
16	0	19	31
17	10	28	49
18	20	37	49
19	25	40	67
Average	16	33	Total 196

Source: Barbara Boland, "Identifying Serious Offenders," in Dealing with Dangerous Offenders, vol. 2: Selected Papers, ed. Daniel McGillis, Susan Estrich, Mark H. Moore, and William Spelman (Cambridge, Mass.: John F. Kennedy School of Government, Harvard University, 1983).

a. Chronic offenders are those with five or more arrests.

criminal justice system should be allowed to review the record of *serious* offenses he committed while a juvenile in order to determine whether he should be treated as a dangerous offender.[13] This position is far short of approving routine access to juvenile records; access is allowed only if a person is arrested for a dangerous offense shortly after reaching adult age. Even then the adult system would have access only to the record of *serious* juvenile offenses.

This limited intrusion into juvenile records is justified because it is in the interests of justice and effectiveness to focus on unusually dangerous offenders, and serious juvenile offenses are relevant to determining dangerousness. Moreover, the interests that originally barred access to juvenile records have not been violated by that limited intrusion. If the juvenile offender has committed several serious offenses, some of the presumed innocence of "youthful indiscretions" has been lost, and with it our desire to protect the youth from guilt and undeserved punishment. If the person commits serious offenses as an adult, then the utilitarian interest in sealing juvenile records has already been lost because he continued to commit offenses. So, this compromise position strikes a proper balance between the opposing principles.

READY AVAILABILITY

It is important that criminal records be available to criminal justice officials at the time when they are making consequential decisions on given offenses and offenders. Availability should not be a problem during sentencing, the last stage of the criminal justice system. Sentencing usually occurs so long after an arrest is made that there is plenty of time to complete a careful identification process and conduct a relatively broad search of local, state, and national criminal justice records. But that time is not necessarily used for this purpose. Judges often have "rap sheets" when they determine sentences, but they often lack disposition data for prior offenses. The rap sheets may be local or state, rather than national. The judge may have some informal information about juvenile offenses, but it is not systematically gathered or documented. So the problems at the sentencing stage are the inaccuracy and incompleteness of criminal justice records rather than lack of ready availability.

There is little pressure for even inaccurate and incomplete records to be available at the front end of the system, the police patrol stage. As noted in Chapter 7, it is possible to imagine focusing patrol attention on dangerous offenders by investing in an analytic process that identified them and circulating that information to patrol units. But there is no time pressure associated with this process; it can be done any time. Perhaps for this reason it is rarely done, or done very slowly and sporadically, even when resources and administrative pressure are directed toward this goal.

The place where there is a great deal of pressure on the availability of criminal justice records is in the middle of the system, where much of the consequential action now occurs. In the first twenty-four to thirty-six hours following an arrest, a great many important decisions must be made. The police must decide how much investigative effort to devote to the case, how comprehensive they must be in locating witnesses, how careful in preparing documents for the court case, and so on. The prosecutor must decide what charge to make and what bail to ask for. And the judge must decide whether there is probable cause for the arrest and how much bail to set. Obviously, these decisions are important for the future of the case and the offender. If the system is going to become selective then, it must know in these few hours if it is dealing with an unusually dangerous offender.

In the best situation a local or state system with online computer capabilities can produce a relatively complete record within an hour or two, once they have a positive idenification.[14] The crucial step determining the speed of response is ordinarily the difficult one of making a positive identification, which often requires a fingerprint. The transmission and analysis of fingerprints is a lengthy process, a matter of several hours even in states with the most sophisticated systems.[15] This means that local information is usually available in time for charging and bail decisions, but usually *not* in time for stepping up the investigative effort on a case. As a result, many opportunities to elaborate the investigation will be lost. For some cases this is not a problem, of course. Cases built on prior investigative efforts often include information about suspects that has been developed well before an arrest is made. But for the many arrests that occur at the scene of the offense or very shortly thereafter, the availability of records may be very important.

In more ordinary systems the situation is worse; it may take several hours to get incomplete *local* information, and statewide information may take a day or two. It is also worth noting that all requests for *national* information based on fingerprint identification from the FBI must be submitted and returned by mail: this implies a turnaround time of thirty days at least — well past the time when this information could be used in charging and bail decisions.[16] In sum, a slow record system affects investigative, charging, and bail decisions, except when the police have already gathered information about the defendant as part of an investigation. The best that can now be done is to get local information several hours after an arrest and national data thirty days later. The average timetable is worse.

A fourth area of concern involves controls on the accessibility of records to people outside the criminal justice system, such as licensing boards, potential employers, lenders, and so on. We are not particularly expert in this area, but it seems to us that much of the concern about labeling people arises because criminal records circulate too freely in the world outside the criminal justice system.[17] We would propose tighter restrictions on the circulation of records. Offenders should not be protected from the consequences of their prior criminal conduct by sloppy record-keeping, but this information should *not* be easily available outside the system. This may allow us to gain some benefits in identifying unusually dangerous offenders without paying too great a price for labeling people in the broader social and economic world.

SHORTCOMINGS OF CURRENT SYSTEMS

Measured against these performance requirements, current record-keeping systems seem to suffer from three major weaknesses. Although not all states have the same degree of difficulty, the identified weaknesses seem to be characteristic of most state systems.

The greatest weakness of the current system is the difficulty of obtaining access to juvenile records of serious offending. For the reasons indicated earlier, we think these policies should be loosened to allow access to information about serious juvenile offending by those who are arrested for a serious offense within a year after graduating from the juvenile system.

However, we are skeptical about how large the effects of such a policy change would be. It is possible that juvenile records are already available to the adult criminal justice system. This is almost certainly true within police agencies, and it may also be true for prosecutors and courts. To the extent that this information is already available, a formal change in policy will have little practical effect. A second concern is that juvenile records are in such bad shape that access to them will mean very little. The informality of juvenile court processes have prevented formal findings of guilt for specific offenses and discouraged the creation of papers and files. It may be impossible to assemble an accurate record of serious juvenile offending, or so expensive and time-consuming as to be practically impossible.[18] So, although we think that there should be some access to juvenile records and that pressure should be put on the juvenile system to keep better records, the immediate effects of such actions may be smaller than our analysis of the importance of this information indicates.

COMPLETENESS OF CRIMINAL RECORDS

The second significant weakness in the current record-keeping system is the erratic coverage of data on the *disposition* of arrests. We are uneasy about basing a policy of selective incapacitation on either arrests (since they give too inadequate a characterization of seriousness of the offense and the weight of the evidence against a suspect) or limited data on convictions (since this information is both weak and unfair in identifying dangerous offenders). It would be much better if our record systems included data as to arrest, charge, bail set, disposition, sentences, and actual time served, as well as the arrest. Such information helps us weigh both the seriousness of the offense and the strength of the evidence against the offender, which helps us gauge his dangerousness more precisely.

Improving the reporting of disposition data is not a simple matter, however. It depends on developing some central record-keeping agency that spans the organizational and jurisdictional boundaries of *local* police, *county* prosecutors, and *state* courts, and providing that agency with enough power and resources to strengthen the capacity of these other agencies, particularly prosecutors and courts, to feed information to them. We realize that much effort has already gone into the development of system-wide offender-based information systems. But an additional reason for strengthening this area is that selective incapacitation cannot operate decently and effectively without such systems.

INTERJURISDICTIONAL RECORDS

The third weakness of current record-keeping systems is the limited access to interjurisdictional records. The national system is now wisely restricted to reports of felonies and serious misdemeanors.[19] But selective incapacitation policies could be effective even with tighter restrictions on the kinds of offenses reported to the national level. One problem with the national system is that some jurisdictions report no information, and others report incomplete information. More importantly, the federal government responds slowly to local inquiries.

One possible improvement would be to improve the FBI's computerized career criminal file, which provides criminal records online for a limited number of offenders who have serious criminal histories. The file now includes 1.9 million records, which is probably too many. A decade ago, the system included fifteen states, but controversy about its appropriateness has cut participation to eight states currently.[20] Since about one-third of known offenders commit crimes in more than one state, we think it is important to improve the accessibility of national-level records for offenders who commit serious offenses often.

RECOMMENDATIONS FOR IMPROVEMENTS AND RESEARCH

A policy of selective incapacitation would place great operational demands on criminal record-keeping systems. Moreover, the success of these policies depends crucially on the accuracy and completeness of the records and the speed with which they can be retrieved. A fully computerized federal system linking local, state, and national records is the only way we know how to ensure that accurate, complete records are speedily available to all levels of the criminal justice system. We urge the federal government to support the development of such a system.

We also think that a system of limited access to juvenile records is of central importance in any effort to identify dangerous offenders early enough to make the crime control benefits of such policies worth the long-run institutional risks.

Finally, states should move as quickly as possible to develop offender-based records. In a world where computers make it easy to track billions of banking transactions with great accuracy and security, it is a disgrace that we know as little as we now do about the processing of people charged with criminal offenses.

9

A Qualified Endorsement of Selective Policies

In a world of increasing crime, more arrests, and fixed prison capacity, the promise to punish contained in our criminal codes exceeds our current capacity to actually administer the punishment. Thus we must ration our use of imprisonment. One obvious solution is to reserve the limited capacity now available for offenders who most deserve punishment and whose incarceration would do the most good to society by reducing crime in the future. How we do this is the question.

We have been exploring proposals to accomplish this goal by sharpening the focus on dangerous offenders at each stage of the criminal justice system. We imagine judges sentencing, prosecutors trying, and police investigating with special attention to those who have committed crimes violently, persistently, and frequently. Such proposals promise some obvious practical benefits. If the most violent and active offenders were arrested, prosecuted, and sentenced more vigorously than others, crime might be reduced. If crimes of violence among strangers were reduced, and if it were clear that the criminal justice system responded adequately to the most callous criminal offenders, then the debilitating sense of public danger might also subside.

It is often assumed that these practical benefits would be won only at some price to justice, but we think that selective proposals may enhance justice as well as produce practical benefits. Selective policies could compensate for a natural bias in the criminal justice system in favor of the most dangerous offenders. Moreover, we think that explicit tests designed to discriminate among offenders on the basis of past criminal records would improve the justice of decisions now made arbitrarily by criminal justice officials. Discretion would be reduced in favor of guide-lines based on an individual's prior criminal conduct.

At the same time, however, our deliberations and the public opposition to such policies have made us mindful of the risks as well as the benefits. The hoped-for benefits, reduced victimization, fear, and sense of danger might not materialize because offending is not so concentrated in a small group, because incapacitation fails to control crime, or because the system is already operating selectively enough that there is little more to be gained.

The policy also risks injustice to individuals. If offenders are exposed to special liabilities and punishments on the basis of predictions of future conduct, both they and we may feel that they have been unjustly treated, especially when one notes that the predictions are wrong as often as they are right. Perhaps the greatest risk, though, is the erosion of our tradition of restraint in confronting criminal offenders. By focusing attention on a small group who seem more deserving of our indignation, we create conditions in which corrosive *ad hominem* motivations may intrude into the operations of the system. Among criminal justice officials, indigna-tion might slide into hostility; and among the general citizenry, an inter-est in justice might be transformed into the passions of a lynch mob.

Despite the risks, we are prepared to give the idea of selective justice a qualified endorsement. We think it points the way toward some signifi-cant improvements, not only in terms of reducing crime and allaying fears, but also in producing justice for offenders, victims, and the general citizenry. Our endorsement is qualified because we think that the bene-fits and risks of an explicit focus on dangerous offenders, in both the short and long run, depend a great deal on the spirit in which the concept is introduced, the concrete ways in which it is made operational, and the provisions for gathering additional information to resolve key uncertain-ties. So it is crucial to keep in mind the qualifications, because without them, the risks of the policy are exacerbated for little practical gain.

GUIDING PRINCIPLES

Three broad principles qualify our endorsement of selective policies. First, they should be guided by a very narrow definition of dangerous offenders. Second, we should think of selective policies as primarily retributivist rather than utilitarian, targeted on those whose acts have revealed them to be particularly blameworthy rather than on those who are predicted to behave badly in the future. Third, these policies should not be considered a comprehensive solution to the problems of the criminal justice system. They address only a portion of the overall problem.

We advocate a narrow definition of dangerous offenders primarily because of our interest in preserving justice. We concluded that to be categorized as dangerous, an offender must have committed crimes at an unusually high rate and deliberately, rather than through accidental circumstances. His record of offending would have to show violence, a high rate, and persistence; without the evidence of all three characteristics, we could not be sure about his durable criminal intentions, and we could not be sure that he was a major contributor to the overall crime problem. As it turns out, this definition is much narrower than those in existing habitual-offender statutes or the administrative practices now followed by prosecutors and police.

Practical interests in controlling crime and using prison space economically also support a narrow definition. Much of the interest in selective policies derives from the potential benefits of being able to distinguish those whose incapacitation would have the maximum impact on crime. If the definition of dangerous offenders becomes too broad, much of the reason for creating the category disappears.

Interests in protecting the integrity of criminal justice institutions also counsel a narrow, firm, and exact definition. It is natural for police, prosecutors, and other agencies to imagine that the right way to proceed is to establish special units whose sole purpose is to incapacitate dangerous offenders. But the bureaucratic zeal and enthusiasm of such units, stimulated by the conviction that their targets are truly evil, could pose a threat to the civil liberties of all offenders. The natural bureaucratic tendency to expand the definition of dangerous offenders risks both the justice and the practical value of selective policies.

To avoid this risk the policy should be implemented through a procedure established for the whole system and triggered whenever an offender appears who meets the established definition. The advantages of a general procedure and a firm definition rather than a special unit are that many officials implement the policy, none becomes specialized in attacking dangerous offenders, and the definition tends to stay narrow.

For purposes of future discussion and analysis, we propose to define a dangerous offender as someone who has been convicted twice for violent crimes within a three-year period of street time and has had two additional arrests for violent offenses or two additional convictions for property offenses within the same period. We estimate that fewer than 5 percent of the offenders currently in the criminal justice system would qualify under this standard, and that they would be primarily the most dangerous offenders in the system. Obviously, some dangerous offenders would be wrongly excluded from this definition, but that is the necessary consequence of a narrow rather than a broad definition.

The second qualification, that selective policies should be backward-looking and retributivist rather than forward-looking and utilitarian, is also proposed primarily to enhance individual justice. The fundamental problems are the injustice of basing criminal liabilities on predictions of future conduct and the occurrence of errors in the identification of dangerous offenders. If we distinguish among offenders by predicting which ones will be most active in the future, individuals are exposed to additional punishment without proof that they have committed criminal acts, even if the predictions are wrong.

If we distinguish the most dangerous offenders on the basis of past acts, however, the problem of mistaken predictions disappears. No one is being punished for predictions about the future, erroneous or otherwise. Instead, they are being punished for an accumulated record of past acts revealing bad character. Of course, there can be errors in this process as well. A person may be wrongly convicted for a particular offense, or the inference of incorrigible character may be wrong even if an offender has been properly convicted. But the familiar problem of uncertainty about past actions is less threatening than the unfamiliar problem of inaccurate predictions.

The retributivist perspective also has implications for the practical benefits of selective policies, but unfortunately, the effects are negative. Only information about prior criminal conduct can be used in discriminating among offenders, because no other variables provide a just basis for punishment. Inevitably, this restriction costs something in the accuracy of discriminations. Because more errors will be made in deciding which offenders are unusually dangerous, some justice and some practical benefits will be lost. Still, the tests themselves will be more just and easier to understand. Individual justice is enhanced by the retributivist perspective, so it is desirable to accept these restrictions. Indeed, the fact that we sacrifice some practical benefit may be a virtue, for it keeps reminding us of the depth of our commitment to the retributivist view.

Conceiving of selective policies as retributivist also keeps such policies at the center of our traditional legal purposes: to distinguish the innocent from the guilty on the basis of past acts and to punish the guilty. True, the issue of guilt has changed from asking whether a defendant committed a criminal act to asking whether he has engaged in a pattern of acts that identifies him as unusually dangerous. But the basic philosophy of judging people on the basis of past acts has been preserved. In contrast, if selective policies were justified in terms of crime control, the system could become more vulnerable over time to appeals to extend social controls on the basis of improved prediction methods.

Perhaps the most important qualifying principle governing our endorsement of selective policies is that they cannot be considered a complete solution to the crime problem. They cannot even be considered a comprehensive policy guiding the operations of the criminal justice system. Crimes emerge from situations other than those provoked by the determined efforts of dangerous offenders. Public fear is stimulated by disorder and uncivil conduct as well as by violent offenses. So coping with the crime problem requires that we also address many types of conduct that are not violent and many offenders who are not particularly dangerous.

This qualification reminds us that to reduce victimization, dispel fears, and allay the broad sense of public vulnerability, selective policies must be complemented by policies for dealing with lesser offenses and offenders. It reminds us that justice is served by distinguishing offenses that are clearly caused by the determined intentions of the offender rather than by circumstances or temporary impulses, and by understanding that much of the work of the criminal justice system involves cases of the second type.

But most important, this qualification emphasizes that by endorsing selective policies we are not necessarily making an ideological statement about crime. We do not have to believe that all crime is the product of dangerous offenders. We do not even have to believe that dangerous offenders are truly incorrigible. Instead, we can retain the notion that much crime and fear emerges from situations in which ordinary human feelings become exaggerated, and we can continue to see potential for rehabilitation in even the most dangerous offenders.

PROPOSALS

The potential for practical gains and enhanced justice of selective policies is likely to be greater at the front end of the criminal justice system than at the back end, the sentencing stage, which is already quite selective. As we have seen, even though the philosophy of rehabilitative sentencing is quite different from the philosophy of selective incapacitation, the procedures are nearly identical. Hence there is probably little more to be gained by now sharpening the focus at this stage.

Pretrial detention decisions also lack the potential for significant practical gains. Adopting explicit standards might bring about some gains in fairness; large numbers of people now being detained might be released because they would fail to qualify as dangerous offenders. But in all likelihood, selective pretrial detention would have little impact on overall crime, because crimes committed by people out on bail cannot be reduced without dramatically increasing the population now being detained.

The greatest potential benefits of a sharpened focus on dangerous offenders are likely to come from the operations of police and prosecutors. Up until now, these groups have been discouraged from knowing too much about the backgrounds of suspects and defendants lest that knowledge inappropriately bias the investigation and prosecution of crimes. Such worries are clearly appropriate when a case reaches the trial stage. They are also appropriate if we think that prosecutors and police may violate guarantees of due process and equal protection. But the potential for abuse need not bar the introduction of selective policies at the police and prosecutorial stages. After all, they have long given special attention to significant figures in organized crime, drug trafficking, and gambling. Why shouldn't the same sort of intelligence systems and targeted investigations be developed for unusually active armed robbers?

One idea that seems promising is for the police to make greater use of postarrest investigations to clear additional offenses and to complete these investigations with multiple indictments. Police agencies will argue that such efforts do little good because the courts are likely to treat the robber with multiple charges against him the same way they would a robber with only one charge. Besides, there are always so many new cases to be investigated that it is hard to justify continued attention to a case that has, for all practical purposes, been solved. But there are three arguments in favor of looking for additional crimes.

First, continuing the investigation ensures that high-rate offenders are not treated more leniently than low-rate offenders. Second, if prosecutors are willing to indict on additional counts, and the judges to sentence consecutively rather than concurrently, the additional cases might result in longer prison terms. Third, even if the additional charges do not produce longer sentences the first time around, the charges against the offender would distinguish him from less active offenders the next time he appears. In short, further investigations and indictments can provide a just and useful basis for distinguishing dangerous offenders.

In prosecutors' offices we propose that special care be given to preserving evidence in cases involving dangerous offenders, that these cases be charged at the highest possible offense warranted by the evidence, and that the prosecutors be more willing to go to trial with these cases. By preservation of evidence we mean clear and convincing documentation of cases in files and sufficient protection for and assistance to victims and witnesses in the case to ensure their continued interest and involvement. We urge the highest charges consistent with the evidence and a tough stance on plea bargaining partly to increase the sentences meted out to dangerous offenders and partly to preserve the information about their patterns of offending, but also to involve the courts in the adjudication of their cases. Indeed, having virtually all cases involving dangerous offenders go to trial would protect the interests of those offenders and would allow the courts to fulfill their function of formally condemning criminal offenders.

Central to all efforts to enhance selectivity is the development of record-keeping procedures that allow officials throughout the system to know when they are dealing with a suspect, defendant, or convicted offender who qualifies as unusually dangerous. Essentially this means system-wide, offender-based records that are readily available to police, prosecutors, and court officials.

Some people may worry that centralized, offender-based records could threaten interests in due process and equal protection for particular suspects and defendants. And one might even consider such records a threat to the rehabilitative opportunities for some defendants. But there are reasons to be worried about the justice and practical consequences of *not* having such records as well. It seems unjust that some offenders escape the consequences of their prior acts because the records are slovenly or inaccessible. It also seems unjust that some offenders escape the consequences and others do not, depending on the vagaries of an inadequate record-keeping system. The fact is that most criminal justice records are disgracefully incomplete. And while we might appreciate the fact that the state's confusion enhances individual privacy, it also means that the state is denied the capacity to act precisely with respect to individual offenders. If it is just and effective to use an offender's past record to shape discretionary decisions in investigation, prosecution, and sentencing, then that record ought to be accurate for individuals and readily available to criminal justice officials.

Moreover, we think that the records should include information about serious juvenile offenses if the offender has committed a serious crime shortly after graduating from the juvenile system. The practical interest in protecting him from the stigma of a criminal record has already been lost, and we can regard his juvenile offenses, along with the adult offense, as evidence of criminal character and orientation rather than impressionability.

UNCERTAINTIES AND EXPERIMENTS

The strategy we have recommended for introducing a selective focus is not without uncertainties. In fact, both the justice and utility of such proposals depend critically on the hypotheses that there are enormous differences among offenders, that these differences may be discerned by examining the records of prior offenses, and that the procedures of the criminal justice system can be redesigned to notice and respond to the observed differences. All these should be understood as hypotheses of uncertain accuracy, not as demonstrated truths. It would be wise to undertake experiments to learn more about the risks to justice and the practical potential of selective policies.

In thinking about which experiments would be most valuable we first considered which hypotheses justifying a selective focus were most uncertain and most consequential for estimates of the overall benefits. We next considered how easy it would be to conduct the different experiments in the context of the evolving policy. Third, and perhaps most important, we weighed how the process of experimentation itself would shape the evolution of the policy by requiring innovations in the criminal justice system and by producing new facts to be interpreted and accommodated in the future.

The most important empirical uncertainties seem to lie in the feasibility of a sharpened focus on dangerous offenders rather than in the estimate of their importance to the crime problem. In short, the picture of the crime problem that puts a small number of unusually dangerous offenders at its center is probably not inaccurate. But if the criminal justice system already allows for differences among criminal offenders and cannot be made to focus more selectively, our judgments about the potential efficacy of a selective policy could be quite wrong. Ironically, then, we may be more ignorant about the society's current and potential response to the crime problem than about the nature of crime.

We also seem to know less about the potential of selective policies at the investigative and prosecutorial stages than at the sentencing stage because less experimentation and research have been conducted at those stages. It is important to learn more about the effects of selective procedures at the earlier stages, where focusing attention on dangerous offenders may be most valuable.

DESIGNING DISCRIMINATING TESTS

By far the most important research concerns the development and evaluation of specific tests to distinguish dangerous offenders from others. So far efforts in this area have been ad hoc: researchers have used available information to construct the best possible test. We propose something more ambitious and systematic, a sustained effort to construct a just and useful definition that could be used at each stage of the criminal justice system.

To do this, it is important to first gather together all the different tests that are now being used at different stages, to determine how much variety currently exists. One would examine the attributes used in making the distinctions, and the definition of the criterion, in the areas of parole decision making, habitual-offender statutes, sentencing guidelines, presentencing reports, bail guidelines, criteria for inclusion in career criminals programs in prosecutors' offices, and even criteria for inclusion in habitual-offender programs in police departments.

Second, the discriminating power of some portion of the tests should be carefully evaluated in terms of differences in mean rates of serious offending among the classified groups *and* rates of false positives and false negatives in assignments to the dangerous offender group. The aim would be to see how well the proposed tests, based on currently available information, perform on relevant dimensions.

In addition, however, efforts should be made to design superior discriminating tests for the future. Part of this effort would involve developing model tests that are nowhere used now but are quite attractive for theoretical reasons. Specific theoretical issues that should be resolved in the design of an optimal test include 1) the problem of weighting offenses so that we have a good measure of the rate of "serious" offending; 2) the problem of estimating the "time available" for committing offenses, given ambiguity in the definition of a "criminal career" and practical problems in capturing information about time under state supervision; 3) the appropriateness and value of using information about less serious offenses as a way of distinguishing high-rate violent offenders from low-rate violent offenders earlier in their careers than would be possible by relying only on serious offenses; 4) the amount of discriminating power that could be added if juvenile records were used. These questions look to the design of better discriminating tests than we now employ.

A second part of the effort, however, is simply to work hard at increasing the quantity and quality of information in the tests. If future tests could be based on *improved* crime solving and record keeping, their discriminating power might be much greater. The only way to find out whether the tests get better as the system performs better is to improve the performance of the system. Thus, to evaluate an improved test, one may have to make important operational changes in the system that produces the information.

DIAGNOSING SELECTIVITY

Given the major uncertainty about the present degree of selectivity in local criminal justice systems, it should also be a high priority to develop and use protocols for diagnosing selectivity. For each stage of criminal justice system processing, the protocols would require analyzing whether there is explicit or implicit authorization of a focus on dangerous offenders, whether there are procedures that produced (or failed to produce) such a focus, and the actual results of processing dangerous offenders. For police organizations, for example, the protocol might include a search for policies governing investigative priorities that properly reflect concerns about dangerous offenses and dangerous offenders; an analysis of clearance rates by crime classification (for example, violence among strangers, risk of violence among strangers, and so on); an examination of procedures governing postarrest investigations and clearances, and how that information is incorporated in police, prosecution, and court records; and analysis of arrest rates of designated dangerous offenders over the course of a year; and an analysis of the preparation of cases of dangerous offenders within the overall activity of the department.

Developing systematic protocols for analyzing selectivity is a high-priority research task for three reasons. First, knowing the present level of selectivity would help resolve the question of how much room for improvement exists. We would know whether current systems were biased against or in favor of unusually dangerous offenders. Second, if we develop convenient protocols and encourage their use beyond the duration of the research project, some incentives would be created to enhance selectivity. Third, if we could routinely analyze the selectivity of a given system, we would have the basis for powerful *aggregate* analyses of the effect of enhanced selectivity on the levels of serious crime. As a result, we could exploit the natural variation in local criminal justice operations for research purposes.

EXPERIMENTING WITH PROGRAMS

We also think it would be desirable to do experiments geared toward improving selectivity at various stages or, somewhat less ambitiously, to explore current operations candidly with an eye to recommending new procedures that could enhance selectivity and could become the focus of experimental investigation. The following operational concepts merit field testing:

1. At the sentencing stage
    Improve the completeness and accuracy of information concerning prior record that is available to sentencing judges.
    Design, implement, and evaluate explicit guidelines governing the use of concurrent and consecutive sentencing.
    Draft model "dangerous offender" statutes to replace existing "habitual offender" statutes.

2. At the prosecution stage
    Enhance police-prosecutor collaboration in the identification, arrest, and prosecution of dangerous offenders.
    Enhance selectivity through general procedures rather than special units.

3. At the investigation stage
    Improve police intelligence concerning dangerous offenders.
    Increase postarrest investigative activity in cases involving dangerous offenders.

4. Criminal justice records
    Develop offender-based records throughout the criminal justice system.
    Develop procedures allowing limited access to juvenile records.

We recommend focusing on programs that could increase the quality of the information available about offenders' criminal activity. This means improving record systems and police capacity to gather evidence and make cases, and instituting procedures at each stage to ensure that those who make decisions have convenient access to accurate information on offenders' prior criminal activity.

Of all possible programs geared to increasing selectivity, however, we think that the most important and most interesting would be to determine if a joint police-prosecutorial focus on dangerous offenders could be effective in dealing with violence among strangers in a major metropolitan area. There is an analogy here to federal "strike forces" that focus on organized crime. But there is the additional benefit to be gained from having two organizations collaborate. It would force the development of *explicit* criteria and procedures for designating people as dangerous offenders. Police intelligence capacities might be improved, prosecutorial reluctance to take on difficult cases overcome, and in general, relationships between the two agencies improved.

FURTHER INVESTIGATION OF RATES OF OFFENDING

Although much has been learned about rates of offending through analyses of arrest records, cohort studies, and prison surveys, much remains to be done. Important methodological tasks include improving methods of validating self-report information, learning how to estimate rates of offending from arrest data, weighting the seriousness of offenses, and developing a conceptual basis for "periods of activity." Important substantive issues involve the following questions: To what extent do distributions of rates of serious offending vary across states and what could account for the differences? To what extent does an individual's rate (and pattern) of offending vary over his career and what seems to account for differing career trajectories? To what extent are patterns of offending within age cohorts varying across time, and what factors explain this trend?

Probably the best way to design research in this area is to let the established researchers who have pioneered the methods and are deeply involved in these questions propose the next round of projects.

EXPERIMENTAL PROGRAMS FOR LESS DANGEROUS OFFENDERS

A potential weakness of selective incapacitation policies is the lack of provisions for less serious offenders. This may grant implicit license to less serious offenders, resulting in higher rates of serious offending. We consider this an important possibility, so it becomes desirable to find less expensive and, ideally, less restrictive forms of incapacitation than jails and prisons that are almost as effective in suppressing crimes while the offender is under state supervision.

We can imagine at least three possible programs. One would be house arrest, which would restrict individuals to their homes and require them to report their movements to police or probation officials on threat of jail time if they cannot be found. A second program would be very intensive probation; an offender's attendance at a job, a sheltered workshop, or some other program would be checked several times a day. A third, a community correction program, would involve both close checks on job holding and program participation during the day, and residence at night. Such programs that have been tried have been evaluated in terms of their *rehabilitative* effectiveness. These programs should be reviewed and reevaluated in terms of their *incapacitation* effects. We think that such programs may produce significant, though not perfect, incapacitation results for less serious offenders at much lower cost and with more decency than jails and prisons.

A CONCLUDING OBSERVATION

Much of what we learned about the risks and benefits of selective policies has reminded us of the importance of truths about the criminal justice system we already know but may have forgotten. We rediscovered the importance of solving crimes — not only to ensure that justice is done in particular circumstances, but to allow us to justly distinguish the unusually dangerous offenders from all others. We also reaffirmed the notion that punishment is just when it is administered in a deliberate way to those who willfully commit a serious crime. Consequently, punishment is particularly appropriate for those few offenders who set themselves apart, not only from the rest of society but even from other offenders, by committing crimes violently, often, and persistently. The purpose of the criminal justice system is not primarily to rehabilitate offenders, nor to control crime through deterrence and incapacitation. Instead, its purpose is to satisfy victims, offenders, and the general citizenry that in adjudicating guilt and innocence and meting out punishment, justice has been done. Such rediscoveries are terribly important because they focus our attention on some basic steps that must be taken to restore the criminal justice system to high standing in the community.

Beyond these traditional concerns, however, our discussion has identified a special new challenge confronting the criminal justice system. It is the challenge of noticing and responding to great differences among offenders in the seriousness of their offenses, their rate and persistence in offending, and even our judgments about how much of their offending can be accounted for by circumstance and momentary pressures rather than basic character and intentions. If there were no important differences among offenders in terms of both the justice and the practical value of punishing them, there would be little to gain from selective policies.

But because there are great differences, the criminal justice system faces a task that has become unfamiliar, that of responding justly and effectively to each of the widely varying situations that present themselves.

In many ways the simplest problem to solve is at the farthest end of this spectrum, where the most dangerous offenders are. True, there are major problems in identifying them and in keeping our response measured and deliberate. But there should be little debate about the correct disposition of their cases. If they are found guilty, prison is the appropriate and useful place.

But those at the other end of the spectrum, including occasional violent offenders, persistent property offenders, and obnoxious troublemakers, represent a far greater challenge to the criminal justice system. After all, they represent the largest portion of the workload of the system, the portion for which the system does not now have an adequate response. Terms in prison and jail seem useless and inappropriate for many of these offenders, and yet the system has no other response. Compared to the ambiguities of domestic assault, persistent disorderly conduct, or even chronic shoplifting, the questions concerning unusually dangerous offenders seem remarkably straightforward.

So the search for dangerous offenders eventually leads us back to the central ambiguities and dilemmas confronting our system of justice: whom do we intend to punish, for what purpose, in what ways? We have given a partial answer to that question. We ought to punish the most violent, active, and persistent offenders with extended terms in prison. And to make this policy just and useful, we must improve our ability to solve the crimes they commit. We have also warned of the risks. But we haven't answered the question of what to do about all the rest of the human misery that shows up in the criminal justice system. And that may be the harder, more important, and more urgent problem to solve.

Appendixes
Notes
Index

Appendix A

Estimating $\bar{\lambda}$

MUCH EFFORT has been put into estimating $\bar{\lambda}$, the rate of offending of the average street criminal. If this number were known, the number of street offenders could be estimated and compared to the prison population. In this way a baseline for the incapacitative effects of present policies could be determined. A reliable estimate of $\bar{\lambda}$ could also be used to identify the probable effects of prison expansion on the crime rate; at least one attempt to do this has been made.[1]

Knowing the average offense rate would help indicate how skewed the distribution of offense rates across offenders is. Since there is plenty of anecdotal evidence that at least some criminals commit serious crimes at high rates—as often as once a day—a very low average rate would suggest that these high-rate offenders are an important part of the crime problem. Most criminals would be part-time, sporadic offenders, but most crimes would be committed by highly motivated career criminals. Similarly, a high average rate would indicate a more homogeneous offending population and a lesser impact for the selective policies presented in the text.

Despite the attention given to the offense rate, there is no consensus as to the average value. One review of five studies, conducted in 1978 by Jacqueline Cohen, examined the assumptions behind each estimate. Cohen was able to reconcile the disparate estimates somewhat by accounting for differences in the assumptions made. But she was able to narrow the range only to two to ten index offenses per year.[2] Moreover, some estimates of $\bar{\lambda}$ since 1978 are much lower than two crimes per year; others are much higher than ten. Fortunately, more information is now available; as we will show, the appropriate range may be narrowed to between three and six index crimes per year, but $\bar{\lambda}$ is probably larger for some populations. First, however, let us consider estimates of $\bar{\lambda}$ as presented in the literature.

TWO SOURCES OF BIAS

Several researchers have attempted to estimate the average offense rate;[3] their results are shown in Table 22. These estimates differ greatly, ranging from a low of 0.22 crimes per year to a high of 142.3 crimes. Two reasons for the differences are particularly important.

First, some estimates were obtained through inspection of official arrest and conviction records, and some from sample surveys of offenders. Because the police do not clear a large proportion of crimes by arrest, and because the courts do not convict a large proportion of offenders who are arrested, the estimates based on official records will understate the average offense rate. Although the jury is still out on the validity of self-report data, there is evidence that low-rate offenders slightly underreport their

Table 22. Unadjusted estimates of $\bar{\lambda}$.

Estimate source[a]	All index offenses	Property crimes	Personal crimes
1. Wolfgang, Figlio and Sellin, 1972	0.22	0.16	0.06
2. Greenberg, 1975	0.5–3.3	—	—
3. Shinnar and Shinnar, 1975	6–14	—	—
4. Williams, 1979	0.34	—	—
5. Boland and Wilson, 1978	2.7	—	—
6. Collins, 1977	1.1	0.7	0.4
7. Blumstein and Cohen, 1979	24.7	16.6	5.1
8. Petersilia, Greenwood, and Lavin, 1978	11.9	10.1	1.8
9. Peterson, Braiker, and Polich, 1980	12.4	7.6	4.8
10. Chaiken and Chaiken, 1983	142.3	125.4	16.9

a. The studies listed here are cited in full in note 3 to Appendix A.

rates of offending, and high-rate offenders overreport.[4] These errors probably offset one another and are probably not very large in the first place.[5] So it makes sense to consider estimates based on self-report data to be more or less correct and estimates from official records to be too low.

The second reason is a bit less obvious. The estimates of $\bar{\lambda}$ shown in Table 22 are obtained from samples of three slightly different populations: studies 1 through 4 apply to all offenders who have ever been arrested; 5, 6, and 7 apply only to offenders who have been arrested two or more times; 8, 9, and 10 apply only to offenders who are incarcerated. If we want to estimate the average offense rate for all street offenders, and thus account for all crimes, each of these estimates will overestimate the true value of lambda. This is because offenders who are never arrested are likely to be those who commit only a few crimes, since with each succeeding crime they leave themselves vulnerable to arrest. (This is not true if there exists a cadre of very skilled chronic offenders who are able to avoid arrest. However, numerous studies have shown that this is very unlikely.)[6] So those who are never arrested and are thus excluded from all of these estimates, are likely to be those who commit crimes at very low rates.

Estimates of $\bar{\lambda}$ that apply to the population of twice-arrested offenders will exclude mostly low-level offenders who are arrested only once; because most first-offense criminals are dealt with leniently by the courts and because frequent offenders are more likely to be caught and imprisoned, the average incarcerated offender will probably have a higher rate still. Of course, it may be very useful to know the average offense rate for recidivists, or for imprisoned offenders. But the point is that the estimates derived to apply to each of these populations should be systematically different and too high for some purposes.

Inspection of Table 23 indicates that we may be able to reconcile these vastly differing estimates by accounting for differences in data and population. First let us consider differences in data collected, attempting to reconcile official records with self-reports.

ADJUSTING OFFICIAL RECORDS

The problem with official records is that the police clear only a small proportion of crimes by arrest. Although arrest rates vary from one jurisdiction to another, a reasonable estimate is that someone will be arrested in about 5 percent of index crimes. Thus an offender who has been arrested five times has almost certainly committed more than five crimes.

If he or she is neither more nor less likely to be arrested than the average criminal, this offender has committed roughly 5 arrests $\times$ (1/.05) crimes/arrest = 100 crimes. This is only the most likely value. If the distribution of offense rates were known, then this figure would represent the mean of the *a posteriori* distribution of offenses, given that five arrests had been made.[7]

It is relatively easy to obtain arrest records; many authors have examined the FBI career criminal file, for example, which includes a record of each arrest made in Washington, D.C., in recent years.[8] If one can determine the rate at which offenders are arrested during the period in which they are active, and divide by the clearance rate, the result will be an unbiased estimate of $\bar{\lambda}$. Thus the reciprocal of the clearance rate may be thought of as an "arrest multiplier."

Boland and Wilson used an arrest multiplier of 5, that is, 1/.20, which they obtained by dividing the number of reported crimes by the number of arrests in Washington, D.C.[9] But many crimes are committed by more than one person; thus the probability that any of the people involved in a given crime would be arrested is less than one in five. Probably more important, most serious crimes are not reported to the police. According to victimization surveys, only about one-third of all serious crimes are reported. Thus the actual arrest multiplier must also be adjusted upward.

Blumstein and Cohen broke down clearance rates by crime type while correcting for the fact that many crimes are not reported to the police and that several offenders are involved in many crimes.[10] Their basic result: an offender was caught about once every twenty-two times he or she committed a crime. Thus each arrest represented roughly twenty-two different offenses. These researchers take victimization survey data at face value, but many have speculated that the data are inflated. Some respondents telescope events into the survey time period that in fact happened earlier, while others inflate the seriousness of the offense. So the Blumstein and Cohen multipliers probably result in estimates for lambda that are too high.

In adjusting estimates to account for incompleteness of official records, it is helpful to establish both an upper and a lower bound. We use an upper-bound multiplier identical to that computed by Blumstein and Cohen. For a lower-bound multiplier, we assume that half of the unreported victimizations would *not* be considered index crimes by police or were not committed during the survey period. However, we correct for multiple-offender crimes. Thus the upper bound of $\bar{\lambda}$ will be 50 percent higher than the lower bound.[11] The mix of crimes committed by offenders in each sample is somewhat different, and arrest, reporting, and multiple-offender commission rates are different for each crime type. Thus a different multiplier was used for each crime type. A few other corrections and additions were made to reconcile the estimates of $\bar{\lambda}$; these are detailed below.

Wolfgang, Figlio, and Sellin (1972).[12] Career length is assumed to be the entire period between the first arrest ("age of onset") and the offender's eighteenth birthday. We assume that the mix of nonviolent and violent crimes committed by these juveniles is the same as the mix of these crimes committed by people arrested two or more times (for example, we assume that the proportion of all nonviolent crimes that are larcenies is the same for the two populations). Then violent and nonviolent arrest rates may be multiplied by the upper- and lower-bound multipliers for violent and nonviolent offenses.

Williams (1979).[13] The data set obtained from the Washington, D.C., Prosecutor's Management Information System includes information on 72,510 arrests of 45,575 offenders, made over a 56-month period. Thus the number of arrests per year for this one-arrest population is .341. There is evidence that five years is a reasonable approximation for the average criminal career,[14] so we assumed that 56 months encompassed the offender's entire career. Some 46.9 percent of these arrests are for index offenses, so the simplest measure of $\bar{\lambda}$ would be: $\bar{\lambda} = (.469)(.3410)M$, where M is the arrest multiplier. This assumes that all offenders committed index offenses at an identical rate, however, and Williams gives evidence that many offenders commit mostly index offenses, while others commit almost entirely nonindex crimes. The practical significance of this is that in theory index offenders might make up 46.9 percent of the criminal population, but they might commit index crimes at the same rate as nonindex offenders commit nonindex crimes. But in practice this could not be true, since people who commit index offenses also commit some nonindex crimes.

The arrest rate was defined as the long-run equilibrium rate consistent with the crime-switch matrix Williams gives in her table 7 (p. 43). This is equal to: rate $= \bar{\lambda} \times q = (.341)(.566) = .193$, where .566 is the likelihood that the next crime committed will be an index crime, given that the offender commits some index crimes. This estimate assumes that the chances of arrest are no different, on average, for index and nonindex offenses.

Greenberg (1975).[15] Greenberg's method is an attempt to correct known FBI arrest rates for people with two or more arrests by adding expected arrest rates for people with only one arrest. The problem is to estimate what proportion of all arrests are of people who have not been arrested before. Greenberg brings evidence to suggest that the upper limit of this proportion is roughly .30; he shows that $\bar{\lambda}$ is roughly 3.3 for a "reasonable" proportion of .25. As Cohen shows, however, $\bar{\lambda}$ varies greatly with small changes in this proportion: expected $\bar{\lambda}$ is nearly 6 if the proportion of "virgin" arrests is as small as .15.[16]

In order to adjust the estimates, the lower bound of $\bar{\lambda}$ was set as follows: reporting rate .75; virgin arrest rate .30; virgin index arrest rate .25. For the upper bound of $\bar{\lambda}$, the following parameters were used: reporting rate .50; virgin arrest rate .15; virgin index arrest rate .10. In addition, the estimates have been adjusted to reflect time spent in prison.[17]

Collins (1977).[18] This study includes both arrest and self-report data. Eighteen offenders said they had committed more than 100 crimes and are not included in Collins's estimates, since they made mean λs between small categories incomparable. Since we are interested only in the aggregate $\bar{\lambda}$, offenders committing more than 100 crimes were assumed to have committed exactly 100. The exact number of crimes reported by these offenders is unavailable.

Blumstein and Cohen (1979).[19] Although the expected $\bar{\lambda}$ for people who committed crimes of all types was 24.7 (adding up the diagonal numbers of their table 19, p. 582), a number of index offenders committed only a few of these crime types during the study period. Thus the appropriate $\bar{\lambda}$ for offenders who committed one or more index crimes of *any* type is the λ for each crime type i, given that an offender committed that crime type, multiplied by the probability that an offender in the sample was arrested for that crime. That is, $\bar{\lambda} = \Sigma_i \lambda(i) \cdot p(i)$, where the $\lambda(i)$ matrix is given as table 19, and the $p(i)$ matrix is derived from table 18, p. 582.

Petersilia, Greenwood, and Lavin (1978).[20] This is self-report information from prison inmates. The authors did not obtain self-report information on offense rates for larcenies. We have assumed that for this sample, larcenies are committed in the same proportions relative to burglaries and auto thefts as they were for the offenders sampled by Blumstein and Cohen.[21]

Peterson, Braiker, and Polich (1980).[22] Here again we have assumed that larcenies are committed in the same proportion relative to other nonviolent crimes as that reported in Blumstein and Cohen.

Chaiken and Chaiken (1983).[23] These are trimmed means of self-reported offense rates, in which the rates of the 10 percent of offenders reporting the highest rates have been truncated to the figure for the tenth percen-

Table 23. Estimates of $\bar{\lambda}$, adjusted for data collection.

Estimate source[a]	All index offenses	Property crimes	Personal crimes
Wolfgang, Figlio, and Sellin, 1972	4.2–5.6	3.6–4.8	0.6–0.8
Greenberg, 1975	4.0–5.4	—	—
Shinnar and Shinnar, 1975	5.0–11.0	—	—
Williams, 1979	3.0–4.4	1.0–3.4	0.4–1.0
Boland and Wilson, 1978	9.2–12.2	—	—
Collins, 1977	12.6	—	—
Blumstein and Cohen, 1979	10.2–13.6	7.9–10.5	2.4–3.2
Petersilia, Greenwood, and Lavin, 1978	11.9	10.1	1.8
Peterson, Braiker, and Polich, 1980	—	11.0	—
Chaiken and Chaiken, 1983	55.0	49.6	5.4

a. The studies listed here are cited in full in note 3 to Appendix A.

tile. The figures were derived by weighting λs for each of the three offense rate groups in their table i-1 (p. xii) by the proportion of offenders in each.

Estimates of $\bar{\lambda}$, adjusted for differences in data collected, are shown in Table 23. The range of estimates is much smaller than before: the earlier very small and very large estimates, in particular, now are closer to the average value. However, the range is still wide. As one would expect, the estimates obtained from the higher-rate populations of recidivists and incarcerated offenders are considerably higher than those designed to apply to all offenders. The next step, then, is to account at least partially for these differences among populations.

ADJUSTING FOR POPULATION

It is more difficult to reconcile estimates of $\bar{\lambda}$ derived from different populations, mostly because there is little good information as to how the groups differ. In particular, two kinds of information are required. To reconcile estimates of $\bar{\lambda}$ for all arrestees with those of recidivists, it is necessary to determine the proportion of the entire identified criminal population that is arrested two or more times. This is very difficult to do, and available estimates are either highly unreliable or population-specific. To reconcile estimates of $\bar{\lambda}$ for recidivists with estimates obtained from surveys of prison inmates, it is necessary to know the probability that a recidivist will be in jail at any given time. Although this is also difficult to determine, it may be estimated from available criminal justice records.[24]

Reasonably reliable information is available only for the second adjustment; still, it is important to ensure that the estimates are consistent. Thus the following compromise seems reasonable: first, we adjust estimates from the prison population, comparing them to available estimates from the recidivist population; second, we use what figures are available to ensure that the recidivist estimates are (at least tentatively) consistent with estimates for the entire offending population.

The rate of offending for the average prison inmate is higher than that for the average street offender because high-rate, violent offenders are more likely to be caught, convicted, and sent to prison than others and because they are sentenced to longer terms. Thus the occasional burglars and thieves who are by chance caught and given stiff sentences are probably more typical of street offenders than the high-rate, violent criminals who make up the bulk of the prison population at any given time. In order to estimate the population of recidivists from prison data, these relatively low-rate offenders are weighted more heavily, using what information is available on their probability of arrest and conviction, and the average sentence they serve.

Although this technique could be used to adjust the estimates obtained from any of the prison studies, sufficient information to allow the adjustment was available only for Peterson, Braiker, and Polich (1980). After adjustment, their data show that the average street offender commits violent crimes at the rate of 2.1 per year and property offenses at an average rate of 10.9 per year. Thus the average street offender commits 13.0 index crimes each year he is free to commit them.[25] This estimate is well within the range of the others available. We may conclude that among offenders who are arrested twice or more (alternatively, among offenders who are like the ones who go to prison), the average rate of index offending lies between 9 and 14 index crimes per year. The best single estimate is probably about 12 crimes per year, or one a month.

The estimate for one-time arrestees, including recidivists as well as offenders caught only once, is about 5 crimes per year. Although we cannot reliably reevaluate the recidivist estimates to apply to the lower-rate population, some information is available that can help us check the consistency of the two groups of estimates. A reanalysis of the second

Rand prison survey found that 82 percent of robberies and 92 percent of burglaries may be accounted for by offenders who are like those in prison; the rest are committed by first-time or infrequent offenders who are unlikely to be sentenced to prison if they are caught.[26] If we assume that robbery and burglary are representative of all personal and property crimes, then the proportion of crimes accounted for by these occasional offenders is: $.15 (.82) + .85 (.92) = .90$, since 85 percent of index crimes are committed against property, and the remainder against persons. So recidivists commit about 90 percent of the crimes.

This estimate is pretty speculative, but its reliability is enhanced by a similar finding from the Philadelphia cohort studies. Researchers found that 90 percent of index crimes in one cohort and 91 percent of index crimes in the other were committed by offenders who had been arrested twice or more by the police; the remainder were committed by one-time offenders.[27] So the figure seems fairly robust.

Now, if we take 5 as the appropriate estimate of $\bar{\lambda}$ for the whole population of offenders, and 12 as the average $\bar{\lambda}$ for the recidivists, then: $5 = 12 \cdot p + \lambda_o(1 - p)$, where λ_o is the rate of offending for criminals who are arrested once and only once, and p is the proportion of offenders who are recidivists. Thus the proportion of offenses committed by recidivists will be: $12p /5 = .90$, and p will be equal to .375. That is, about 40 percent of index offenders should be arrested more than once for index crimes. Further, λ for the other 60 percent should be roughly: $5 - 12 (.375) / (1 - .375) = .80$, or one crime every 15 months.

It is difficult to check this estimate of the offense rate for very casual offenders empirically, since for persons who commit crimes at such low rates the entire concept of a criminal career is of dubious validity. But it is roughly as large as one would expect, given the results of surveys of criminal offending among the general population.[28]

The other conclusion, that 40 percent of index offenders are arrested more than once, may be checked directly and empirically from the Philadelphia cohort studies. In Philadelphia the probability that an individual who had been arrested for a violent crime would be arrested again for any index crime was .33 for persons born in 1945 and .42 for persons born in 1958; for individuals arrested for property crimes, the rearrest probabilities for each cohort were .43 and .51. Thus our best guess for the proportion of offenders who are arrested for two or more index crimes is about 40 percent, and the estimates of $\bar{\lambda}$ obtained from the two populations are at least roughly consistent with one another.

CONCLUSIONS

The average offender commits about five crimes per year. However, some 60 percent of these are very low-level offenders who commit very few offenses. About nine of every ten index crimes are committed by recidivists who comprise only 40 percent of the offending population.[29] Recidivists commit about twelve crimes per year.

However, as the prison surveys and countless anecdotes tell us, there are a few offenders — those in the right tail of this right tail — who commit crimes far more frequently, on the order of once a day. The contribution of these very frequent criminals to the total crime problem is still a matter of some controversy and will continue to be for some time. But the fact that they commit crimes at rates much higher than the average offender suggests that their contribution is large.

Appendix B

Indirect Estimates of Bias in Criminal Justice Agencies

ONE OF THE STRONGEST objections to enhancing the criminal justice system's focus on frequent, violent offenders is that the present system is already sharply focused. If agencies are already concentrating on the most dangerous offenders, it will do little good and conceivably some harm to urge still greater concentration. Because this is a potentially serious problem, it is important to develop some sense of whether the system is now biased in favor of or against high-rate, violent offenders. We can investigate this question by looking directly at the operations of criminal justice agencies or by looking at the results of their operations.

DIRECT MEASURES OF SELECTIVITY

It is fairly easy to determine how selective most criminal justice agencies try to be. When a judge passes sentence on a convicted defendant, he has at least part of the defendant's prior record, some information on social and status variables such as drug and employment history, and perhaps the personal opinions of the probation officer who prepared the report, and of the defendant's acquaintances, neighbors, and employers. If the judge is being selective, the form of the selectivity will be fairly obvious: all else being equal, if three-time robbers receive longer sentences than first offenders, the judge is using the number of prior offenses as an indication of offense frequency or blameworthiness or something else that merits incarceration. By comparing how each agency processes cases of offenders with different records and backgrounds, it is also possible to identify the selectivity of judges in deciding to set bail, of parole boards in deciding to grant parole, of prosecutors in deciding what to charge or whether to bargain, and of police in deciding how much effort to put into the investigation of specific cases. This method works because information of each offender and the agency's response is readily available. Evidence developed through direct observations of the criminal justice system is presented in Chapters 4, 5, 6, 7, and 8.

The problem with this straightforward method, however, is that all direct observations assume that the records on which courts, prosecutors, and police base their decisions are unbiased reflections of individual patterns of offending, that high-rate offenders' records are quite different from those of low-rate offenders. But there are many reasons to doubt that this is true. Whether it is true depends crucially on how effective the criminal justice system is in attributing crimes to offenders. There is no direct way to investigate this question except through surveys and self-reports, but there is an indirect method.

AN INDIRECT METHOD FOR ESTIMATING BIAS

The aggregate measure of bias with respect to rates of offending relies on what might be termed "filtering." By this we mean that at each stage of criminal processing, the worst offenders appear to take on added importance. The worst offenders account for a large percentage of crimes, a larger percentage of arrests, and still larger percentages of convictions and incarcerations.[1] In effect, even a totally nonselective system appears to act as a filter, letting through the most dangerous criminals while keeping out the sporadic offenders as a natural consequence of probabilistic mechanisms. Even more important, this filtering effect is measurable and predictable and therefore can provide a benchmark for estimating the direction and magnitude of bias in the system. Although the reasoning behind filtering is rather subtle, measurements of filtering are potentially quite useful.

To understand why an unbiased criminal justice system will naturally focus most of its attention on the most dangerous offenders, consider a simple example. Suppose there are two kinds of offenders — intensives and casuals. Intensives, which are 10 percent of the offending population, commit twenty crimes per year; the other 90 percent commit only four crimes each year.[2] Thus it might be said that the worst 10 percent of offenders have 36 percent of the motivations to commit crimes.

If each offender committed crimes at exactly the same rate, year after year, they would also commit 36 percent of the crimes each year. But even offenders with strong motivations may not commit some crimes for various reasons—illness, lack of opportunities, or quarrels with accomplices, for instance. So λ—the rate at which the offender commits crimes—is an average rate. In any given year the actual number of crimes an offender commits will vary, but in the long run it will average out to his λ. If this is true, then the proportion of crimes actually committed that are attributable to the worst 10 percent of offenders must be greater than 36 percent: a few temporarily motivated casuals would commit many crimes and be counted among the 10 percent worst offenders in place of temporarily unmotivated intensives. If crimes are committed according to a Poisson process (that is, if the chances that an offender will commit a crime tomorrow do not depend on whether he committed one today), then the most active 10 percent of the criminals commit 39 percent of all crimes.

Now suppose that the police are successful in arresting offenders 10 percent of the time and that this percentage applies equally to all offenders and crimes. That is, the police are unbiased with respect to the *rate* of offending. Because arrests are made randomly, some offenders who commit many crimes will get lucky and never be caught; others who commit fewer crimes will be arrested several times. Since unlucky low-rate offenders will replace lucky high-rate offenders in the right tail of the arrest distribution, the 10 percent of most-arrested offenders will account for more than 39 percent of all arrests. In fact, if the chances of arrest for each crime are constant across all offenders, then calculations indicate that the most-arrested 10 percent of the offenders will account for 46 percent of all arrests.

Finally, say that 50 percent of all arrests result in conviction and incarceration. Just as unfortunate lower-rate offenders replaced lucky higher-rate crooks in the right tail of the arrest distribution, offenders with few arrests who happen to be convicted several times will replace luckier offenders with more arrests. Thus the 10 percent of offenders with the most convictions will account for more than 46 percent of convictions. If the chances of conviction do not depend on the number of prior arrests, they will account for 54 percent of convictions.

Figure 11 shows the proportion of λs or "motivations," crimes, arrests, and convictions that would be accounted for by the top 10 percent of each distribution if the system were unbiased with respect to rates of offending. This proportion might be thought of as the concentration of each outcome among the offenders in the right tail of the distribution. The higher the proportion, the more important is the right tail. The

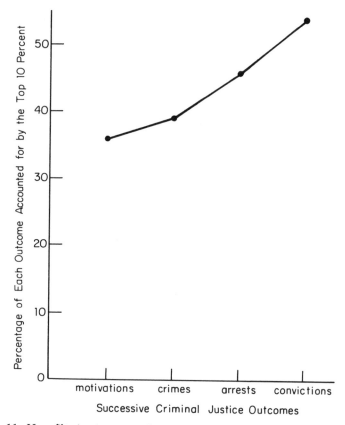

Figure 11   How filtering increases the importance of the right tail of the distribution.

obvious result—that outcomes become more and more concentrated among the worst offenders as one proceeds through the system—is perfectly general and can be relied upon to help measure the selectivity of criminal justice agencies.

The results do not change much when the distribution of λ is taken to be continuous and when nonselective incapacitation through incarceration is taken into account. Incarceration falls disproportionately on the most active offenders because of filtering, so these offenders on the right tail are off the street more than the less active offenders, and the concentration of crimes, arrests, and convictions is somewhat reduced. Note, however, that no matter what the original distribution of λ, the proportions increase as we move through the system, so long as the police, prosecutor, and judge are not being selective. So filtering works predictably.

Now suppose that we wish to test the hypothesis that the system is unbiased or to measure the bias of any given agency, say the police department. In addition to the nonselective case, there are two possibilities. The agency may be biased against active offenders: that is, the police may focus their activities on offenders who have been previously arrested, by checking modus operandi files, distributing mug shots, and surveilling offenders known to be active. As a result of this focus, the more arrests an offender has, the more likely he is to be arrested again. The other possibility is that the agency is biased in favor of active offenders. Experienced offenders may learn to avoid capture by leaving fewer clues, working alone more often, and more carefully planning their escape. Thus the more crimes an offender has committed, the less likely he is to be arrested for the next one. In either case the police continue to clear 10 percent of crimes.[3]

When each of these two scenarios was applied to our simulated cohort, the concentration of outcomes among offenders changed dramatically. As shown in Figure 12, by focusing on the actions of offenders with prior records, the police greatly increased the proportion of arrests (and with it, the proportion of convictions and incarcerations) accounted for by the 10 percent of offenders with the most arrests. (Incidentally, the concentration of crimes among criminals decreased, since the most frequent offenders were incapacitated more of the time.) When experienced offenders learned to avoid arrests, however, exactly the opposite results were obtained. The proportion of arrests, convictions and incarcerations accounted for by the worst 10 percent of offenders all decreased; because frequent offenders were less often punished, they committed proportionately more crimes. In effect, selective police programs *stretched* the tail of the arrest, conviction, and incarceration distributions, while offender actions leading to negative police selectivity suppressed the right tail.

This result suggests that it might be possible to determine whether the police are positively or negatively selective in making arrests, simply by comparing estimates of the distribution of λ, crimes committed, and arrests made. If arrests are much more concentrated among offenders than crimes, then the police are picking out the worst offenders (or at least they are picking out *some* of the worst offenders); if the distribution of arrests is no more skewed than the distribution of crimes — and especially if it is *less* skewed — then we can be sure that the police are being negatively selective.

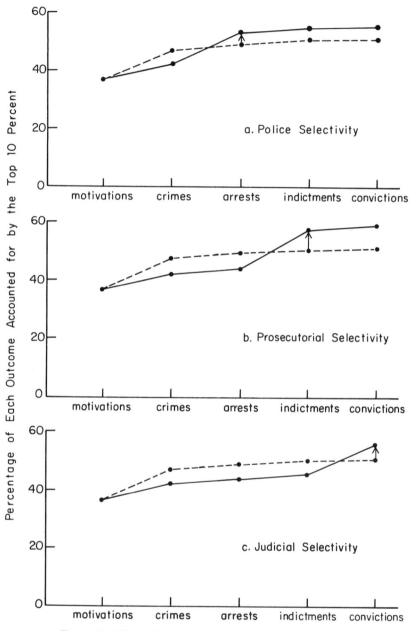

Figure 12   How selectivity changes the filtering process.

ESTIMATES OF POLICE SELECTIVITY

A definitive answer to the question of police selectivity would require extensive data collection within a particular jurisdiction, including a survey of offenders to determine their offense history and offense rates and a comprehensive review of arrest, conviction, and prison records. Because existing data were not collected for this purpose, and because complete distributional information is not available for any single jurisdiction (or even any single state), it is somewhat premature to use existing data to estimate selectivity. However, we will try it anyway, partly to demonstrate the method and partly to show that police practices may be so *counterselective* that a particularly careful analysis is unnecessary.

The data used were gleaned from a variety of studies. The distributions of λ and of crimes committed were obtained from the Rand inmate surveys.[4] The distribution of arrests was gleaned from the first and second Philadelphia cohort studies, from a cohort study of youths in Columbus, Ohio, and from career criminal files in the United States and

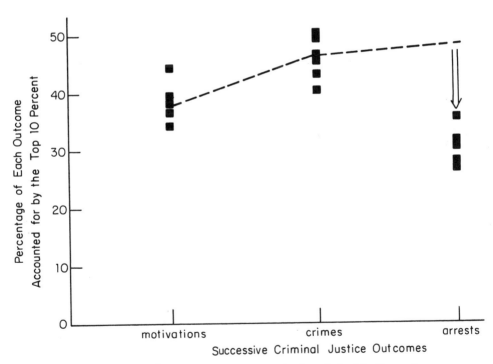

Figure 13 Empirical estimates of filtering in the criminal justice system.

Denmark.[5] Needless to say, there is no particular reason that these distributions, drawn from vastly differing populations, will be consistent with one another. We ask that our results be taken as suggestive, at best.

Figure 13 shows the proportion of λs, crimes, and arrests accounted for by the worst 10 percent of offenders in each distribution studied. The results are striking: the right tail of the distribution of offenders is consistently responsible for 35 to 40 percent of the lambda, and some 45 percent of the crimes committed. By contrast the top 10 percent of offenders arrested account for only about 30 percent of the arrests. Compared to the results simulated above (shown here as a dotted line), it is clear that the distribution of arrests is markedly less skewed than one would expect if police were selective or neutral with respect to frequent and violent offenders. In fact, the police seem remarkably counterselective. Police selectivity programs appear to be desperately needed, if only to make the system neutral with regard to the most dangerous offenders.

Notes

INTRODUCTION

1. If the seriousness of offenses is accounted for, the most criminally active 6.3 percent of individuals committed 56.4 percent of the seriousness-weighted offenses. Marvin E. Wolfgang, Robert M. Figlio, and Thorsten Sellin, *Delinquency in a Birth Cohort* (Chicago: University of Chicago Press, 1972), 88, 95.

2. This is suggested by distributional parameters for the Rand Second Inmate Study, given in John E. Rolph, Jan M. Chaiken, and Robert L. Houchens, *Methods for Estimating the Crime Rates of Individuals* (Santa Monica, Calif.: Rand, 1981), 26.

3. Peter W. Greenwood and Allan Abrahamse demonstrate this in *Selective Incapacitation* (Santa Monica, Calif.: Rand, 1982), 47–66.

4. Greenwood, in *Selective Incapacitation* and numerous other publications, has led the charge for selective sentencing policies.

5. The continuing nationwide movement to establish career criminal units began in the mid-1970s. A history of this movement, and an evaluation of the usefulness of these units in ensuring convictions of the worst offenders, may be found in Eleanor Chelimsky and Judith Dahmann, *Career Criminal Program National Evaluation: Final Report* (Washington, D.C.: U.S. Government Printing Office, 1981).

6. Police experiments began at a local level with "location-oriented" and "perpetrator-oriented" patrols and other "serious habitual offender" programs; see Tony Pate, Robert A. Bowers, and Ron Parks, *Three Approaches to Criminal Apprehension in Kansas City: An Evaluation Report* (Washington, D.C.: Police Foundation, 1976). They became the vogue when federal funding began with the Integrated Criminal Apprehension Program (ICAP). See for example, Thomas Beall, *A Case Study Evaluation of the Implementation of the Integrated Criminal Apprehension Program in Stockton, California* (Washington, D.C.: University City Science Center, 1981).

7. For example, in 1977 the Law Enforcement Assistance Administration sponsored a conference for project directors of police ICAP and prosecutors' Career Criminal programs, and it published a guide for the benefit of jurisdictions involved in both efforts. *Program Guide, Integrated Criminal Apprehension Program and Career Criminal Program* (Washington, D.C.: Law Enforcement Assistance Administration, 1977). A similar conference, focusing on repeat offenders and attracting a national audience, was held on October 6–7, 1982, at the University of Maryland.

8. For two accounts of this information-integration process, see Charles Lindblom, *The Intelligence of Democracy: Decision Making through Natural Adjustments* (New York: Free Press, 1965), and Donald T. Campbell, "Reforms as Experiments," in *Handbook of Evaluation Research*, vol. I, ed. Elmer L. Struening and Marcia Guttentag (Beverly Hills, Calif.: Sage, 1975).

1. PUBLIC DANGER AND THE PROBLEM OF CRIME

1. U.S. Department of Justice, Bureau of Justice Statistics, "Households Touched by Crime, 1982", (Washington, D.C.: Bureau of Justice Statistics, 1983), 1.

2. Charles E. Silberman, *Criminal Violence, Criminal Justice* (New York: Random House, 1978), 3.

3. U.S. Department of Justice, Federal Bureau of Investigation, *Uniform Crime Reports for the United States, 1980* (Washington, D.C.: U.S. Government Printing Office, 1981), 7–13.

4. U.S. Department of Commerce, Bureau of the Census, *Criminal Victimization in the United States, 1980* (Washington, D.C.: U.S. Government Printing Office, 1982), 22.

5. FBI, *Uniform Crime Reports, 1980*, 41.

6. Census Bureau, *Criminal Victimization, 1980*, 22.

7. Census Bureau, *Criminal Victimization, 1980*, 62–63.

8. A victim who resists an attacker is sometimes able to deter the offender, reducing the chances that the crime will be completed. But resistance is a risky strategy, since it increases the chances of injury by as much as three times. Marvin E. Wolfgang, "Victim Intimidation, Resistance and Injury: A Study of Robbery," paper presented to the Fourth International Symposium on Victimology, Tokyo, Japan, August 1982; Philip J. Cook, "A Strategic Choice Analysis of Robbery," in *Sample Surveys of the Victims of Crime*, ed. Wesley Skogan (Cambridge, Mass.: Ballinger, 1974).

9. For a striking group of anecdotal accounts of mugging, emphasizing the humiliation and powerlessness of victims, see Robert Lejeune and Nicholas Alex, "On Being Mugged: The Event and Its Aftermath," *Urban Life and Culture* 2 (1973) 259–287.

10. FBI, *Uniform Crime Reports, 1980*, 41.

11. In 1980, 84.8 percent of all index crimes committed were against property; thus 5.58 times more property crimes were committed than personal crimes. Census Bureau, *Criminal Victimization, 1980*, 22.

12. In 1976 the Joint Economic Committee of Congress estimated the aggre-

gate cost of crimes against property to be $4 billion. See "That Costly White Collar Mob," *New York Times*, January 2, 1977, 15. The most recent FBI estimate was about $6.4 billion. FBI, *Uniform Crime Reports, 1980*, 179.

13. The median economic loss from theft and damage for a property crime is about $50. Census Bureau, *Criminal Victimization, 1980*, 15. Although auto thefts are only about 3 percent of all index crimes, they account for 48 percent of all crimes resulting in theft of property worth $1,000 or more. Census Bureau, *Criminal Victimization, 1980*, 22, 64, 67.

14. Norval Morris and Gordon Hawkins, *The Honest Politician's Guide to Crime Control* (Chicago: University of Chicago Press, 1970), 102; Census Bureau, *Criminal Victimization, 1980*, 66.

15. Victimization surveys indicate that 8 percent of property and damage losses from larcenies, 19 percent of losses from burglary, and 66 percent of auto theft losses are at least partially covered by insurance. Census Bureau, *Criminal Victimization, 1980*, 66–67. This understates the proportion of large losses that are covered, since most policies covering burglary and theft include a deductible of $100 or more. Insurance Information Institute, *Insurance Facts: 1982–83* (New York: Insurance Information Institute, 1982).

16. A-T-O Incorporated, *The Figgie Report on Fear of Crime: America Afraid, I, The General Public* (New York: A-T-O, 1980), 30.

17. "Fears of Crime in Rocky Mountain States," *Current Opinion* 5 (1977), 136.

18. "One Household in Four Hit by Crime; Many Afraid to Walk Alone in Neighborhoods," *Gallup Report* 210 (1983), 3–9.

19. Freud, for example, considered anxiety to be "the fundamental phenomenon and the central problem of neurosis." Sigmund Freud, *The Problem of Anxiety* (New York: Norton, 1936). Although anxiety itself poses few serious psychological problems, the psychic and physical defenses people adopt to allay their anxieties do, because they tend to backfire. Examples include obsessive rituals, depression, and drug and alcohol dependency. Worse, these defenses can actually increase levels of fear if they seem to be working poorly, leading to "pyramiding of defenses." See generally Karen Horney, *The Neurotic Personality of Our Time* (New York: Norton, 1937), and Erich Fromm, *Man for Himself* (New York: Rinehart, 1947).

20. The seminal work on the medical effects of prolonged stress is Hans Selye's *The Stress of Life* (New York: McGraw-Hill, 1956). More recent research is reviewed in O. Carl Simonton, Stephanie Matthews-Simonton, and James Creighton, *Getting Well Again* (Los Angeles: Tarcher, 1978), and *Selye's Guide to Stress Research*, ed. Hans Selye (New York: Van Nostrand Reinhold, 1980).

21. This figure, which includes home and business security patrols and night watchers, burglar alarm maintenance and monitoring, and private investigators, is collected by the Census Bureau as SIC code 7393. It does not include manufacture of alarms, lights, or other protective equipment. U.S. Department of Commerce, Bureau of the Census, *1977 Census of Service Industries: Geographic Area Series: United States* (Washington, D.C.: U.S. Government Printing Office, 1979), 52-8–52-9.

22. Fred DuBow, Edward McCabe, and Gail Kaplan, *Reactions to Crime: A*

Critical Review of the Literature (Washington, D.C.: National Institute of Law Enforcement and Criminal Justice, 1979), 42–44.

23. *New York*, February 8, 1982, 37.

24. DuBow, McCabe, and Kaplan, *Reactions to Crime*, 43.

25. George L. Kelling, Tony Pate, Duane Dieckman, and Charles E. Brown, *The Kansas City Preventive Patrol Experiment: Technical Report* (Washington, D.C.: Police Foundation, 1974); Market Opinion Research, *The Michigan Public Speaks Out on Crime* (Detroit: Market Opinion Research, 1977); Stephanie Greenberg, *Characteristics of High and Low Crime Neighborhoods in Atlanta, 1980*, ICPSR codebook 7951 (Ann Arbor: Inter-University Consortium for Political and Social Research, 1983), 193.

26. Leonard D. Savitz, Michael Lalli, and Lawrence Rosen, *City Life and Delinquency: Victimization, Fear of Crime, and Gang Membership* (Washington, D.C.: U.S. Government Printing Office, 1977).

27. Institute for Social Research, *Public Safety: Quality of Life in the Detroit Metropolitan Area* (Ann Arbor: University of Michigan, Survey Research Center, 1975).

28. Larry Springer, "Crime Perception and Response Behavior," Ph. D. dissertation, Pennsylvania State University, 1974.

29. Charles T. Clotfelter, "Urban Crime and Household Protective Measures," *Review of Economics and Statistics* 59 (1977) 499–503; Michael G. Maxfield, "Reactions to Fear," working paper, Reactions to Crime Project (Evanston, Ill.: Northwestern University, Center for Urban Affairs, 1977), quoted in DuBow, McCabe, and Kaplan, *Reactions to Crime*, 46.

30. *New York Times*, October 11, 1981, 23.

31. *New York*, February 8, 1982, 27–31.

32. Jane Jacobs, *The Death and Life of Great American Cities* (New York: Vintage, 1961).

33. Matthew G. Yeager, Joseph D. Alviani, and Nancy Loving, *How Well Does the Handgun Protect You and Your Family?* (Washington, D.C.: U.S. Conference of Mayors, 1976).

34. Kansas City Police Department, *Response Time Analysis: Executive Summary* (Kansas City, Mo.: Board of Police Commissioners, 1977), 26.

35. Isaac Ehrlich and Gary Becker, "Market Insurance, Self-Insurance, and Self-Protection," *Journal of Political Economy* 80 (1972), 623–648.

36. A-T-O, *Figgie Report*, 30; *Current Opinion* 5 (1977), 136.

37. Arthur L. Stinchcombe, Rebecca Adams, Carol A. Heimes, Kim Lane Scheppele, Tom W. Smith, and D. Garth Taylor, *Crime and Punishment in Public Opinion: 1948–1974* (Chicago: National Opinion Research Center, 1977), 52–53.

38. John L. Conklin, *The Impact of Crime* (New York: Macmillan, 1975), 113.

39. Erving Goffman, *Relations in Public: Microstudies of the Public Order* (New York: Harper and Row, 1972), 11.

40. Nathan Glazer, "On Subway Graffiti in New York," *The Public Interest* 54 (1979), 4.

41. Wasserman Associates, *Security in Public Housing: A Report for the Boston Housing Authority* (Harvard, Mass.: Wasserman Associates, 1980). See also James Q. Wilson, "The Urban Unease: Community vs. City," *The Public Interest* 12

(1968), 25–39; James Q. Wilson and George L. Kelling, "Broken Windows: The Police and Neighborhood Safety," *Atlantic* (March 1982), 29–38; William Spelman, "Reactions to Crime in Atlanta and Chicago: A Policy-Oriented Reanalysis" Final Report to the National Institute of Justice (Cambridge, Mass.: John F. Kennedy School of Government, 1983), 208–222.

2. DANGEROUS OFFENDERS

1. This idea seems to appear naturally and inevitably whenever public concern about crime reaches a certain level. For an outstanding account of the form it has taken in England, see Leon Radzinowicz and Roger Hood, "Incapacitating the Habitual Criminal: The English Experience," *Michigan Law Review* 78 (August 1980), 1305–1389. For a recent exposition, see Peter W. Greenwood and Allan Abrahamse, *Selective Incapacitation* (Santa Monica, Calif.: Rand, 1982).

2. For a penetrating analysis raising these basic questions, see Alan Dershowitz, "The Origins of Preventive Confinement in Anglo American Law," *University of Cincinnati Law Review* 43 (1974), 1–60, 781–846.

3. In searching for explanations for the fact that many felony arrests in New York City never reached felony convictions, the Vera Institute of Justice found that the fact situations that lay behind felony arrests were often ambiguous. Many robberies, felonious assaults, and so on seemed to be the product of disputes in which it was hard to see who was at fault. Only a few of the felonies resembled our image of a violent, unprovoked attack by one stranger against another. See Vera Institute of Justice, *Felony Arrests: Their Prosecution and Disposition in New York City Courts* (New York: Vera Institute, 1977).

4. For analyses of the question of imprisonment as criminal punishment, see Norval Morris, *The Future of Imprisonment* (Chicago: University of Chicago Press, 1974), or Michael Sherman and Gordon Hawkins, *Imprisonment in America* (Chicago: University of Chicago Press, 1981).

5. For a literary treatment of the issue of the role of guilt in crime and punishment, see Herman Melville, *Billy Budd: Foretopman* (1924; reprint ed., New York: Bobbs-Merrill, 1975).

6. For empirical evidence on the success of rehabilitation programs, see Robert Martinson, "What Works: Questions and Answers about Prison Reform," *The Public Interest* 35 (1974), 22–54.

7. Jan M. Chaiken, Marcia R. Chaiken, and Joyce E. Peterson, *Varieties of Criminal Behavior: Summary and Policy Implications* (Santa Monica, Calif.: 1982), 20.

8. See, for example, Walter Miller, *Violence by Youth Gangs and Youth Groups as a Crime Problem in Major American Cities* (Washington, D.C.: National Institute of Justice, 1981), or more generally, Maynard L. Erickson, "The Group Context of Delinquent Behavior," *Social Problems* 19 (1971), 114–129.

9. For a classic study indicating the role of alcohol and victim provocation in homicides, see Marvin Wolfgang, "Victim Precipitated Criminal Homicide," *Journal of Criminal Law, Criminology and Police Science* 48 (1957), 1–11. For a provocative analysis suggesting the phenomenon of "victim-proneness" (and therefore victim complicity in causing crime), see Michael Hindelang, Michael R.

Gottfredson, and James Garofalo, *Victims of Personal Crime: An Empirical Foundation of a Theory of Personal Victimization* (Cambridge, Mass.: Ballinger, 1978).

10.   Mark H. Moore, "Controlling Criminogenic Commodities: Drugs, Guns, and Alcohol," in *Crime and Public Policy,* ed. James Q. Wilson (San Francisco: Institute for Contemporary Studies, 1983), 125–144.

11.   For more examples of how the built environment creates and stifles opportunities for crime, see Oscar Newman, *Defensible Space: Crime Prevention through Environmental Design* (New York: Collier, 1973).

12.   Lawrence E. Cohen and Marcus Felson, "Social Change and Crime Rate Trends: A Routine Activity Approach," *American Sociological Review* 44 (1979), 588–608; Glenn Collins, "Study Finds Child Abduction by Parents Exceeds Estimates," *New York Times,* October 23, 1983, 63.

13.   For an anecdotal account of the background of an armed robber that seems to emphasize the role of casual violence in the family setting, see John Allen, *Assault with a Deadly Weapon: The Autobiography of a Street Criminal* (New York: Pantheon, 1977).

14.   For empirical evidence about the contribution of guns to the violent crime problem, see Philip J. Cook, "The Effect of Gun Availability on Violent Crime Patterns," *The Annals* 456 (1981), 63–79; for a spectrum of interpretations and implications, see the other articles in that issue, and Mark H. Moore, "The Bird in Hand: A Feasible Strategy for Gun Control," *Journal of Policy Analysis and Management* 2 (1983), 185–195.

15.   Although the cultural origins of *mens rea,* the "guilty mind," are muddled, the concept was thoroughly entrenched by at least the eighteenth century. Consider Blackstone: "To constitute a crime against human laws, there must be, first, a vicious will; and secondly, an unlawful act consequent upon such vicious will.' Sir William Blackstone, *Commentaries on the Laws of England,* vol. 4 (1769; reprint ed., London: Dawsons, 1966), 21. It remains the central idea in present considerations of criminal responsibility, as noted by both its proponents — for example, Jerome Hall, *General Principles of Criminal Law* (Indianapolis: Bobbs-Merrill, 1960), 70–77; and H. L. A. Hart, "Negligence, Mens Rea and Criminal Responsibility," in *Punishment and Responsibility: Essays in the Philosophy of Law* (New York: Oxford University Press, 1968), 136–157 — and its detractors, most notably Gary V. Dubin, "*Mens Rea* Reconsidered: A Plea for a Due Process Concept of Criminal Responsibility," *Stanford Law Review* 18 (1966), 322–395.

16.   Of course, acts are involved in prosecutions for conspiracies and attempts. To prove a conspiracy under common law, the prosecutor must show an overt agreement between the conspiring parties to commit a harmful act. In some states it must be shown that the conspirers have done some act (which need not be a civil or criminal wrong) to effect the agreed-to wrong. *State* v. *Carbone,* 10 N.J. 329 (1952); *People* v. *Hines,* 284 N.Y. 93 (1940). To be guilty of an attempt, meanwhile, the offender must take a "substantial step toward the commission of the offense." *People* v. *Paluch,* 78 Ill. App. 2d 356 (1966). In most states the act must be so nearly harmful that there is a "dangerous proximity" to success. *Hyde and Schneider* v. *U.S.,* 225 U.S. 347 (1911), 388. So in both conspiracy and attempt some act is required, but the act in itself need not be harmful.

17. According to Dubin, "Blackstone implied that . . . evil intent alone should be punished if proof of such thoughts were possible without any investigation into the outward manifestations of intention (the accompanying act)." Dubin, *"Mens Rea* Reconsidered," 354.

18. Vera Institute, *Felony Arrests*, 135–136.

19. Information on individual rates of offending has been constructed from two kinds of sources: self-reports by the offenders themselves, as described by Jan M. Chaiken and Marcia R. Chaiken, *Varieties of Criminal Behavior* (Santa Monica, Calif.: Rand, 1982); and inferences drawn from official records, as described by Alfred Blumstein and Jacqueline Cohen, "Estimation of Individual Crime Rates from Arrest Records," *Journal of Criminal Law and Criminology* 70 (1979), 561–585.

20. Strictly speaking, λ refers to an individual's propensity to commit offenses; the actual number committed per unit of time is generally assumed to be subject to random fluctuation. For a full description and some interesting implications of this view, see John E. Rolph, Jan M. Chaiken, and Robert L. Houchens, *Methods for Estimating Crime Rates of Individuals* (Santa Monica, Calif.: Rand, 1981). As with most individual propensities, λ is usually assumed to be constant in the short run but changeable in the long run. For empirical evidence on changes in propensities over the course of an offender's career, see James J. Collins, "Offender Careers and Restraints: Probabilities and Policy Implication," mimeographed, University of Pennsylvania, 1977.

21. Thorsten Sellin and Marvin E. Wolfgang originally developed their seriousness measure through sample surveys of college students, police officers, and judges; it reflects the seriousness of the victim's financial, physical, and psychological losses. See Sellin and Wolfgang, *The Measurement of Delinquency* (New York: John Wiley and Sons, 1964). The seriousness scores have been successfully replicated with a variety of samples, including samples drawn from several foreign countries. The measure seems remarkably robust: the correlation between scores for different samples ranges from .85 to .95. Charles F. Wellford and Michael Wiatrowski, "On the Measurement of Delinquency," *Journal of Criminal Law and Criminology* 66 (1975), 175–188.

22. The Police Executive Research Forum is experimenting with a crime classification system for use in police departments that includes information on the legal charge, the nature and size of the victim's loss, the relationship between victim and offender, and the location of the crime. This scheme has great appeal. See Gregory A. Thomas, *Summary Report on the Crime Classification System for the City of Peoria, Illinois* (Washington, D.C.: Police Executive Research Forum, 1982).

23. According to the best available calculations, the likelihood that someone who commits a robbery will be arrested for his crime is about 7 percent; the likelihood that a burglar will be caught is even lower, about 5 percent. Blumstein and Cohen, "Estimation of Individual Crime Rates," 579.

24. Probable cause—"reasonably trustworthy information . . . sufficient . . . to warrant a man of reasonable caution in the belief" that a crime has been committed—is typically needed for an arrest. *Carroll* v. *U.S.,* 267 U.S. 132

(1924), 162; see also *Locke* v. *U.S.*, 7 Cranch 339 (1813), 348; *Stacey* v. *Emery*, 97 U.S. 642 (1878), 645; and more recently *Draper* v. *U.S.*, 358 U.S. 307 (1959); *Ker* v. *California*, 374 U.S. 23 (1963). Although the exact definition of probable cause depends on the circumstances, it is roughly equivalent to a better-than-even chance of guilt.

25.   Although most offenders who participate in self-report surveys report many more crimes than they have been arrested for, the average offender probably underestimates his criminal history. One indication of this is the proportion of crimes reported by convicted offenders that resulted in their arrest; if offenders were reporting all their crimes, the proportion should be about the same as the probability of arrest obtained from analysis of official records. However, it is substantially lower. Compare Mark A. Peterson, Harriet B. Braiker, and Suzanne M. Polich, *Who Commits Crimes: A Survey of Prison Inmates* (Cambridge, Mass.: Oelgeschlager, Gunn, and Hain, 1981), 56, with Blumstein and Cohen, "Estimation of Individual Crime Rates," 579. Similar results are obtained with noninstitutionalized youths; see Michael J. Hindelang, Travis Hirschi, and Joseph G. Weis, "Correlates of Delinquency: The Illusion of Discrepancy between Self-Report and Official Measures," *American Sociological Review* 44 (1979), 995–1014. Still, some respondents probably overestimate the number of offenses, and it is clear that self-report data account for a much higher fraction of the offenses committed than official records do.

26.   An analysis of the reliability of the Rand self-report data found that though much of the information was inconsistent with official records, there was no evidence of systematic bias. Kent H. Marquis and Patricia Ebener, *Quality of Prisoner Self-Reports: A Record Check Evaluation of Bias and Reliability in Arrests and Conviction Responses* (Santa Monica, Calif.: Rand, 1981).

27.   The sources for the estimates in Table 2 are: Marvin E. Wolfgang, Robert M. Figlio, and Thorsten Sellin, *Delinquency in a Birth Cohort* (Chicago: University of Chicago Press, 1972); David Greenberg, "The Incapacitative Effect of Punishment: Some Estimates," *Law and Society Review* 2 (1975), 541–580; Shlomo Shinnar and Reuel Shinnar, "The Effects of the Criminal Justice System on the Control of Crime: A Quantitative Approach," *Law and Society Review* 2 (1975), 581–611; Kristen M. Williams, *The Scope and Prediction of Recidivism,* PROMIS Research Project Publication 10 (Washington D.C.: Institute for Law and Social Research, 1979); Barbara Boland and James Q. Wilson, "Age, Crime and Punishment," *The Public Interest* 51 (1978), 22–34; Collins, "Offender Careers and Restraints"; Blumstein and Cohen, "Estimation of Individual Crime Rates," 561–585; Mark A. Peterson, Harriet B. Braiker, and Suzanne M. Polich, *Doing Crime: A Survey of California Prison Inmates* (Santa Monica, Calif.: Rand, 1980). Details as to how these estimates were made are provided in Appendix A.

28.   In the typical burglary committed in 1980, the thief made off with property valued by the victim at about $150. U.S. Department of Commerce, Bureau of the Census, *Criminal Victimization in the United States, 1980* (Washington, D.C.: U.S. Government Printing Office), 65. If the offender commits burglaries at the much higher than average rate of twenty per year, he will still gross only $3,000. Because most offenders do not use the goods they steal but must fence

them for a fraction of their value, the net income for the average burglar is much less; see Marilyn E. Walsh, *The Fence: A New Look at the World of Property Theft* (Westport, Conn.: Greenwood, 1977).

29. According to a study conducted by Abt Associates, the average annual operating costs of a prison cell range from a low of $2,241 per adult prisoner in Texas to a high of $15,946 per adult prisoner in New Hampshire, with an average of about $9,000. Each new cell costs between $32,000 and $40,000 to construct. Joan Mullen, Kenneth Carlson, and Bradford Smith, *America's Prisons and Jails*, vol. I: *Summary and Policy Implications of a National Study* (Washington, D.C.: U.S. Government Printing Office, 1980), 67, 119.

30. See the discussion in Chapter 1.

31. Jacqueline Cohen, "The Incapacitative Effect of Imprisonment: A Critical Review of the Literature," in *Deterrence and Incapacitation: Estimating the Effects of Criminal Sanctions on Crime Rates*, ed. Alfred Blumstein, Jacqueline Cohen, and Daniel Nagin (Washington, D.C.: National Academy of Sciences, 1978), 187–243.

32. Floyd H. Allport, "The J-Curve Hypothesis of Conforming Behavior," *Journal of Social Psychology* 5 (1934), 141–183.

33. Kettil Bruun, Griffith Edwards, Martti Lumio, Klaus Mäkelä, Lynn Pan, Robert E. Popham, Robin Room, Wolfgang Schmidt, Ole-Jørgen Skog, Pekka Sulkunen, and Esa Österberg, *Alcohol Control Policies in Public Policy Perspective* (Helsinki: Finnish Foundation for Alcohol Studies, 1975), 30–45; Denise Kandel, "Stages in Adolescent Involvement in Drug Use," *Science* 190 (1975), 912–914.

34. Wolfgang, Figlio, and Sellin, *Delinquency in a Birth Cohort*; Collins, "Offenders' Careers and Restraints"; Marvin E. Wolfgang and Paul Tracy, "The 1945 and 1958 Birth Cohorts: A Comparison of the Prevalence, Incidence and Severity of Delinquent Behavior," in *Dealing with Dangerous Offenders*, vol. 2: *Selected Papers*, report to the National Institute of Justice, ed. Daniel McGillis, Susan Estrich, Mark H. Moore, and William Spelman (Cambridge, Mass.: Harvard University, John F. Kennedy School of Government, 1983).

35. Wolfgang and Tracy, "1945 and 1958 Birth Cohorts," 16; Wolfgang, Figlio, and Sellin, *Delinquency in a Birth Cohort*, 88.

36. Wolfgang and Tracy, "1945 and 1958 Birth Cohorts," 16; Wolfgang, Figlio, and Sellin, *Delinquency in a Birth Cohort*, 102.

37. Wolfgang and Tracy, "1945 and 1958 Birth Cohorts," 19.

38. Wolfgang and Tracy, "1945 and 1958 Birth Cohorts," 17–18.

39. Rand's first self-report survey was of forty-nine armed robbers incarcerated in California in the mid-1970s; the results are described in Joan Petersilia, Peter W. Greenwood, and Marvin Lavin, *Criminal Careers of Habitual Felons* (Santa Monica, Calif.: Rand, 1977). A more general survey of California prisoners, based on a survey questionnaire rather than in-person interviews, was completed two years later (Peterson, Braiker, and Polich, *Doing Crimes*). Rand's third and most ambitious effort applied this questionnaire to 2,600 offenders incarcerated in jails and prisons in California, Michigan, and Texas. See Greenwood and Abrahamse, *Selective Incapacitation;* Chaiken and Chaiken, *Varieties of Criminal Behavior.* Juv. S.

40. Ten percent of prison inmates who commit robberies commit eighty-seven or more each year. Chaiken and Chaiken, *Varieties of Criminal Behavior*, 206.

41. Alfred Blumstein and Richard Larson, "Models of a Total Criminal Justice System," *Operations Research* 17 (1969), 119–132, used arrest data from the Minnesota Board of Corrections and the Federal Bureau of Prisons to determine the likelihood that an offender would be arrested for any of a list of index crimes, given the crime type of his last arrest. Williams, in *Scope and Prediction*, computed a similar matrix from FBI career criminal records, and Blumstein and Cohen, "Estimation of Individual Crime Rates," combined the same data set with information from victimization surveys to give more reliable results. Peterson, Braiker, and Polich, *Doing Crime*, used self-report data to draw correlations between rates of offending for different crime types.

42. Blumstein and Larson, "Models of a Total Criminal Justice System," 224–225; Williams, *Scope and Prediction*, 77; Blumstein and Cohen, "Estimation of Individual Crime Rates," 582; Peterson, Braiker, and Polich, *Doing Crime*, 39.

43. If offending patterns were random, an offender's past history would give no clues as to his future conduct. For example, the probability that a given offender will commit a burglary will not change, even if the last thirteen crimes he has committed were burglaries. Chaiken and Chaiken, *Varieties of Criminal Behavior*, 20–23.

44. Chaiken and Chaiken, *Varieties of Criminal Behavior*, 62–63.

45. Allport, "The J-Curve Hypothesis"; Bruun and others, *Alcohol Control Policies*; Kandel, "Stages in Adolescent Involvement."

46. Chaiken and Chaiken, *Varieties of Criminal Behavior*, 68.

47. Greenwood and Abrahamse, *Selective Incapacitation*, 45.

48. Charles E. Silberman, *Criminal Violence, Criminal Justice* (New York: Random House, 1978), 77–78.

49. Greenwood shows that 82 percent of robberies and 92 percent of burglaries are committed by offenders who have been arrested at least once. See Greenwood and Abrahamse, *Selective Incapacitation*, 118.

50. These studies are considered in detail in Chapters 4, 5, and 6.

51. Many assaults, rapes, and murders are easy to solve because the offender is known to the victim; stranger-to-stranger crimes are much more difficult to solve because the offender can be identified only if he is apprehended while escaping the scene or if he leaves physical traces at the crime scene. See generally, John E. Eck, *Solving Crimes: Police Investigation of Burglary and Robbery* (Washington, D.C.: Police Executive Research Forum, 1983).

52. That is, the proportion of arrests, prosecutions, and convictions accounted for by the most dangerous and frequent offenders (say, the worst 10 percent) is much lower than the proportion of crimes they claim to have committed.

53. Wolfgang, Figlio, and Sellin, *Delinquency in a Birth Cohort*; I. J. McKissack, "The Peak Age for Property Crimes: Further Data," *British Journal of Criminology* 13 (1973) 253–261; Donald J. West and David P. Farrington, *Who Becomes Delinquent?* (London: Heinemann, 1973).

54. Marvin E. Wolfgang, "Crime in a Birth Cohort," in *Crime, Criminology, and Public Policy: Essays in Honour of Sir Leon Radzinowicz*, ed. Roger Hood (New

York: Free Press, 1974), 79–92; Mildred R. Chaitin and H. W. Dunham, "The Juvenile Court in Its Relationship to Adult Criminality: A Replicated Study," *Social Forces* 45 (1966) 114–119. There is evidence that this is a relatively recent phenomenon; sixty years ago 60 percent of juvenile offenders went on to accumulate criminal records as adults. Henry McKay, "Report on the Criminal Careers of Male Delinquents in Chicago," in President's Commission on Law Enforcement and Administration of Justice, *Task Force Report: Juvenile Delinquency and Youth Crime* (Washington, D.C.: U.S. Government Printing Office, 1967).

55. Thorsten Sellin, "Recidivism and Maturation," *NPPA Journal* 4 (1958), 241–250; Preben Wolf, "A Contribution to the Topology of Crime in Denmark," in *Scandinavian Studies in Criminology*, vol. 1, ed. Karl O. Christiansen (London: Tavistock, 1965); Donald J. West and David P. Farrington, *The Delinquent Way of Life* (London: Heinemann, 1977).

56. Marvin E. Wolfgang, "Crime in a Birth Cohort," *Proceedings of the American Philosophical Society* 117 (1973) 410.

57. For a succinct account of the origins of the juvenile justice system, see President's Commission on Law Enforcement and Administration of Justice, *Task Force Report: Juvenile Delinquency*.

58. This "labeling perspective" was first presented in Edwin Lemert, *Social Pathology* (New York: McGraw-Hill, 1951), and has been developed and evaluated extensively since then. See, for example, Edwin M. Schur, *Labelling Deviant Behavior: Its Sociological Significance* (New York: Harper and Row, 1971); Bernard A. Thorsell and Lloyd W. Klemke, "The Effect of Labeling upon Youths in the Juvenile Justice System: A Review of the Evidence," *Law and Society Review* 8 (1974), 583–614.

59. Wolfgang, "Crime in a Birth Cohort," *Proceedings of the American Philosophical Society* 117.

60. Radzinowicz and Hood, "Incapacitating the Habitual Criminal," 1328.

61. Norval Morris, *The Habitual Criminal* (London: London School of Economics and Political Science, 1951), 63–65.

62. Note, for example, that the courts take more time to process homicides and rapes than robberies and burglaries, as shown by Kathleen B. Brosi, *A Cross-City Comparison of Felony Case Processing* (Washington, D.C.: Institute for Law and Social Research, 1979); prosecutors take longer to prepare violent crime cases than property cases, see Brian Forst and Kathleen B. Brosi, "A Theoretical and Empirical Analysis of the Prosecutor," *Journal of Legal Studies* 6 (1977), 177–191; and police work harder to solve violent crimes, shown by Eck, *Solving Crimes.*

63. Chaiken and Chaiken, *Varieties of Criminal Behavior*, 56.

64. To get a rough handle on the proportion of offenders who might be subsumed under this definition, suppose that lambda for violent crimes were gamma-distributed with a mean of 2.0 and a skew of between 2.0 and 3.0. (These assumptions are derived from empirical estimates of offense rates obtained from both self-reports and official records. See William Spelman, "The Crime Control Effectiveness of Selective Criminal Justice Policies," in *Dealing with Dangerous Offenders*). Then two violent crimes in three years of street time, at an 8.3 percent chance of arrest per crime, implies an expected lambda of about $2/[3(.083)] = 8.0$, which is approximately four times the average lambda. For a skew of 2.0, the

probability that lambda will be greater than or equal to four times the average is about .016; for a skew of 2.5, the probability is .035; for a skew of 3.0, the probability is .050.

3. THRESHOLD OBJECTIONS TO SELECTIVE POLICIES

1. Norval Morris, *The Future of Imprisonment* (Chicago: University of Chicago Press, 1974), 62–73.

2. John Monahan, *Predicting Violent Behavior* (Beverly Hills, Calif.: Sage, 1981), 31–36.

3. Herbert Packer, *The Limits of the Criminal Sanction* (Stanford: Stanford University Press, 1968), 37–55. See also Gerald Gardiner, "The Purposes of Criminal Punishment," *Modern Law Review* 21 (1958), 117–129, 221–235; Francis A. Allen, "Criminal Justice, Legal Values and the Rehabilitative Ideal," *Journal of Criminal Law, Criminology and Police Science,* 50 (1959), 226–232; and Johannes Andenaes, "The General Preventive Effects of Punishment," *University of Pennsylvania Law Review* 114 (1966), 949–983.

4. Packer, *Limits of the Criminal Sanction,* 37–55.

5. Alan Dershowitz, "The Law of Dangerousness: Some Fictions about Predictions," *Journal of Legal Education* 23 (1970), 24–27.

6. Twentieth Century Fund Task Force on Criminal Sentencing, *Fair and Certain Punishment* (New York: McGraw-Hill, 1976), reviews both the genesis of discretionary sentencing and its effects in producing inequitable and uncertain punishment.

7. Parole boards have used actuarial techniques to measure the likelihood of recidivism since at least the late 1920s, and this practice seems to be increasing. For examples of methods used in several states, see Donald M. Gottfredson, Colleen A. Cosgrove, Leslie T. Wilkins, Jane Wallerstein, and Carol Rauh, *Classification for Parole Decision Policy* (Washington, D.C.: U.S. Government Printing Office, 1978).

8. See, for example, the "salient factor scores" described by Donald M. Gottfredson, Leslie T. Wilkins, and Peter B. Hoffman, *Guidelines For Parole and Sentencing* (Lexington, Mass.: Lexington Books, 1978).

9. For an example of such a strict position, see Ernest van den Haag, *Punishing Criminals* (New York, Basic Books, 1975).

10. The most complete and eloquent arguments supporting the notion that recedivists deserve greater punishment have been made by Andrew von Hirsch. See, generally, his *Doing Justice: Report of the Committee for the Study of Incarceration* (New York: Hill and Wang, 1976), and more specifically his recent response to critics of this notion, "Desert and Previous Convictions in Sentencing," *Minnesota Law Review* 65 (1981), 591–634.

11. For evidence on the "trajectories" of criminal ability over a lifetime career, see Marvin E. Wolfgang, "Crime in a Birth Cohort," *Proceedings of the American Philosophical Society* 117 (1973), 410.

12. Police solve between 20 and 30 percent of robberies, and between 15 and 20 percent of burglaries. U.S. Department of Justice, Federal Bureau of Investigation, *Crime in the United States,* annual (Washington, D.C.: U.S. Government Printing Office, 1975–1980). Because many crimes are not reported to the police,

and many offenders work in teams, the probability that a participant in a robbery will be arrested by police is considerably lower.

13. It would not be accepted by van den Haag. See *Punishing Criminals.*

14. Morris, *Future of Imprisonment,* 62–73.

15. Monahan, *Predicting Violent Behavior,* 58.

16. As Monahan remarks, "Rather than we know it is impossible to accurately predict violent behavior under any circumstances, I believe a more judicious assessment of the research to date is that we know very little about how accurately violent behavior may be predicted under many circumstances." Monahan, *Predicting Violent Behavior,* 37.

17. Sir Leon Radzinowicz and Roger Hood argue that the failure of selective incapacitation policies in England is rooted in the failure to be precise about who is to be included in the dangerous group—those who commit serious offenses or those who commit offenses often. See Radzinowicz and Hood, "Incapacitating the Habitual Criminal: The English Experience," *Michigan Law Review* 78 (1980), 1305–1389. Morris also sees that the great risks associated with selective incapacitation are in the "plasticity" of the concept of dangerous offenders. See Morris, *Future of Imprisonment,* 62.

18. Peter W. Greenwood and Allan Abrahamse, *Selective Incapacitation* (Santa Monica, Calif.: Rand, 1982); Kristen M. Williams, *The Scope and Prediction of Recidivism* (Washington, D.C.: Institute for Law and Social Research, 1978); Gottfredson, Wilkins, and Hoffman, *Guidelines For Parole.*

19. Donald Black, *On the Manners and Customs of the Police* (New York: Academic, 1980), 85–108.

20. See Chapter 8.

21. Eric D. Wish, Kandace A. Klumpp, Amy H. Moorer, Elizabeth Brady, and Kristen M. Williams, *An Analysis of Drugs and Crime Among Arrestees in the District of Columbia* (Washington, D.C.: U.S. Department of Justice, 1981).

22. Mark H. Moore, "Criminogenic Commodities: Drugs, Guns and Alcohol," in *Crime and Public Policy,* ed. James Q. Wilson (San Francisco: Institute for Contemporary Studies, 1983), 125–144.

23. The studies listed in Table 9 are: Ernst A. Wenk and Robert L. Emrich, "Assaultive Youth: An Exploratory Study of the Assaultive Experience and Assaultive Potential of California Youth Authority Wards," *Journal of Research in Crime and Delinquency* 9 (1972), 171–196; Ernst A. Wenk, James O. Robinson, and Gerald W. Smith, "Can Violence Be Prevented?" *Crime and Delinquency* 18 (1972), 393–402; Harry L. Kozol, Richard J. Boucher, and Ralph F. Garofalo, "The Diagnosis and Treatment of Dangerousness," *Crime and Delinquency* 18 (1972), 371–392; Terrence Murphy, *Michigan Risk Prediction: A Replication Study,* final report (Lansing, Mich.: Department of Corrections Program Bureau, 1980); Mark A. Peterson, Harriet B. Braiker, and Suzanne M. Polich, *Who Commits Crimes: A Survey of Prison Inmates* (Cambridge, Eng.: Oelgeschlager, Gunn, and Hain, 1982); Wright Williams and Kent S. Miller, "The Role of Personal Characteristics in Perceptions of Dangerousness," *Criminal Justice and Behavior* 4 (1977), 241–252; Peter B. Hoffman, Don M. Gottfredson, Leslie T. Wilkins, and Guy E. Pasela, "The Operational Use of An Experience Table," *Criminology* 12 (1974), 214–228.

24. The classic comparison of these two approaches is contained in Paul E.

Meehl, *Clinical versus Statistical Prediction: A Theoretical Analysis and a Review of the Evidence* (Minneapolis: University of Minnesota Press, 1954).

25. Evidence suggests that although clinicians are not so good as statistical models at making predictions, they are quite good at selecting the appropriate characteristics for making a prediction. See the research summarized by Robyn M. Dawes, "The Robust Beauty of Improper Linear Models in Decision Making," *American Psychologist* 34 (1979), 571–582; see also Hillel J. Einhorn, "Expert Measurement and Mechanical Combination," *Organizational Behavior And Human Performance* 7 (1972), 86–106.

26. As John Monahan states, "The principal impediment to progress in the area of prediction is that most of the difficult problems hide behind a screen of 'professional judgment.' What are we trying to predict? Assault? Property damage? No. We predict 'dangerousness.' What factors do we use in making this prediction? Race? Socioeconomic status? No. We rely on 'clinical experience.' " Monahan, *Predicting Violent Behavior*, 40.

27. In fact, all studies comparing clinical and actuarial/statistical predictions have found that statistical predictions are more accurate. Meehl, *Clinical versus Statistical Prediction*; John Sawyer, "Measurement *and* Prediction, Clinical *and* Statistical," *Psychological Bulletin* 66 (1966), 178–200; others are cited in Dawes, "Robust Beauty."

28. As Meehl illustrates, case-specific information will in some cases show convincingly that an offender who is statistically predicted to be dangerous is not dangerous at all. Paul Meehl, *Psychodiagnosis: Selected Papers* (Minneapolis: University of Minnesota Press, 1973), 85. Some psychologists—Meehl among them—argue that such useful case-specific information will exist in all cases though it may be difficult or impossible to collect and validate it through statistical analysis. Thus an individual would be punished at the same level as others in some important way. Meehl, *Psychodiagnosis*, 130; Meehl, *Clinical versus Statistical Prediction*, 20. Perhaps a more straightforward objection is that it is unjust to base an individual's punishment partly on the fact that he belongs to a group, if he has limited control of being in the group. See Barbara Underwood, "Law and the Crystal Ball: Predicting Behavior with Statistical Inference and Individualized Justice," *Yale Law Journal* 88 (1979), 1432–1447; James Q. Wilson, "The Political Feasibility of Punishment," in *Justice and Punishment*, ed. J. B. Cederblom and William L. Blizek (Cambridge, Mass.: Ballinger, 1977), 107–123.

29. See Chapter 8.

30. For an analysis of how restricted access to juvenile records and low arrest and conviction rates can reduce the value of incapacitation policies, see Mark H. Moore, James Q. Wilson, and Ralph Gants, "Violent Attitudes and Chronic Offenders," mimeographed, John F. Kennedy School of Government, 1978.

31. Groups such as youth gangs or larger networks that work through fences or organized criminal syndicates may well recruit new members to replace those in prison. Alfred Blumstein, "Research Perspectives on Selective Incapacitation as a Means of Crime Control," in *Dealing with Dangerous Offenders*, vol. 2: *Selected Papers*, ed. Daniel McGillis, Susan Estrich, Mark H. Moore, and William Spelman (Cambridge, Mass.: Harvard University, John F. Kennedy School of Government, 1983), 5–6, points out that replacement is most likely for crimes

associated with these groups, such as drug sales and property offenses. In addition, to the degree that the supply of controlled substances such as drugs is relatively inelastic, the incapacitation of old users will lead to addition of new users; if drugs are an important criminogenic commodity, a crime replacement effect will result.

32. Radzinowicz and Hood, "Incapacitating the Habitual Criminal," 1377. See also Michael E. Smith, "Alternative Forms of Punishment and Supervision for Convicted Offenders," in McGillis et al., *Dealing with Dangerous Offenders*, vol. 2.

33. Greenwood and Abrahamse, *Selective Incapacitation*, 108–118. This is strictly true only if the offenders who are imprisoned commit offenses at the same rates as those who are not. Common sense suggests that at least a few offenders never make it to jail or prison and probably commit crimes at lower rates. However, Greenwood and Abrahamse show that offenders like those incarcerated account for between 80 and 90 percent of street crimes.

34. See William Spelman, "The Crime Control Effectiveness of Selective Criminal Justice Policies," in *Dealing with Dangerous Offenders*, vol. 2: *Selected Papers*, for results of experiments with a slightly different model. One benefit of Spelman's approach is that, unlike Greenwood's, it does not require that certain unrealistic assumptions be made. They are described in Reuel Shinnar and Shlomo Shinnar, "The Effects of the Criminal Justice System on the Control of Crime: A Quantitative Approach," *Law and Society Review* 9 (1975), 581–611. The most important of Greenwood's assumptions is that the average prison sentence is short relative to the length of the average criminal career. In order to reduce robbery rates by 20 percent, the Greenwood model indicates that the average sentence for a convicted robber with a predicted high rate of offending must be increased from 2.5 years to 10.0 years; thus this assumption is pushed to (and probably beyond) its limits.

35. About 500,000 robberies are reported to the police each year; about three-fifths of reported robberies are committed against persons, about two-fifths against commercial businesses. FBI, *Crime in the United States, 1980,* 19. Not all robberies are reported; some 60 percent of robberies against persons are reported, and about 80 percent of robberies against businesses. U.S. Department of Commerce, Bureau of the Census, *Criminal Victimization In the United States, 1980* (Washington, D.C.: U.S. Government Printing Office, 1982) 71, and Census Bureau, *Criminal Victimization in the United States, 1975,* 73. Thus some 750,000 robberies are committed each year; 20 percent of this is 150,000.

36. Kathleen B. Brosi, *A Cross-City Comparison of Felony Case Processing* (Washington, D.C.: Institute for Law and Social Research, 1979); Brian Forst and Kathleen B. Brosi, "A Theoretical and Empirical Analysis of the Prosecutor," *Journal of Legal Studies* 6 (1977), 177–191; John E. Eck, *Solving Crimes: Police Investigation of Burglary and Robbery* (Washington, D.C.: Police Executive Research Forum, 1983).

37. A large majority of the most serious offenses, and particularly the stranger-to-stranger violent crimes the public finds so frightening, are committed in groups; see, for example, Maynard L. Erickson, "The Group Context of Delinquent Behavior," *Social Problems* 19 (1971), 114–129. For both theory and empir-

ical evidence of recruitment by and role assignment within the most active groups, youth gangs, see the classic study by James F. Short, Jr., and Fred L. Strodtbeck, *Group Process and Gang Delinquency* (Chicago: University of Chicago Press, 1965); Malcolm W. Klein's manual for gang workers, *Street Gangs and Street Workers* (Englewood Cliffs, N.J.: Prentice-Hall, 1971); or Joan W. Moore's case studies, *Homeboys: Gangs, Drugs and Prison in The Barrios of Los Angeles* (Philadelphia: Temple University Press, 1978).

38. This is an intuitively appealing hypothesis, but there is no direct empirical demonstration of this effect yet. All the demonstrations of an incapacitative effect are simply analytic models that assume crimes are suppressed while an offender is in jail.

39. The Rand survey results suggest that the worst 10 percent of offenders account for about 45 percent of index crimes. See Appendix B.

40. Certainly there is interest in optimizing the allocation of investigative and prosecutorial resources. See, for example, Bernard Greenberg, Carola V. Elliott, Lois P. Kraft, and H. Steven Proctor, *Felony Investigation Decision Model — An Analysis of Investigative Elements of Information* (Menlo Park, Calif.: Stanford Research Institute, 1975); John E. Eck, *Managing Case Assignments: The Burglary Investigation Decision Model Replication* (Washington, D.C.: Police Executive Research Forum, 1979); Judith S. Dahmann and James L. Lacy, *Criminal Process in Four Jurisdictions: Departures From Routine Processing in the Career Criminal Program,* Technical Report 7550 (McLean, Va.: MITRE, 1977).

41. Although the courts have taken an active part in regulating police interrogations, for example, in *Miranda* v. *Arizona,* 384 U.S. 436 (1966) and *Terry* v. *Ohio,* 392 U.S. 1 (1968), and searches and seizures, for example, *Mapp* v. *Ohio,* 367 U.S. 643 (1961), they have been silent on issues relating to postarrest investigation. If the courts' regulation of prosecutorial discretion is any indication, detectives have wide latitude to focus their efforts as they want, so long as they do not allocate resources according to a classification such as race or religion, *Oyler* v. *Boles,* 368 U.S. 448 (1962), *Yick Wo* v. *Hopkins,* 118 U.S. 356 (1886); focus on individuals for purposes of intimidating or harassing them, *United States* v. *Falk,* 479 F.2d 616 (1973), *United States* v. *Steele,* 461 F.2d 1148 (1972); or select cases arbitrarily or capriciously, *State* v. *Vadnais,* 295 Minn. 17 (1972), *People* v. *Acme Markets, Inc.,* 37 N.Y. 2d 326 (1975).

42. Many have already. See Chapters 6 and 7.

43. Smith, "Alternative Forms."

44. We are indebted to George L. Kelling and Alan Dershowitz for emphasizing this point.

4. SENTENCING

1. In nine states — California, Colorado, Connecticut, Illinois, Indiana, Maine, Minnesota, New Mexico, and North Carolina — the legislature has stripped the parole board of discretionary releasing power and required judges to pass determinate sentences. Nationwide, about 70 percent of offenders released from prison are released after serving only a portion of an indeterminate sen-

tence, however. U.S. Department of Justice, Bureau of Justice Statistics, *Probation and Parole 1982* and *Probation and Parole 1981* (Washington, D.C.: Bureau of Justice Statistics, 1983, 1982).

2. For an extensive description of the parole decision-making process in seven states and in the federal system, see Donald M. Gottfredson, Colleen A. Cosgrove, Leslie T. Wilkins, Jane Wallerstein, and Carol Rauh, *Classification for Parole Decision Policy* (Washington, D.C.: U.S. Government Printing Office, 1978).

3. The most celebrated of these is presented in Peter W. Greenwood and Allan Abrahamse, *Selective Incapacitation* (Santa Monica, Calif.: Rand, 1982).

4. Alfred Blumstein and Jacqueline Cohen, "Estimation of Individual Crime Rates from Arrest Records," *Journal of Criminal Law and Criminology* 70 (1979), 561–585; Vera Institute of Justice, *Felony Arrests: Their Prosecution and Disposition in New York City's Courts* (New York: Vera Institute, 1977).

5. Eugene Doleschal, "Rate and Length of Imprisonment: How Does the United States Compare with the Netherlands, Denmark and Sweden?" *Crime and Delinquency* 23 (1977), 52.

6. For a statement of the basic retributivist position, see Andrew von Hirsch, *Doing Justice: Report of the Committee for the Study of Incarceration* (New York: Hill and Wang, 1976). For an analysis of prison policies on almost entirely utilitarian grounds, see Alfred Blumstein, Jacqueline Cohen, and Daniel Nagin, ed. *Deterrence and Incapacitation: Estimating the Effects of Criminal Sanctions on Crime Rates* (Washington, D.C.: National Academy of Sciences, 1978).

7. Von Hirsch, *Doing Justice*, 45–55.

8. Blumstein, Cohen, and Nagin, *Deterrence and Incapacitation*, 3–14.

9. Early Christian communities justified punishment for its therapeutic value as early as the second century, A.D. See Charles Guignebert, *Ancient, Medieval, and Modern Christianity: The Development of a Religion* (New Hyde Park, N.Y.: University Books, 1961), 160.

10. Although the early deterrence theorists, notably Beccaria and Bentham, evolved their theory largely in response to the needless length and harshness of the average criminal sentence of that time, the hallmark of classical penology is that punishment should be exactly as large as needed to achieve the lowest crime rate. See Cesare Beccaria, *On Crime and Punishments* (1764; reprint ed., New York: Oxford University Press, 1964).

11. Enrico Ferri, a central figure in the "positive" school of rehabilitation, put it starkly: "The historical mission of the Classical School (the deterrence theorists) consisted in a reduction of punishment . . . We now follow up the practical and scientific mission of the classical school with a still more noble and fruitful mission by adding to the problem of the diminution of penalties the problem of the diminution of crime." Quoted in Ian Taylor, Paul Walton, and Jack Young, *The New Criminology: For a Social Theory of Deviance* (New York: Harper and Row, 1973), 10; see pp. 10–30 for more substantiation of this point.

12. The early enthusiasm for prison rehabilitation is described by W. David Lewis, *From Newgate to Dannemora: The Rise of the Penitentiary in New York, 1796–1848*, (Ithaca, N.Y.: Cornell University Press, 1965); for a more recent set of

high-minded recommendations, see President's Commission on Law Enforcement and Administration of Justice, Task Force on Corrections, *Corrections* (Washington, D.C.: U.S. Government Printing Office, 1967).

13. Robert Martinson, "What Works: Questions and Answers about Prison Reform," *The Public Interest* 35 (1974), 22–54.

14. Twentieth Century Fund Task Force on Criminal Sentencing, *Fair and Certain Punishment* (New York: McGraw-Hill, 1976).

15. See, for example, Andrew A. Bruce, "The History and Development of the Parole System in Illinois," in *The Workings of the Indeterminate Sentence Law and the Parole System in Illinois,* by Andrew A. Bruce, Ernest W. Burgess, and Albert J. Harno (Springfield: Illinois Parole Board, 1928), 54.

16. A particularly interesting proposal of this type is presented in John Monahan, "The Case for Prediction in the Modified Desert Model of Criminal Sentencing," *International Journal of Law and Psychiatry* 5 (1982), 103–113.

17. Joan Mullen, Kenneth Carlson, and Bradford Smith, *American Prisons and Jails,* vol. 1: *Summary Findings and Policy Implications of a National Survey* (Washington, D.C.: National Institute of Justice, 1980).

18. See Michael Sherman, "Strategic Planning and Focused Imprisonment," in *Dealing with Dangerous Offenders:* vol. 2, *Selected Papers,* ed. Daniel McGillis, Susan M. Estrich, Mark H. Moore, and William Spelman (Cambridge, Mass.: John F. Kennedy School of Government, 1983); see also Michael Sherman and Gordon Hawkins, *Imprisonment in America* (Chicago, University of Chicago Press, 1981).

19. Sherman and Hawkins, *Imprisonment in America,* 109.

20. Sherman and Hawkins, *Imprisonment in America,* 110.

21. Sherman and Hawkins, *Imprisonment in America,* 110.

22. Peter Greenwood, "Trade-Offs Between Prediction Accuracy and Selective Incapacitation Effects," in McGillis, et al., *Dealing with Dangerous Offenders.*

23. Greenwood and Abrahamse, *Selective Incapacitation,* 50.

24. *Williams* v. *New York,* 337 U.S. 241, 247 (1949).

25. *Pennsylvania* v. *Ashe,* 302 U.S. 51, 55 (1937).

26. *Williams* v. *New York,* 337 U.S. 241, 247 (1949).

27. Whether or not *Williams* remains good law in the death penalty area, its approach and reasoning were cited with approval and relied upon as recently as 1978, in *United States* v. *Grayson,* 438 U.S. 41, where the Court upheld a trial judge's discretion to increase a sentence (within statutory limits) based on his judgment that the defendant had lied during his trial.

28. Marvin E. Frankel, *Criminal Sentences: Law without Order* (New York: Hill and Wang, 1973), 21.

29. California, Florida, Louisiana, and Tennessee included mandatory statutes for drug offenders. Idaho, Iowa, Maine, Montana, New Mexico, Ohio, Tennessee, and West Virginia took similar action for repeat offenders. Violent offenses such as kidnaping, arson, rape, murder, and armed robbery were singled out for mandatory sentences in Arkansas, Arizona, California, Illinois, Iowa, Kansas, Louisiana, Montana, Nevada, New Mexico, North Carolina, Ohio, Oregon, and Tennessee. Twenty-seven states now have mandatory sentencing laws,

including the following enacted in 1977 and 1978: for drug offenders, Hawaii and Iowa; repeat offenders, Alabama, Arizona, Florida, Louisiana, Maryland, Mississippi, Nebraska, New Hampshire, New York, North Carolina, and Texas. Nicholas N. Kittrie and Elyce H. Zenoff, *Sanctions, Sentencing, and Corrections* (Mineola, N.Y.: Foundation Press, 1981), 539.

30. See Ernest Van den Haag, *Punishing Criminals: Concerning a Very Old and Painful Question* (New York: Basic Books, 1973), 194.

31. See, for example, *Coker* v. *Georgia*, 433 U.S. 584 (1977): rapist cannot be sentenced to capital punishment.

32. See *Rummel* v. *Estelle*, 445 U.S. 263 (1980), life sentence upheld for three-time petty thief; *Hutto* v. *Davis*, 102 S. Ct. 703, 454 U.S. 370 (1982), forty-year sentence upheld for possession of marijuana with intent to distribute.

33. Greenwood and Abrahamse, *Selective Incapacitation*, 79–80.

34. Jan M. Chaiken and Marcia R. Chaiken, *Varieties of Criminal Behavior* (Santa Monica, Calif.: Rand, 1982), 113–117.

35. Gottfredson et. al., *Classification for Parole*.

36. Edward Green, *Judicial Attitudes in Sentencing: A Study of the Factors Underlying the Sentencing Practices of the Criminal Court of Philadelphia* (London: Macmillan, 1961).

37. Edward Green, "Inter and Intra-Racial Crime Relative to Sentencing," *Journal of Criminal Law, Criminology and Police Science* 55 (1964), 348–358.

38. Barbara L. Johnston, Nicholas P. Miller, Ronald Schoenberg, and Laurence Ross Weatherly, "Discretion in Felony Sentencing: A Study of Influencing Factors," *Washington Law Review* 48 (1973), 857–880.

39. Lawrence P. Tiffany, Yakov Avichai, and Geoffrey W. Peters, "A Statistical Analysis of Sentencing in Federal Courts: Defendants Convicted after Trial, 1967–1968," *Journal of Legal Studies* 4 (1975), 369–390.

40. Peter W. Greenwood, Sorrel Wildhorn, Eugene Poggio, Michael Strumwasser, and Peter De Leon, *Prosecution of Adult Felony Defendants* (Santa Monica, Calif.: Rand, 1976); Johnston et al., "Discretion in Felony Sentencing."

41. Charles J. Judson, James J. Pandell, Jack B. Owens, James L. McIntosh, and Dale L. Matschullat, "A Study of the California Penalty Jury in First Degree Murder Cases," *Stanford Law Review* 21 (1969), 1297–1497.

42. Green, *Judicial Attitudes*. Judson et al., "California Penalty Jury."

43. James Eisenstein and Herbert Jacob, *Felony Justice: An Organizational Analysis of Criminal Courts* (Boston: Little, Brown, 1977).

44. Tom Hawkinson, "The Effect of Pre-Trial Release, Race, and Previous Arrest on Conviction and Sentencing," *Creighton Law Review* 8 (1975), 930–937.

45. Johnston et al., "Discretion in Felony Sentencing."

46. A discussion of the genesis of the parole system in Illinois, written in 1928, is instructive: "When fixed sentences alone are imposed [offenders] rely not merely upon the probability that perhaps a lesser plea will be accepted, but on the kindheartedness of the individual judge and on the appeal that may be made to him by family and often political influences . . . So, too, usually at the trial and almost always where a plea of guilty is entertained, there is no inquiry into or an opportunity to investigate the prior record of the defendant, his past crimes, or

his associates . . . So, too, any system which places the discretion entirely in the trial judge must result in glaring inconsistencies and in a rankling sense of injustice." Bruce, "History and Development," 51, 54.

47. In Illinois the average felony sentence served increased from 1.5 to 2.1 years after parole was introduced. Bruce, "History and Development," 49.

48. Consider this turn-of-the-century description of a determinate sentence law that had been recently scrapped in favor of an indeterminate parole system: "The old law was as vicious a piece of legislation as was ever enacted. It was vicious because its enforcement gave the most gross inequality in sentences . . . It was vicious because it gave the habitual offenders a short sentence while the first offender most frequently received a long term." Quoted in Bruce, "History and Development," 53. Ironically, one of the reasons California replaced its indeterminate sentencing statutes with a determinate sentence law was a widespread feeling that the parole boards were letting habitual or serious offenders off with inadequate sentences. Messinger and Johnson, "California's Determinate Sentence," 21–24.

49. Terrence Murphy, "Michigan Risk Prediction: A Replication Study," Final Report no. AP-0 (Lansing: Michingan Department of Corrections, 1980).

50. Michael Smith, "Alternative Forms of Punishment and Supervision for Convicted Offenders," in McGillis et. al., Dealing with Dangerous Offenders.

51. In New York City the Vera Institute of Justice currently administers a program of 1,000 community service sentences each year. Those sentenced to the program have an average of seven prior adult arrests and more than four prior adult convictions. Fifty-eight percent were arraigned on felony charges, and 45 percent had been sentenced to jail or prison on their last conviction. The program requires community service work in a supervised framework. For those who fail to comply, jail is an immediate and direct prospect, which is not the case for offenders on probation. So far, only 10 percent of those assigned to the program have failed to complete it, and everyone in that 10 percent was resentenced to a jail term. See Vera Institute of Justice, The New York Community Service Sentencing Project: Development of the Bronx Pilot Project (New York: Vera Institute of Justice, 1981).

5. PRETRIAL DETENTION

1. For example, see Attorney General's Task Force on Violent Crime, Final Report (Washington, D.C.: U.S. Department of Justice, 1981), pp. 50–53; American Bar Association, Criminal Justice Section, Task Force on Crime, Final Report to the Association (Washington, D.C.: American Bar Association, 1981), 11–13.

2. California Assembly, Committee on Criminal Justice, Analysis of Proposition 8: The Criminal Justice Initiative (Sacramento: California Legislature, 1982), 22–27.

3. Hudson v. Parker, 156 U.S. 277 (1895), 285; Stack v. Boyle, 342 U.S. 1 (1951), 2.

4. See generally Daniel J. Freed and Patricia M. Wald, Bail in the United States, 1964 (Washington, D.C.: U.S. Department of Justice and Vera Institute, 1964).

5. Lazar Institute, *Pretrial Release, A National Evaluation of Practices and Outcomes: Summary and Policy Analysis* (Washington, D.C.: U.S. Government Printing Office, 1981), 10–11.

6. As of May 1982, twenty-nine states were operating either individual jails and prisons or entire prison systems under orders from federal judges to remedy existing conditions. Most judges cited crowding, lack of adequate medical care and sanitation and poorly trained, violent staff in declaring these states in violation of the Eighth Amendment right to freedom from cruel and unusual punishment. See Wendell Rawls, Jr., "Judges' Authority in Prison Reform Attacked," *New York Times*, May 18, 1982, 1. For more complete information on the situation in April 1980, see Joan Mullen, Kenneth Carlson, and Bradford Smith, *American Prisons and Jails* vol. I: *Summary and Policy Implications of a National Survey* (Washington, D.C.: U.S. Government Printing Office, 1980), 35–36.

7. Lazar Institute, *Pretrial Release*, 6.

8. Lazar Institute, *Pretrial Release*, 7.

9. Lazar Institute, *Pretrial Release*, 16, 20.

10. Lazar Institute, *Pretrial Release*, 15.

11. Lazar Institute, *Pretrial Release*, 20.

12. Attorney General's Task Force, *Final Report*, 50–53.

13. See American Bar Association, *Final Report*, 11–13. The District of Columbia's preventive detention statute is reviewed in Nan C. Bases and William F. McDonald, *Preventive Detention in the District of Columbia: The First Ten Months* (New York: Vera Institute of Justice, 1972).

14. See Kenneth Feinberg, "Promoting Accountability in Making Bail Decisions: Congressional Efforts at Bail Reform," in *Dealing with Dangerous Offenders*, vol. 2: Selected Papers, ed. Daniel McGillis, Susan M. Estrich, Mark H. Moore, and William Spelman (Cambridge, Mass.: John F. Kennedy School of Government, 1983), for a discussion of the Criminal Code Reform Act of 1981. Senators Strom Thurmond and Joseph Biden introduced S. 2572 on May 26, 1982. The bill was designed to amend the Bail Reform Act of 1966 and to allow for consideration of dangerousness in setting bail. On the same day Rep. Robert McClory introduced H.R. 6497, which was identical to S. 2572. The bills would require hearings to decide on pretrial detention.

15. See *The Pretrial Reporter* 6 (December 1982), 4, for a discussion of the Illinois and Colorado referenda.

16. *Pretrial Reporter* 6 (July 1982), 5; *Pretrial Reporter* 6 (September 1982), 4.

17. This proposal has been adopted explicitly in Philadelphia, where judges set bail according to a schedule that rates the risks of flight or pretrial arrest. See John Goldkamp, "Room for Improvement in Pretrial Decisionmaking: The Development of Judicial Bail Guidelines in Philadelphia," in McGillis et al., *Dealing with Dangerous Offenders*.

18. California Assembly, *Analysis of Proposition 8*, 22.

19. California Assembly, *Analysis of Proposition 8*, 22; emphasis added.

20. State of Wisconsin, *Amendments to Wisconsin Statutes* (1982), chapter 969.

21. John Goldkamp, Michael Gottfredson, and Susan Mitchell-Herzfeld, *Bail Decisionmaking: A Study of Policy Guidelines* (Washington, D.C.: National Institute of Corrections, 1981).

22. Goldkamp, "Room for Improvement," reviews the guidelines study. See also Goldkamp, Gottfredson, and Mitchell-Herzfeld, *Bail Decisionmaking.*

23. Daniel Freed, "Dangerous Offenders and the Bail Process: Protecting Public Safety without Preventive Detention," unpublished manuscript, Yale University, 1982, provides an interesting discussion of improved approaches to establishing conditions of release, including the notion of having respected individuals serve as sureties for defendants.

24. Freed, "Dangerous Offenders and the Bail Process." See also John Goldkamp, *Two Classes of Accused: A Study of Bail and Detention in American Justice* (Cambridge, Mass.: Ballinger, 1979), 15–31, for a discussion of this issue.

25. See *Pretrial Reporter* 6 (March 1982), 13, for a discussion of this issue.

26. Chief Justice Frederick M. Vinson noted in the majority opinion in *Stack* v. *Boyle,* 342 U.S. 1 (1951), at 5, "Like the ancient practice of securing the oaths of responsible persons to stand as sureties for the accused, the modern practice of requiring a bail bond or the deposit of a sum of money subject to forfeiture serves as an additional assurance of the presence of an accused. Bail set at a figure higher than an amount reasonably calculated to fulfill this purpose is 'excessive' under the Eighth Amendment." However, the Court replied explicitly on legislatively determined rules in making its decision, and at the time federal rules justified bail *only* on the grounds that it helped ensure the presence of the defendant. (p. 5). Thus denial of bail under a preventive detention statute was not precluded; in fact, in June 1984 the Supreme Court ruled that preventive detention laws *are* permissible in juvenile cases. *Schall* v. *Martin,* No. 82-1248, slip. op. Because the Court relied heavily on the juvenile court's "special status," however, it is doubtful that the ruling will apply to preventive detention of adults.

27. Goldkamp, *Two Classes of Accused,* 16–17.

28. Caleb Foote, "The Coming Constitutional Crisis in Bail: I, " *University of Pennsylvania Law Review* 113 (1965), 959–999; Neil Fabricant, "Bail as a Preferred Freedom and the Failures of New York's Revision," *Buffalo Law Review* 18 (1968), 303–315.

29. *United States* v. *Edwards,* 430 A.2d 1321, *cert.* denied, 102 S.Ct. 1721, 455 U.S. 1022 (1982).

30. *United States* v. *Edwards,* 1330–1331.

31. *United States* v. *Edwards,* 1331–1343.

32. The preventive detention amendment had been upheld by the Supreme Court of Nebraska in *Parker* v. *Roth,* 278 NW 2d 106 (1979). See also *Murphy* v. Hunt, 648 F.2d 1148, *cert.* denied, 102 S.Ct. 1181 455 U.S. 478 (1982).

33. *Hunt* v. *Roth,* 648 F. 2d 1148, 1981.

34. *Murphy* v. *Hunt,* 102 S.Ct. 1181, at 1182.

35. *Pretrial Reporter* 6 (March 1982), 13.

36. Lazar Institute, *Pretrial Release,* 20.

37. Lazar Institute, *Pretrial Release,* 21.

38. Jeffrey A. Roth and Paul B. Wice, *Pretrial Release and Misconduct in the District of Columbia* (Washington, D.C.: Institute for Law and Social Research, 1980).

39. Goldkamp, "Room for Improvement," 11.

40. Mary A. Toborg, "Potential Value of Increased Selectivity in Pretrial De-

tention Decisions," in McGillis et al., *Dealing with Dangerous Offenders*, vol. 2, p. 24.

41. Toborg, "Potential Value," 2.

42. Goldkamp, "Room for Improvement," 11.

43. Toborg, "Potential Value," 4.

44. *U.S. News and World Report*, Feb. 22, 1982, 38.

45. Feinberg, "Promoting Accountability," 7.

46. Several of these studies are cited in Goldkamp, Gottfredson, and Mitchell-Herzfeld, *Bail Decision-Making.*

47. Roth and Wice, "Pretrial Release and Misconduct".

48. Roth and Wice, "Pretrial Release and Misconduct," 63–64.

49. Roth and Wice, "Pretrial Release and Misconduct," 64–65.

50. Roth and Wice, "Pretrial Release and Misconduct," 64–65.

51. Donald E. Pryor, *Program Practices: Release* (Washington, D.C.: Pretrial Services Resource Center, 1982), quoted in Toborg, "Potential Value," 7.

52. Pryor, *Program Practices*, quoted in Toborg, "Potential Value," 7.

53. Goldkamp, Gottfredson, and Mitchell-Herzfeld, *Bail Decisionmaking.*

54. See Lazar Institute, *Pretrial Release*, for an examination of the pattern of bail crime over time.

55. Attorney General's Task Force, *Final Report*, also recommends harsher sentences for persons convicted of jumping bail.

56. Freed, "Dangerous Offenders."

6. PROSECUTION

1. See generally Frank Miller, *Prosecution: The Decision to Charge a Suspect with a Crime* (Boston: Little, Brown, 1969); Arthur Rosett and Donald Cressey, *Justice by Consent* (Philadelphia: Lippincott, 1976); Kenneth Culp Davis, *Discretionary Justice* (Baton Rouge: Louisiana State University Press, 1969); and James Vorenberg, "Narrowing the Discretion of Criminal Justice Officials," *Duke Law Journal* (1976), 651–697.

2. See James Vorenberg, "Decent Restraint of Prosecutorial Power," *Harvard Law Review* 94 (1981), 1521–1573. Vorenberg notes (p. 1539) "It says something about the wide berth the judiciary has given prosecutorial power that the leading case invalidating an exercise of prosecutorial discretion is the nearly century-old decision in *Yick Wo* v. *Hopkins.*" Thus only the most invidious policies and decisions are invalidated. Vorenberg continues (p. 1540), "Unless based on a constitutionally impermissible criterion such as race, sex, or exercise of first amendment rights, the exercise of prosecutorial discretion has been routinely upheld by the courts." See, for example, *United States* v. *Batchelder*, 442 U.S. 114 (1979), 123–124.

3. See generally Philip J. Cardinale and Steven Feldman, "The Federal Courts and the Right of Nondiscriminatory Administration of the Criminal Law: A Critical View," *Syracuse Law Review* 29 (1978), 659–692; Vorenberg, "Decent Restraint," states (p. 1542), "In any event, the problems involved in proving that a prosecutor had an impermissible motive or personal animus are enormous. Rarely will a prosecutor explicitly signal improper motives. Unless he does, the

defendant must try to draw a clear inference of discrimination by comparing his case with those of persons who were not charged, at which point he is met with the almost unbroken line of cases upholding a prosecutor's discretion to determine whom and how he will charge."

4. Joan Jacoby has conducted a series of studies exploring the varying philosophies of prosecutors' offices. See, for example, Jacoby, *The Prosecutor's Charging Decision: A Policy Perspective* (Washington D.C.: U.S. Government Printing Office, 1977), and Jacoby, *Prosecutorial Decision Making* (Washington D.C.: U.S. Government Printing Office, 1982).

5. The President's Task Force on Victims of Crime, *Final Report* (Washington, D.C.: U.S. Government Printing Office, 1982), documents the prosecutor's need for close cooperation with victims and suggests strategies for improving such cooperation. Research by the Vera Institute of Justice has illustrated the high attrition of felony prosecutions because of noncooperation of victims. See Vera Institute of Justice, *Felony Arrests: Their Prosecution and Disposition in New York City's Courts* (New York: Vera Institute of Justice, 1977).

6. Andrew von Hirsch, speech given in Denver, Colorado, Nov. 10, 1983.

7. The prosecutor must be satisfied that a case meets a standard of "probable cause" before he initiates a prosecution. Given the discretionary judgment involved in such a decision, differences routinely occur in individual prosecutors' assessments of specific cases. Most observers would be likely to agree upon cases that are highly frivolous and without merit; the difficulties arise when one moves from cases on the margin to ones that are less flagrantly frivolous but still far from clear candidates for charging.

8. The impact of resource constraints upon prosecutorial selectivity in case processing is discussed in Jacoby, *Prosecutorial Decision Making*. Vorenberg, "Decent Restraint of Prosecutorial Power" notes (p. 1543), "Funding levels determine how many cases can be brought and inevitably force prosecutors' offices to give little or no attention to many chargeable crimes."

9. The Institute for Law and Social Research (INSLAW) conducted an intensive study of patterns of case processing in the District of Columbia's court system, and their research notes that the seriousness of the offense and strength of the evidence are critically important. See Institute for Law and Social Research, *Curbing the Repeat Offender: A Strategy for Prosecutors* (Washington, D.C.: U.S. Government Printing Office, 1977).

10. See Peter Greenwood, Sorrel Wildhorn, Eugene Poggio, Michael Strumwasser, and Peter De Leon, *Prosecution of Adult Felony Defendants in Los Angeles County: A Policy Perspective* (Santa Monica, Calif.: Rand, 1973), for a discussion of the differential resources provided for felony prosecution in one jurisdiction.

11. See Institute for Law and Social Research, *Case Screening,* briefing paper no. 2 (Washington, D.C.: INSLAW, 1976), and *Uniform Case Evaluation and Rating,* briefing paper no. 3 (Washington, D.C.: INSLAW, 1976). The Law Enforcement Assistance Administration funded many case screening practices.

12. Institute for Law and Social Research, *Curbing the Repeat Offender,* 17.

13. Such statistics are calculated only after elimination of cases that do not proceed to disposition. Case attrition is substantial. For example, the INSLAW study of case processing in Washington indicated that "of all felonies received by

prosecutors in 1973, 23 percent were refused prosecution; 30 percent, nolled or dismissed; 2 percent ignored by the grand jury; 3 percent found not guilty; and 31 percent found or pled guilty. (About 12 percent were still open by the end of 1973.)" INSLAW, *Curbing the Repeat Offender,* 15. Over 90 percent of cases proceeding to disposition in Washington, D.C., resulted in convictions but far less than half of the cases proceed to disposition. The large amount of case attrition raised questions about prosecutorial effectiveness.

14. Only 15 percent of a sample of 75,661 felony arrest cases resulted in a felony conviction and "only 4 percent went to disposition without a reduction or dismissal of the original charge or acquittal at trial."Vera Institute, *Felony Arrests, rests,* 6. Only 9 percent of guilty pleas resulted in felony time sentences (of over one year) in the Vera Institute sample (p. 134). Following guilty pleas in 41,488 cases, 3,675 defendants received felony time; 16,421 received misdemeanor time of less than one year. Following trials in 1,744 cases, 136 defendants received felony time and 271 defendants received misdemeanor time (p. 7).

15. Vera Institute, *Felony Arrests,* 19–20.

16. See Edward Banfield and Martin Anderson, "Court Processing in Chicago," mimeographed, Harvard University, Department of Government, 1968.

17. Witnesses become weary of repeating their story to the numerous prosecutors in a horizontal prosecution structure. Institute for Law and Social Research, *Curbing the Repeat Offender,* reports (p. 15) that "according to prosecutors, witness noncooperation accounted for nearly 40 percent of the cases refused prosecution or subsequently dropped by prosecutors or dismissed by the court."

18. James McMullin, *The Development of the Career Criminal Concept,* paper presented at the Career Criminal Workshop, National Institute of Justice, 1979, provides an excellent account of how defendants can take advantage of the many weaknesses of the criminal justice system. The particular problem of delay has been studied intensively in recent years by the National Center for State Courts. See Thomas Church, *The Pace of Justice: Court Delay in Urban Trial Courts* (Williamsburg, Va.: National Center for State Courts, 1980).

19. For a review of the history and scope of federal support of such programs, see Eleanor Chelimsky and Judith Dahmann, *Career Criminal Program National Evaluation: Final Report* (Washington, D.C.: U.S. Government Printing Office, 1981); and Andrew Halper and Daniel McGillis, *The Major Offense Bureau: An Exemplary Project* (Washington, D.C.: U.S. Government Printing Office, 1977). The Halper and McGillis report presents a summary of the characteristics of the first nineteen career criminal programs.

20. See Joan Petersilia and Martin Lavin, *Targeting Career Criminals: A Developing Criminal Justice Strategy* (Santa Monica, Calif.: Rand, 1978), for a discussion of major program goals.

21. Peter Greenwood, "Career Criminal Prosecution: Potential Objectives," *Journal of Criminal Law and Criminology* 71 (1980), 85–88, provides an interesting discussion of collateral goals of career criminal programs, such as improvement of general office morale.

22. A detailed discussion of the selection criteria is presented in William Rhodes, Herbert Tyson, James Weekley, Catherine Conly, and Gustave Powell, *Developing Criteria for Identifying Career Criminals* (Washington, D.C.: INSLAW,

1982). Halper and McGillis, *Major Offense Bureau*, provides a summary of the case selection criteria used in nineteen career criminal programs.

23. See Debra Whitcomb, *Major Violator Unit, San Diego, California: An Exemplary Project* (Washington, D.C.: U.S. Government Printing Office, 1980), for a discussion of the variations in selection criteria among major career programs, including Dallas, San Diego, and New Orleans.

24. See Halper and McGillis, *Major Offense Bureau*, for a discussion of the impact of open discovery procedures.

25. See Chelimsky and Dahmann, *Career Criminal Program*, for a discussion of the impacts of plea bargaining restrictions. See also Office of Criminal Justice Planning, *California Career Criminal Prosecution Program: Second Annual Report to the Legislature* (Sacramento, Calif.: Office of Criminal Justice Planning, 1980).

26. The Bronx County, New York, District Attorney's Office reported favorable results with this procedure. Halper and McGillis, *Major Offense Bureau*, 24–28.

27. Efforts to encourage assistance from victims and witnesses have been supplemented in many prosecutors' offices by victim-witness assistance units, which provide a wide variety of services to victims and seek to reduce case attrition, as discussed earlier in this chapter. See, for example, American Bar Association, Section of Criminal Justice, Victim Witness Assistance Project, *Bar Leadership on Victim Witness Assistance* (Washington, D.C.: American Bar Association, 1980).

28. Detailed workload data are available for the career criminal programs in California. See Office of Criminal Justice Planning, *California Career Criminal Prosecution*. In some programs the caseloads of career criminal unit attorneys are only one-fourth as large as those of attorneys in other felony divisions of the office.

29. Judith Dahmann and James Lacy have published four case study reports assessing career criminal program departures for routine case processing and illustrating procedures used to increase the likelihood of pretrial detention of defendants. See Dahmann and Lacy, *Targeted Prosecution: The Career Criminal — Orleans Parish, Louisiana; San Diego County, California; Franklin County (Columbus), Ohio, and Kalamazoo County, Michigan* (McLean, Va.: MITRE, 1977).

30. Some projects have used *crime-specific criteria*. For example, the San Diego program focused upon robbery suspects. To qualify as a career criminal the suspect must also have had a prior robbery conviction (or related conviction) or currently be charged with committing three or more separate robberies at different times and places. It is not clear that the suspects selected for this program would be drawn from the persistent, high-rate offender pool recommended by our criteria in Chapter 2. Some other programs have used *offender history criteria*. For example, the New Orleans project required that to be considered a career criminal a suspect currently charged with either a felony or a misdemeanor must have either two prior felony convictions or five prior felony arrests. These criteria also do not guarantee that violent, persistent, high-rate offenders would be selected. The prior felony convictions could be for nonviolent offenses. Furthermore, the use of arrest data for screening poses serious problems. A third screening approach commonly used involves the *weighted combination of factors* dealing

with the offense, the offender, and the evidence. Some programs (for example, Dallas) even handle cases against first offenders if the crime is sufficiently serious. Kristen Williams, "Selection Criteria for Career Criminal Programs," paper presented at the Career Criminal Workshop, National Institute of Justice, 1979, has discussed the critical importance of using criteria that stress serious repeat offending. Brian Forst, "The Prosecutor's Case Selection Problem: Career Criminals and Other Concerns," in *Dealing with Dangerous Offenders*, vol. 2, *Selected Papers*, ed. Daniel McGillis, Susan Estrich, Mark H. Moore, and William Spelman (Cambridge, Mass.: John F. Kennedy School of Government, 1983), underscored the problems with career criminal selection criteria: "The current procedures for dealing with repeat offenders, which use arbitrary selection criteria and which feature the 'career criminal' unit as a centerpiece, may be largely ceremonial, ineffective, and costly."

31. See the discussion of Vorenberg, "Decent Restraint," in note 2, above.

32. See notes 2 and 3, above.

33. John S. Bartolomeo, "Practitioners' Attitudes toward the Career Criminal Program," *Journal of Criminal Law and Criminology* 71 (1980), 113–117.

34. Chelimsky and Dahmann, *Career Criminal Program.*

35. Office of Criminal Justice Planning, *California Career Criminal Prosecution.*

36. Greenwood, "Career Criminal Prosecution."

37. See, for example, Brian Forst, "The Prosecutor's Case Selection Problem: 'Career Criminals' and Other Concerns," in McGillis et al., *Dealing with Dangerous Offenders;* and Floyd Feeney, "Prosecutorial Selectivity: A View of Current Practices," in McGillis et al., *Dealing with Dangerous Offenders.*

38. Williams, "Selection Criteria."

39. Williams, "Selection Criteria," 93.

40. Table 17 is based on information provided in Rhodes et al., *Developing Criteria.*

41. Floyd Feeney, Forrest Dill, and Adrianne Weir, *Arrests without Convictions: How Often Do They Occur and Why,* final report (Davis, Calif.: University of California, Center on Administration of Criminal Justice, 1982), 129–168.

42. Feeney, Dill, and Weir, *Arrests without Convictions.*

43. Because our estimate of the present effectiveness of the average prosecutor's office is a distribution rather than a point, and because our estimate of the effects of selective policies on prosecutorial effectiveness is also a distribution, there is no avoiding considerable uncertainty as to the benefits of selective policies. These are vague judgments, but they may be specified more precisely to aid in decision making; for an excellent description of a technique for doing this — decision analysis — see Howard Raiffa, *Decision Analysis: Introductory Lectures on Choices under Uncertainty* (Reading, Mass.: Addison-Wesley, 1970).

7. POLICE PRACTICES

1. For a further discussion of this issue, see Mark H. Moore, "Invisible Offenses: A Challenge to Minimally Intrusive Law Enforcement," in *ABSCAM Ethics: Moral Issues and Deception in Law Enforcement,* ed. Gerald M. Caplan (Washington, D.C.: Police Foundation, 1983), 17–42.

2. Moore, "Invisible Offenses," 29–30.

3. For a discussion of the current, largely unenthusiastic response of the criminal justice system to white-collar crime, see John E. Conklin, *"Illegal but not Criminal": Business Crime in America* (Englewood Cliffs, N.J., Prentice-Hall, 1977) and Herbert Edelhertz, *The Nature, Impact and Prosecution of White-Collar Crime* (Washington, D.C.: U.S. Government Printing Office, 1970). There is considerable evidence that the public considers white-collar crimes to be considerably more important than criminal justice agencies do. See, for example, Peter H. Rossi, Emily Waite, Christine E. Bose, and Richard E. Berk, "The Seriousness of Crimes: Normative Structure and Individual Differences," *American Sociological Review* 39 (1974), 224–237.

4. Donald Black, *The Manners and Customs of the Police* (New York: Academic Press, 1980).

5. Although this proposition squares with most people's scenario of the typical index crime, there is evidence that in most cases the victim and the offender are similar in social status. According to the Census Bureau's Victimization Survey, for example, two-thirds of violent crimes are committed by an offender of the same race as the victim; two-thirds of the personal offenses committed against youths are committed by youths; upward of 70 percent of crimes committed against adults are committed by one or more adults. U.S. Department of Commerce, Bureau of the Census, *Criminal Victimization in the United States—1980* (Washington, D.C.: U.S. Government Printing Office, 1982), 51. Moreover, the offender is frequently known to the victim. 17 percent of all robberies, 34 percent of all rapes, and 41 percent of all assaults are committed by friends, relatives, or other acquaintances of the victim. Census Bureau, *Criminal Victimization—1980,* 44. Although victimization survey data are not available for burglaries, New York City arrest data, reported in Vera Institute of Justice, *Felony Arrests: Their Prosecution and Disposition in New York City's Courts* (New York: Vera Institute, 1977), 86–89, suggest that the proportion of burglaries committed by offenders known to the victims is similar to the proportion for robberies, around 17 percent.

6. This view is most frequently advanced in connection with discussions of undue use of force by police. See, for example, William A. Westly, "Violence and the Police," *American Journal of Sociology* 59 (1953), 34–41; Albert J. Reiss, Jr., "Police Brutality—Answers to Key Questions," in *Crime, Criminology and Contemporary Society,* ed. Richard D. Knudten (Homewood, Ill.: Dorsey, 1970), 225–238.

7. Floyd Feeney, "Case Processing and Police-Prosecutor Relations" (mimeographed, 1981); and Peter W. Greenwood, Jan M. Chaiken, and Joan Petersilia, *The Criminal Investigation Process* (Lexington, Mass.: Lexington Books, 1977).

8. John E. Eck, *Solving Crimes: The Investigation of Burglary and Robbery* (Washington, D.C.: Police Executive Research Forum, 1983), 242–244.

9. Jerome E. McElroy, Colleen A. Cosgrove, and Michael Farrell, *Felony Case Preparation: Quality Counts* (New York: Vera Institute of Justice, 1981). See also Feeney, "Case Processing," Brian Forst, *Arrest Convictability as a Measure of Police Performance: Executive Summary* (Washington, D.C.: Institute for Law and Social Research, 1981); and Eck, *Solving Crimes,* 225–228.

10. Note, for example, that 17 percent of reported robberies are committed by a friend, relative, or other acquaintance, but 36 percent of robbery *arrests* are of friends, relatives, and acquaintances. Census Bureau, *Criminal Victimization—1980*, 44, 72; Vera Institute, *Felony Arrests*, 65.

11. Joan Petersilia, Peter W. Greenwood, and Marvin Lavin, *Criminal Careers of Habitual Felons* (Santa Monica, Calif.: Rand, 1977), 113; Mark A. Peterson, Harriet B. Braiker, and Suzanne M. Polich, *Doing Crime: A Survey of California Prison Inmates* (Santa Monica, Calif.: Rand, 1980), 79.

12. Petersilia, Greenwood, and Lavin, *Criminal Careers*, 36–37; Peterson, Braiker, and Polich, *Doing Crime*, 56.

13. Mary Ann Wycoff, Charles E. Brown, and Robert E. Petersen, *Birmingham Anti-Robbery Unit Evaluation Report*, mimeographed draft (Washington, D.C.: Police Foundation, 1980). The hypothesis is also substantiated by the author's observations of police practices and discussions with police officers.

14. Eck, *Solving Crimes*, 268–269.

15. Wycoff, Brown, and Peterson, *Birmingham Anti-Robbery Unit*.

16. This program was described by John Riech, Manhattan assistant district attorney, in an advisory group meeting of the Conference on Public Danger, Dangerousness, and the Criminal Justice System, at Harvard University, October 30, 1981.

17. This strategy was tried with some modest success. See John E. Boydstun, *San Diego Field Interrogation: Final Report* (Washington, D.C.: Police Foundation, 1975).

18. John E. Eck, "Investigative Strategies for Identifying Dangerous Repeat Offenders," in *Dealing with Dangerous Offenders*, vol. 2, *Selected Papers*, ed. Daniel McGillis, Susan Estrich, Mark H. Moore, and William Spelman (Cambridge, Mass.: John F. Kennedy School of Government, 1983), at 18–19.

19. We are indebted to George Kelling for this idea. This was also a key part of England's efforts to incapacitate dangerous offenders. See Sir Leon Radzinowicz and Roger Hood, "Incapacitating the Habitual Criminal: The English Experience," *Michigan Law Review* 78 (August 1980), 1336–1352.

20. The sources listed in Table 18 are: Tony Pate, Robert A. Bowers, and Ron Parks, *Three Approaches to Criminal Apprehension in Kansas City: An Evaluation Report* (Washington, D.C.: Police Foundation, 1976); Eleanor Chelimsky and Judith Dahmann, *Career Criminal Program National Evaluation: Final Report* (Washington, D.C.: U.S. Government Printing Office, 1981); John E. Boydstun, Richard L. Mekemson, Margaret E. Minton, and Ward Keesling, *Evaluation of the San Diego Police Department's Career Criminal Program* (San Diego, Calif.: Systems Development Corporation, 1981); McElroy, Cosgrove, and Farrell, *Felony Case Preparation*; William G. Gay, "The Police Role in Serious Habitual Offender Incapacitation: A Working Paper," in *Dealing with Dangerous Offenders*, vol. 2: *Selected Papers*, ed. Daniel McGillis, Susan Estrich, Mark H. Moore, and William Spelman (Cambridge, Mass.: John F. Kennedy School of Government, Harvard University, 1983); Eck, *Solving Crimes*. *Michigan Law Review* 78 (August 1980), 1336–1352.

21. See generally McElroy, Cosgrove, and Farrell, *Felony Case Preparation*.

22. McElroy, Cosgrove, and Farrell, *Felony Case Preparation*, 12.

23. John E. Boydstun, Richard L. Mekemson, Margaret E. Minton, and Ward

Keesling, *Evaluation of the San Diego Police Department's Career Criminal Program* (Washington, D.C.: Police Foundation, 1981).

24. Boydstun et al., *San Diego Career Criminal Program*, V-22–V-33.

25. Boydstun et al., *San Diego Career Criminal Program*, V-1–V-6.

26. Reported crimes increased to the baseline level, while arrests remained constant. Boydstun et al., *San Diego Career Criminal Program*, V-1–V-6.

27. Tony Pate, Robert A. Bowers, and Ron Parks, *Three Approaches to Criminal Apprehension* in *Kansas City: An Evaluation Report* (Washington, D.C.: Police Foundation, 1976).

28. Pate, Bowers, and Parks, *Three Approaches*, 24.

29. Pate, Bowers, and Parks, *Three Approaches*, 33.

30. William Gay, "The Police Role in Serious Habitual Offenders Incapacitation," in McGillis et al., *Dealing with Dangerous Offenders*, 12–13.

31. Gay, "Police Role," 12.

32. Gay, "Police Role," 12.

33. Gay, "Police Role," 15–16.

8. CRIMINAL JUSTICE RECORDS

1. For a historical account of the development of methods for identifying criminal offenders, see Leon Radzinowicz and Roger Hood, "Incapacitating the Habitual Offender: The English Experience," *Michigan Law Review* 78 (August 1980), 1305–1389.

2. Statement by David Nemecek, chief of the Criminal Identification Division, FBI, at the Conference on Public Danger, Dangerous Offenders, and the Criminal Justice System, February 12, 1982, at Harvard University.

3. Nemecek statement.

4. This is based on research experience that involves looking at rap sheets, which rarely included information on disposition. It was also supported by the testimony of David Nemecek, cited in note 2 above.

5. For surprising accounts of the actual events underlying felony charges, see Vera Institute, *Felony Arrests: Their Prosecution and Disposition in New York City's Courts* (New York: Vera Institute, 1977), especially 65–73, 86–89.

6. Nemecek statement.

7. The literature on youth delinquent activities, in particular, emphasizes the role of socialization and learning and shows how difficult it may be to distinguish between opportunity and motivation when the offender's behavior is linked closely with that of friends and neighbors. See, for example, Richard A. Cloward and Lloyd Ohlin, *Delinquency and Opportunity* (Glencoe, Ill.: Free Press, 1960); David Matza, *Delinquency and Drift* (New York: John Wiley and Sons, 1964); and Albert K. Cohen, *Delinquent Boys: The Culture of the Gang* (New York: Free Press, 1955).

8. There has been an extensive, ongoing national debate about the appropriateness of developing national criminal justice records. The specter of Big Brother hangs heavily over this debate. For a view emphasizing the need for safeguards to prevent impropriety, irrelevance, and secrecy, see the discussion of computerized medical record keeping in Alan F. Westin, *Computers, Health Records, and*

Citizen Rights, National Bureau of Standards Monograph 157 (Washington, D.C.: U.S. Dept. of Commerce, December 1976). The National Advisory Commission on Criminal Justice Standards and Goals, *Criminal Justice System* (Washington, D.C.: Law Enforcement Assistance Administration, 1973), 119–138, recommended similar safeguards.

9. This recommendation is broadly consistent with the recommendations of the Attorney General's Task Force on Violent Crime, and with the current inclinations of the FBI. See Attorney General's Task Force on Violent Crime, *Final Report* (Washington, D.C.: U.S. Dept. of Justice, 1981), 11–12, 18, 23.

10. For a compelling theoretical and empirical development of this idea, see Cloward and Ohlin, *Delinquency and Opportunity.*

11. Jan M. Chaiken and Marcia R. Chaiken, *Varieties of Criminal Behavior* (Santa Monica, Calif.: Rand, 1982), and the other Rand inmate studies are only the most recent supporting the notion that habitual offenders start their careers earlier. See, for example, Thorsten Sellin, "Recidivism and Maturation," *NPPA Journal* 4 (1958), 241–250.

12. Barbara Boland, "Identifying Serious Offenders," in *Dealing with Dangerous Offenders,* vol. 2: *Selected Papers,* ed. Daniel McGillis, Susan Estrich, Mark H. Moore and William Spelman (Cambridge, Mass.: John F. Kennedy School of Government, Harvard University, 1983). See also Barbara Boland and James Q. Wilson, "Age, Crime and Punishment," *Public Interest* 51 (Spring 1978), 22–35.

13. Lloyd E. Ohlin, "Limited Access to Juvenile Records for Adult Felony Prosecution and Sentencing," in McGillis et al., *Dealing with Dangerous Offenders.*

14. Paul M. Wisenand and Tug T. Tamara, *Automated Police Information Systems* (New York: John Wiley and Sons, 1970).

15. Nemecek reported that only seventeen states have centralized record systems, and only some of these are automated. In New York City it takes a minimum of three to five hours to obtain a record from the central file despite the existence of a fairly sophisticated automated system.

16. Nemecek statement.

17. For an account of the possible effect of "labeling" by criminal justice authorities on offenders' access to legitimate opportunities, see Don C. Gibbons, *Society, Crime and Criminal Careers* (Englewood Cliffs, N.J.: Prentice-Hall, 1977), 49–77. See also note 63 in chapter 2.

18. Jan and Marcia Chaiken suggest that records in the juvenile system as they currently exist are probably *inadequate* for identifying dangerous offenders. See Chaiken and Chaiken, *Varieties of Criminal Behavior,* 115–117.

19. Nemecek statement.

20. Nemecek statement.

APPENDIX A

1. Jacqueline Cohen, "The Incapacitative Effect of Imprisonment: A Critical Review of the Literature," in *Deterrence and Incapacitation: Estimating the Effects of Criminal Sanctions on Crime Rates,* ed. Alfred Blumstein, Jacqueline Cohen, and Daniel Nagin (Washington, D.C.: National Academy of Sciences, 1978), 187–243. Throughout Appendixes A and B, $\bar{\lambda}$ will be used to refer to the

average rate of criminal offending over the offending population. The criminal offense rate for some individual, or the rate at which some offending population commits certain, specified crimes, will be referred to as λ (without the overbar), and will occasionally be subscripted to indicate the population or crimes referred to.

2. Cohen, "Incapacitative Effect," 220–224.

3. Marvin E. Wolfgang, Robert M. Figlio, and Thorsten Sellin, *Delinquency in a Birth Cohort* (Chicago: University of Chicago Press, 1972); David Greenberg, "The Incapacitative Effect of Punishment: Some Estimates," *Law and Society Review* 2 (1975), 541–580. Shlomo Shinnar and Reuel Shinnar, "The Effects of the Criminal Justice System on the Control of Crime: A Quantitative Approach," *Law and Society Review* 2 (1975), 581–611; Kristen M. Williams, *The Scope and Prediction of Recidivism*, PROMIS Research Project Publication 10 (Washington, D.C.: Institute for Law and Social Research, 1979); Barbara Boland and James Q. Wilson, "Age, Crime and Punishment," *The Public Interest* 51 (1978), 22–34; James J. Collins, "Offender Careers and Restraints: Probabilities and Policy Implications" (Philadelphia: University of Pennsylvania, 1978); Alfred Blumstein and Jacqueline Cohen, "Estimation of Individual Crime Rates from Arrest Records," *Journal of Criminal Law and Criminology* 70 (1979), 561–585; Joan Petersilia, Peter W. Greenwood, and Marvin Lavin, *Criminal Careers of Habitual Felons* (Santa Monica, Calif.: Rand, 1978); Mark A. Peterson, Harriet B. Braiker, and Suzanne M. Polich, *Doing Crime: A Survey of California Prison Inmates* (Santa Monica, Calif.: Rand, 1980); Jan Chaiken and Marcia Chaiken, *Varieties of Criminal Behavior* (Santa Monica, Calif.: Rand, 1982).

4. See, for example, William Spelman, "The Crime Control Effectiveness of Selective Criminal Justice Policies," in *Dealing with Dangerous Offenders*, vol. 2: *Selected Papers* (Cambridge, Mass.: John F. Kennedy School of Government, 1983), 14.

5. Kent Marquis with Patricia Ebener, *Quality of Prisoners' Self-Reports: Arrest and Conviction Response Errors* (Santa Monica, Calif.: Rand, 1981).

6. See the studies cited by Charles E. Silberman, *Criminal Violence, Criminal Justice* (New York: Random House, 1978), 77–78.

7. This is not strictly true, since if some information is available about the average offense rate over all offenders, the *a posteriori* distribution should be "shrunk" toward this expected value. See John E. Rolph, Jan M. Chaiken, and Robert L. Houchens, *Methods for Estimating the Crime Rates of Individuals* (Santa Monica, Calif.: Rand, 1981).

8. Greenberg, "Incapacitative Effect;" Collins, "Offender Careers"; Boland and Wilson, "Age, Crime and Punishment"; Blumstein and Cohen, "Estimation of Individual Crime Rates."

9. Boland and Wilson, "Age, Crime, and Punishment."

10. Blumstein and Cohen, "Estimation of Individual Crime Rates."

11. This is because M/r is 50 percent higher than $M/\{r+[(1-r)/2]\}$, where M represents the adjustment for multiple-offender crimes and arrest rates, and r is the reporting rate.

12. Wolfgang, Figlio, and Sellin, *Delinquency in a Birth Cohort*.

13. Williams, *Scope and Prediction of Recidivism*.

14. See the discussion and research cited in Spelman, "Crime Control Effectiveness," 17–19; see also Joan Petersilia, "Criminal Career Research: A Review of Current Evidence," in *Crime and Justice—An Annual Review of Research*, vol. 2, ed. Norval Morris and Michael Tonry (Chicago: University of Chicago Press, 1980).

15. Greenberg, "Incapacitative Effect."

16. Cohen, "Incapacitative Effect," 206.

17. See Shinnar and Shinnar, "Effects of the Criminal Justice System," for an explication of the method.

18. Collins, "Offender Careers."

19. Blumstein and Cohen, "Estimation of Individual Crime Rates."

20. Petersilia, Greenwood, and Lavin, *Criminal Careers*.

21. Blumstein and Cohen, "Estimation of Individual Crime Rates," 582.

22. Peterson, Braiker, and Polich, *Doing Crime*.

23. Chaiken and Chaiken, *Varieties of Criminal Behavior*.

24. For a full explanation of this method of reconciliation, see Jan M. Chaiken, "Models Used for Estimating Crime Rates," in Peterson, Braiker, and Polich, *Doing Crime*, 224–252.

25. Peterson, Braiker, and Polich, *Doing Crime*, 28.

26. Peter W. Greenwood and Allan Abrahamse, *Selective Incapacitation* (Santa Monica, Calif.: Rand, 1982), 117–118.

27. Marvin E. Wolfgang and Paul E. Tracy, "The 1945 and 1958 Birth Cohorts: A Comparison of the Prevalence, Incidence, and Severity of Delinquent Behavior," in McGillis et al., *Dealing with Dangerous Offenders*, Tables 10a and 10b.

28. For a review of several studies showing the widespread nature of low-level criminal offending, see Michael J. Hindelang, Travis Hirschi, and Joseph G. Weis, "Correlates of Delinquency: The Illusion of Discrepancy between Self-Report and Official Measures," *American Sociological Review* 44 (1979).

29. Although this result is derived in part from the Philadelphia cohort studies of Wolfgang and his associates, it differs from the more familiar result (18 percent of the offenders committed most of the crimes) because only index crimes, rather than all offenses, are considered here.

APPENDIX B

1. This may not be true if the criminal careers of high-rate offenders are substantially longer than those of casual offenders. Thorsten Sellin, "Recidivism and Maturation," *NPPA Journal* 4 (1958), 241–250, was the first to suggest that the worst offenders start earlier and continue their careers longer than others. Although the theory has been provisionally confirmed, recent evidence suggests that the effect, if it exists, is weak. See, for example, Donna Martin Hamparian, Richard Schuster, Simon Dinitz, and John P. Conrad, *The Violent Few: A Study of Dangerous Juvenile Offenders* (Lexington, Mass.: D.C. Heath, 1978), 56–69, 125.

2. Although this example is intended to demonstrate filtering, rather than to specify its effects with precision, the parameters were chosen to reflect what is known about the activities of offenders and criminal justice agencies. See William

Spelman, "The Crime Control Effectiveness of Selective Criminal Justice Policies," in *Dealing with Dangerous Offenders*, vol. 2: *Selected Papers*, ed. Daniel McGillis, Susan Estrich, Mark H. Moore, and William Spelman (Cambridge, Mass.: John F. Kennedy School of Government, 1983), for a detailed description of the simulation model and the parameters used.

3. In each case the probability of arrest was a power function. For the case of police bias against high-rate offenders, parameters were determined so that offenders who committed more than the median amount of crime would be twice as likely to be arrested, on average, as those who commit less than the median. For the case of police bias in favor of high-rate offenders, parameters were set so that above-median criminals were half as likely to be arrested as below-median offenders.

4. Joan Petersilia, Peter W. Greenwood, and Marvin Lavin, *Criminal Careers of Habitual Felons* (Santa Monica, Calif.: Rand, 1978); Mark A. Peterson, Harriet B. Braiker, and Suzanne M. Polich, *Who Commits Crimes* (Cambridge, Mass.: Oelgeschlager, Gunn, and Hain, 1981); Jan M. Chaiken and Marcia R. Chaiken, *Varieties of Criminal Behavior* (Santa Monica, Calif.: Rand, 1983).

5. Marvin E. Wolfgang, Robert M. Figlio, and Thorsten Sellin, *Delinquency in a Birth Cohort* (Chicago: University of Chicago Press, 1972); Marvin E. Wolfgang and Paul Tracy, "The 1945 and 1958 Birth Cohorts: A Comparison of the Prevalence, Incidence, and Severity of Delinquent Behavior," in McGillis et al., *Dealing with Dangerous Offenders*; Hamparian and others, *The Violent Few*; Preben Wolf, "A Contribution to the Topology of Crime in Denmark," in *Scandinavian Studies in Criminology*, vol. 1, ed. Karl O. Christiansen (London: Tavistock, 1965).

Index

79-89